COYOTE WISDOM

"*Coyote Wisdom* is about *soul* and *mind*—the shared journey of healer and patient toward insights and images that break us out of our frozen-heart places and transform awareness, and thus permit us to let go of suffering. As a physician and one who also strives to *heal* patients, not just *treat* them, I honor Dr. Mehl-Madrona for achieving a practical clinical method in *Coyote Wisdom* that is woven from the artistry of storytelling in the tradition of his elders and his reverence for the healing power of universal myths."

> JAMES LAKE, M.D., CHAIR, AMERICAN PSYCHIATRIC ASSOCIATION
> CAUCUS ON COMPLEMENTARY AND ALTERNATIVE MEDICINE IN
> PSYCHIATRY; CLINICAL PROFESSOR, DEPARTMENT OF PSYCHIATRY,
> STANFORD UNIVERSITY SCHOOL OF MEDICINE;
> AND AUTHOR OF *TEXTBOOK OF INTEGRATIVE PSYCHIATRY*

"*Coyote Wisdom* is a gateway to understanding the importance of stories in rituals and ceremonies. Mehl-Madrona's study of healers is a step forward in explaining the implicit wisdom that healers convey to help people get well. To journey with him is a way to be transformed and healed."

> BARBARA BIZIOU, AUTHOR OF *THE JOY OF EVERYDAY RITUALS*

"In this, his third book, Lewis Mehl-Madrona introduces *systems narrative medicine,* giving professional and lay readers alike a chance to learn the healing secrets of story from a master storyteller. Readers will finish the book inspired by the power of story as a catalyst for healing and enriched with practical guidance on how to access this power."

> PAMELA MILES, AUTHOR OF *REIKI: THE DEFINITIVE GUIDE*

"Lewis Mehl-Madrona has spent many years exploring and developing means of integrating American Indian healing techniques into Western medicine. In *Coyote Wisdom,* he gives fresh insights into the power of the spoken word to bring forth miraculous healings and fulfill other human needs. His views on the psychology of the miraculous serve as an important contribution to our understanding of native medicine powers."

> WILLIAM S. LYONS, PH.D., AUTHOR OF
> *ENCYCLOPEDIA OF NATIVE AMERICAN HEALING*

Also by Lewis Mehl-Madrona

Coyote Medicine:
Lessons from Native American Healing

Coyote Healing:
Miracles in Native Medicine

COYOTE WISDOM

The Power of Story in Healing

Lewis Mehl-Madrona, M.D., Ph.D.

Bear & Company
Rochester, Vermont

Bear & Company
One Park Street
Rochester, Vermont 05767
www.InnerTraditions.com

Bear & Company is a division of Inner Traditions International

Library of Congress Cataloging-in-Publication Data
Mehl-Madrona, Lewis, 1954-
  Coyote wisdom : the power of story in healing / Lewis Mehl-Madrona.
      p. cm.
  Includes bibliographical references.
  ISBN 1-59143-029-1 (pbk.)
  1. Narrative therapy. 2. Mythology—Therapeutic use. 3. Indians of North
America—Mental health. I. Title.

  RC489.S74M44 2005
  616.89'165—dc22

                                                            2004031034

Printed and bound in the United States by Lake Book Manufacturing, Inc.

10 9 8 7 6 5 4 3 2

Text design and layout by Priscilla Baker
This book was typeset in Sabon with BodegaSerif as a display typeface

This book is dedicated to my children,
Sorrel Madrona Isherwood, A. Yarrow Madrona,
Julianna Madrona, and Takoda Madrona,
and to my wife, Morgaine.
I love you all.

Contents

Acknowledgments

I want to thank my friends at Inner Traditions/Bear & Company for their role in making this book happen, including Jeanie Levitan, Susan Davidson, Evelyn Leigh, Cynthia Fowles, and Andy Raymond.

I also want to acknowledge the stimulating and inspiring discussions with faculty and students in the Discursive Therapies Program at Massey University, Palmerston North, New Zealand. I'm especially grateful for feedback and ideas from Andrew Lock, Thomas Strong, and Kenneth and Mary Gergen.

Finally, I'd like to acknowledge my colleagues at the University of Arizona, including Andrew Weil, Anne-Marie Chiasson, Evan Kligman, Linda Larkey, Catherine Coe, Robert Krouse, and others. I want to thank my colleagues in the Department of Psychiatry for their ideas and the comraderie in working together—notably Dr. Ernestina Pelayo de Olivares, Dr. Roger Osterholtz, Dr. Robert McCabe, Dr. Robert Garrett, Dr. Numan Gharaibeh, and Dr. David Stoker.

Preface

Sunset in the Desert,
the kind of colors that seem impossible in a painting
but breathtaking in real life.

Streaks of pink, purple, and orange
against the deepening velvet of night;
awaiting the stars overhead.

Stories abound in the desert —
Coyote stories, rabbit stories, cactus stories;
Every story and even the whispering voices of ancient seas.

The colors are bleeding with the cries of the suffering —
An Asian tsunami wiping clean human shores,
collecting souls in that spot where the sun meets the horizon.

The temperature plunges as the sun disappears;
The suffering have no blankets for the night;
they huddle under bridges, in parks, under palo verde trees.

As the sun disappears and the twilight fades,
the full moon rises above the Eastern Mountains,
hanging large above the peaks.

Coyotes cry for this large, pregnant moon;
Eagles and owls try to fly for it;
Fools climb the peaks to jump onto it.

These stories are for the suffering;
These stories are for those in pain;
These stories are for the sick and the downtrodden.

Coyote sings the stories of healing,
the stories of forgiveness and reconciliation,
the stories of transformation.

They make us generous warriors,
They make us whole,
and we dance with the rising of the moon.

Introduction

I grew up in a culture of stories and storytellers. My grandmother told stories from dawn to dusk—Native American, biblical, family legends, and local gossip. Even my grandfather's beloved country music consisted of stories set to music. In my earlier book, *Coyote Medicine*, I told my story—how I tried to make sense of my life as both Anglo-European and Native American, how I tried to integrate these two sides into my medical practice, and how I came to enrich my work with Native American philosophy and culture. As part of the story of my journey, I described the remarkable healings of people I met along the way. In *Coyote Healing*, I continued this theme to focus upon elements common to stories of healing and to the people who heal. I wrapped the healing journey around the medicine wheel, starting in the East with spirit, moving to the South with emotion, to the West with the physical body, and ending in the North with mind and community. In this book, I pursue the stories healers tell to inspire us to make that journey and to believe that healing is possible.

Through my participation in ceremony and my observations of Native healers, I realized that hearing and telling stories are integral to healing. By hearing stories about healing from people who seem like us, we become inspired to believe that our own healing is possible. The telling and retelling of stories is the powerful means by which cultures of families and communities are formed and maintained, national identities are preserved, problem-solving skills are taught, and moral values are instilled. Stories can inspire, uplift, and transform their listeners, or they can belittle, humiliate, and drive their listeners to despair. Stories get our attention to teach us things we will never forget.

Healers lacking in any formal education often demonstrate a masterful command of language in telling stories. With their stories, they communicate complex ideas about love, forgiveness, faith, hope, and self-transformation. They practice the sophisticated art of a master hypnotherapist without ever demonstrating any awareness of the techniques they are using. They use the ancient art of storytelling—a masterful tool of persuasion and, no doubt, the mother of hypnosis. They tell creation stories, stories about personal transformation and development, stories about stealing fire or stealing summer, and stories about other people who have healed. They use personal stories as example, highlighting similar problems they or other family members and friends have experienced and solved. The wisdom for how to heal is contained in these stories, which serve as an orientation into a culture of faith and hope.

The more I participated in rituals and ceremony, the more I found myself telling stories. I came to understand stories as the glue that binds people together into families and cultures. We know we are in the same family because we tell similar stories when we get together. Likewise, members of a culture share stories, often ritualistically enacting them at specified times. Christians celebrate Easter and the story of Christ's Crucifixion and Resurrection. Jews tell the story of Passover as part of their ritual. The story and the ritual are inseparable.

When I applied what I was learning from healers to my observations of psychotherapy and family therapy, I saw the same process at work—a continual negotiation and reworking of each individual's stories into more balanced and harmonious combinations. Stories appeared to be vehicles that carry the basic, irreducible units of meaning in human life. They contain the secrets for how we transform. They carry the wisdom that teaches us how to change, how to deepen our spirituality, how to have faith, and how to recognize our hidden assumptions about life that prevent us from finding creative solutions to life's problems or lock us in destructive solutions. Hence, my title, *Coyote Wisdom*—this is the wisdom of the stories we tell and that are told to us for healing and transformation.

It is no accident that when asked to explain how they changed, transformed, or got well, people embed their explanation within a story.

Often they tell a story about the time that led up to the transformation, including seemingly innocuous events preceding their sudden change. They tell stories about the aftereffects of that transformation. The more of these stories I heard, the more I realized the importance of appreciating them as meaningful units of instruction about growth and change.

Healers of all cultures are engaged in a similar process with the sick. People come to healers over and over telling stories about how sick they are, that they are dying, that there is no hope. Healers tell them different stories, stories that emphasize hope, that cast sickness as a stage to pass through (a territory, a river to cross, a mountain to climb), that insist that they will live, and that cultivate faith. The healers tell these stories to show their patients what they cannot tell them directly.

Of course, there are situations in which healers recognize that survival is unlikely. Then the emphasis of the stories shifts to the cultivation of peacefulness. Nevertheless, for the average case in which survival is expected, the initial stories are meant to foster faith that recovery will happen. In coming to the healer, the sick person meets or hears of others who got well after working with the healer or with other healers. These people give testimonials. Over and over, a series of competing stories about health and wellness engages the sick person's attention, slowly eroding the certainty of sickness and death with the competing possibility of healing and health. To the extent that the story is incorporated—consumed, digested, internalized—the possibility that it will become true grows.

Sitting in Native American ceremony one day, I realized that, whatever else healing may be, it is a negotiation of story. This led me to want to write about this negotiation, for I recognized it as what I do with people who consult me with problems. I had long ago abandoned the idea that I did therapy. Therapy contains the idea that I can "treat" someone else, an idea that seems specious and patronizing. I preferred the idea that I could tell stories that might inspire people to change. I saw the Native healers engaged in this same negotiation, a process that has been called "reauthoring."

I take this view even for so-called physical problems. I bracket this category with "so-called" because I was raised with a paradigm different from the one held by conventional medicine. Conventional, allopathic medicine rests upon what has been called Cartesian dualism—the idea that mind and body are separate. This idea is so universally accepted within modern Western society that it is rarely questioned, except in philosophy classes or by the counterculture. Nevertheless, only European culture evolved around this idea, regardless of how widespread it has become. Native American culture does not separate mind and body. Much like the French philosopher Maurice Merleau-Ponty, Native Americans see people as mind–body–spirit wholes, lacking any separation between subject and object. This leads me to approach "physical," "mental," and "spiritual" problems in the same way.

(What does that mean? Am I crazy? Don't physical problems require drugs for healing?)

I've managed to avoid the conventional medical (and cultural) bias that "biological" problems are treated by biological means—pharmaceuticals, primarily, or, in alternative medical and cultural circles, herbs and vitamins and diets. While a conventional person would say I lack boundaries, I would say that we define our boundaries in somewhat arbitrary ways. Recent PET scan findings support my argument. Successful psychotherapy for depression, obsessive-compulsive disorder, and anxiety produces the same changes in the brain as medications.[1] The brain doesn't seem to care. When conditions change, it changes. On aesthetic grounds, I tend to prefer non-pharmacological methods of effecting change, believing that they are longer lasting. (Research findings support this argument, also.[2]) From this point of view, medications are just one more tool to support transformation. Given my beliefs, it is not surprising that I prefer to reserve pharmaceuticals for emergencies or extreme cases.

In the story I tell myself about how things work, we begin with a baby born into a sea of entangled and interconnected biology, family, culture, and spirit. The baby evolves into an adult through its relations and connections with all of us (everything). As the ancient Greek philosopher Heraclitus said, "We know that it's impossible to step into the river twice in the same place." This is a metaphorical way of saying that no two humans are the same. No two humans could ever evolve in the same way. Even the milieu in which two brothers live has changed by the time the second brother is born. The context of our lives is constantly in flux.

We evolve through relationships. This idea is central to Cherokee and Lakota healing—the two cultures with which I have genetic connections. Healing involves restoration of "right relationship." I need to hear your story, the story you tell about yourself and your illness, to know where your relationships are disturbed. The unfolding of the story provides the clues about where to restore balance and harmony.

In this book, I advance the importance of the story in medical practice. I want to convey the idea that illness and the story of the illness are as inseparable as mind and body. When we speak about an illness, we engage in a creative act. With our words and gestures, we can augment health or illness. We listen to what we say. We convince others to agree with us. The philosopher George Herbert Mead believed that words have visceral components. We feel in our guts what we say. Even if we consciously use one meaning for a word, our bodies react to all of its meanings. This corresponds to what Hindus mean when they speak about the vibration of a sound and how that vibration resonates within the whole body. Through our social interactions, we learn to feel some words differently than others. Are we speaking healing words or sickness words? We find out by listening to the stories we tell and perceiving their effects upon our bodies and upon our listeners.

Of course, if you don't accept the oneness of mind and body, this idea is crazy. Nevertheless, I will point to emerging evidence from quantum physics to support my argument that we are all connected, that connectivity is fact, that separation is impossible, that doctor and patient become a treatment unit just like mind and body or word and illness. As the philosopher Ashok Gangadean says, "Predication is illusion."[3] By this, he means that the usual linguistic convention of subject–verb–object is incorrect. Our use of language implies that we are separate from what we perceive, when we are actually integrally connected. The idea of predication, meaning that we can turn something into an object that is separate from us, is false. The stories we tell about our illnesses are actions upon the world that result in confirmation of the way we see things.

My goal is to tell healing stories, and to teach people who are telling sickness stories how to sing a different tune. In *Coyote Wisdom*, I ask readers to consider a different paradigm of health and disease than what is familiar, potentially, to think more like Indians or quantum physicists. This would change the way we practice medicine, psychology, and counseling. It would change the way we attempt to solve problems. If story and illness are connected like chicken and egg, then we cannot just diagnose the illness; we must also "diagnose" the story, meaning that we must understand the illness as something created through the mutual entanglements of relationship—entanglements of biology, culture, and spirit. Language is the vehicle for exploring these webs of connection.

Just as creation stories explain our existence by preserving our culture's mutually agreed-upon idea of how we got here (the topic of chapter 1), the stories we tell give us clues about the creation of our illness. Through carefully listening to a person's story about their illness (and the stories told by others in his or her community), we can begin to grasp the imbalances and disturbances of harmony that foster illness. Illness arises as a creative solution to problems created out of our imbalances and disharmonies. The illness can always be seen as a partially successful attempt at healing. We need to know what problems the illness has helped solve and which still need to be addressed.

This "storied" approach to healing can also explain the so-called placebo effect. In this self-healing response, we share in the creation of a story to suggest how I can get well. The story may or not be grounded in biological science, but because we believe it to be true, it serves as a pivot point for changing the story I tell about my illness and its destiny. This approach can make both conventional medicine and alternative medicine adherents uncomfortable. Their structuralist culture seeks specific answers that apply uniformly to everyone. "Mercury is bad. Everyone needs mercury fillings removed." "Coffee prevents colon cancer." "Vitamins are bad for cancer patients. They make the cancer grow." "Macrobiotics will cure cancer." "Everyone needs cholesterol-lowering drugs." "Meat is bad." "Carbohydrates are bad." "Take Prozac." "Drink spring water." "Go get a bee sting." A recent article in *Scientific American* concluded that the only certainty about medical recommendations to prevent heart disease is that they change every two years.

The storied approach to healing makes the radical hypothesis that no pure biological facts exist. Biological investigations without specification of the subject's beliefs (revealed through the stories they tell about themselves), family constellation (revealed through the stories family members tell about each other and the family), culture (revealed through the recurring themes or stories everyone hears—the so-called pop culture of the modern world), and spirituality (revealed through the religious stories people hear and repeat) are incomplete and prone to inaccuracy. This does not mean that clinical trials will not reveal biological trends, given sufficiently large numbers of subjects, but it does suggest that even these trends flow with the flux of culture. It suggests that medical treatment as we conceptualize it may be ineffective because of our lack of grounding in these larger contexts. Herein lies the essence of what I am calling *narrative medicine* (or "Coyote wisdom")—that biology is embedded in larger hierarchies: families, communities, cultures, and historical time periods. Biology cannot be studied apart from the context in which it is embedded.

Modern philosophers are coming to similar conclusions. Wittgenstein, for example, began his career believing that language would lead us to the truth. He ended his career believing that meaning relies on how people use language with one another and is anchored in human communication and evaluation. He came to understand that there is more than one correct way to understand and communicate, that understanding cannot be premapped in a one-size-fits-all manner from which we can assess the accuracies of our communication and understanding. I suggest that similar implications hold for biological medicine—that our efforts to find one-treatment-fits-all-with-that-diagnosis are doomed to fail when we ignore the world in which biology is placed. We can discover that world only by hearing the stories of people who suffer, along with the stories told by their families, their cultures, and their religions. And that world is changed when we "contaminate" those stories with alternate stories suggesting other ways of interpreting and organizing the same experiences to lead to different outcomes—healing, health, and spiritual well-being.

While it remains mysterious that telling stories can change physiology, scientific research is beginning to discover potential explanations for how this happens. Stories affect our states of mind, which are reflected in changes in brain states. When we are happy, PET scans of the brain show patterns of regional blood flow different from when we are sad. These patterns of blood flow are different in states of joy compared with states of depression. The stories we tell ourselves inform us about how to perceive the world around us. They even tell us how to interpret our bodily sensations. Change the stories and perception changes. Changed perception means changed experience, and change in experience alters brain biology. Since the brain regulates everything in the body, including the immune system, the body changes when the brain changes. Here is the beginning of our understanding about how stories can have healing power.

Wittgenstein came to understand that there might be many equally valid ways to understand and relate. He saw that there are multiple realities. He realized that the kind of objectivity science idealizes is not possible. Quantum physics shows that the certainty and objectivity desired by conventional science disappears when we reach a certain level of smallness. Medical science may need to abandon its quest for biological certainty and expand to consider the larger dimensions within which biology operates. We perform autopsies on dead actors without stepping back to grasp the stage upon which they performed, or the audience, or even to wonder what the play was all about. We have to outgrow that.

In our daily life, we assume that objects occupy definite points in space and time. In the mid-1920s, physicist Werner Heisenberg demonstrated that, for the basic units of matter, it is impossible to know both their position and their velocity. The very attempt to measure position and velocity will move the particle about in unpredictable ways and speeds. How we measure determines everything about what we describe. Heisenberg's uncertainty principle further asserts that the basic units of matter cannot be observed apart from the observer. He argued that this operates at all levels of nature, but that we can generally discard the anomalies at our level, that of large objects seen with the naked eye. Nevertheless, as biological medicine moves toward the microscopic, we may discover that knowing everything about one aspect of the body means that we abandon all awareness of other aspects.

Physicists solved this problem by saying that the basic particles of matter exist as probability distributions (describing where they might be found if measured). When applied to medicine, Heisenberg's uncertainty principle might suggest that even when the human genome project reaches its goal of describing the genetic code of all human genes, we may be clueless about how this relates to health and disease, since the function of genes cannot be separated from the social and cultural milieu in which the person operates. What if human health and disease involve many more levels than merely the genetic?

Stories contain and convey the meanings and values of our lives. They tell us how to perceive the world. They give us cultural identity. At weddings and funerals, they tell us about families and lives and what it means to belong. They comfort and heal us, both in the listening and the telling. They contain the living symbols we use to make sense of our world. The characters in these stories vary across cultures, but certain themes remain the same, since our stories arise from and are constrained by our biology, geography, and means of communication. Stories are the units of meaning for a life, and life unfolds through the enactment of those stories. *Coyote Wisdom* shows how the stories we tell, the stories we grow up with, and the stories that inspire us represent blueprints for the ways we conceive of ourselves and our world. In short, we are our stories. We live them as they live us.

John Barth begins his poetic first-person account of a salmon's night journey to spawn with the question, "Is the journey my invention? Do the night, the sea, the sky, exist at all, apart from my experience of them? Do I myself exist, or is this a dream . . . ? And if I am, who am I?"[4] The power of his writing lies in the commonality of these questions. At some time in our journey through life we all ask these questions. Stories contain our answers. They impose order onto the chaos of our experience. They help us organize our experience in time. They provide a beginning, middle, and ending. They locate our experience within cultural contexts and geographies. They tell us who we are, where we are, and what we are.

Barth continues, "Many accounts of our situation seem plausible to me . . . But implausible ones as well, perhaps especially those, I must admit as possibly correct. Even likely." Humans of all cultures and historical periods share this problem of uncertainty, which is uncomfortable. So we construct stories and tell them over and over to establish certainty.

We physicians think that the stories we tell ourselves about health and disease are fact. Unlike the salmon-philosopher's reflections in *Night-Sea Journey*, we swallowed the "only biology" story hook, line, and sinker. We need to mature to a larger perspective that encompasses the role of the stories we tell in helping us to transform and to heal ourselves and our communities. We need to understand the power of our negative stories—for example, the ones in which we tell people that they have only six months to live. We need to understand that the context of our stories is as important as what we talk about.

Stories contain the hidden secrets of transformation, the alchemist's formulas for turning lead into gold. If we hear enough stories about profound transformation, we find ourselves transforming, even in spite of ourselves. While we can't command transformation, we can create an enriched environment that makes it more possible.

The following story about Kata illustrates the healing power of the right story heard at the right time.

Kata was thirty-nine years old when she came to see me for depression, feeling that her life was going nowhere. She was almost out of time to complete the final course required for her graduate degree. She had not yet recovered from the end of a long-term relationship one year prior.

Kata and her fiancé broke up just before closing on their dream house, which she bought anyway (for reasons she couldn't explain). Since moving in, she had felt isolated and alone. Her neighbors had kids and horses. She perceived herself as an anomaly in this neighborhood— single, Jewish, horseless, and truckless. She couldn't find a reason to talk to her neighbors. Their barbeques didn't interest her. She didn't go to their church on Sunday or meet them on horseback in the wash. She didn't like football or pool parties.

For years, she had felt intimidated by men. She had avoided working with or having them as bosses. This was worse since the break-up. Her story was depressing to hear and to live. I wondered if things had always been this sad. Had there been a time when she felt happy? Kata's demeanor changed as she began to remember.

She happily remembered being twelve and running wildly through the countryside outside of Los Angeles, where she had grown up. She remembered her exuberance as a child. She remembered not wanting to grow up and take on the expectations of her parents, telling me that they and their friends could not see her as a success unless she became a doctor or a lawyer, preferably a doctor. She described a childhood friend who first became an accountant, then a lawyer, and next a business school graduate. Now he was finishing medical school. She suffered in being eclipsed by such a towering figure.

Feeling a bit stuck and not knowing where else to go, I asked her if she'd seen any good movies lately. This sometimes dramatically shifts the mood of the room. To my surprise, she began an enthusiastic recount of the movie, *Whale Rider*, whose main character is a young Maori girl who reminded Kata of herself as a child. Nothing changes the mood as quickly as a good story. Suddenly we were drawn into the different reality of this wonderful movie.

A Maori tribal elder has prophesied that the new leader of the people will be born to his son's wife, only to suffer the disappointment of her having a girl, and the double trauma of his son's wife dying in childbirth. In one moment, his vision for a future leader was destroyed.

In his emotional despair, the elder's son abandoned his baby girl to her grandmother, escaping to Germany to start a new life as an artist. The girl, Paikea, remained, to be raised by her grandmother and a reluctant grandfather. She became a constant reminder of his son's failure to provide a male leader for his people.

Paikea had her own vision. Each day, as she walked past the statue of the "whale rider," an ancestor who had come, riding on the back of a whale, to save her people from disaster, she saw herself doing the same. She heard whales singing in her dreams. She heard them singing on her walks along the ocean. She heard them singing as she daydreamed at school. Throughout this time of cultivating her vision, her grandfather ignored her. She was "just a girl."

Eventually, Paikea's grandfather established a school for the traditional healing arts, excluding Paikea, his most avid potential student, because she was female. She disgraced him by secretly watching his classes and teaching herself enough Maori stick-fighting to spar with one of the boys in his school. Grandfather broke her stick and cursed her to never return. Nevertheless, Paikea continued to learn. She convinced her uncle, once a stick-fighting champion, now a beer guzzler, to be her teacher.

Grandfather took the boys out to dive into the ocean to recover his medicine bag, where he had previously dropped it, but they failed. Later, Paikea paddled out to the spot with her uncle, dove deeply down into the water, and brought back the medicine bag. However, to Paikea's great pain, not even this could convince her grandfather to adjust his view of women.

Then the whales came. Paikea heard them. They were beached. The people strained with ropes to pull the whales off the sand and into the ocean but failed. Exhausted and despairing, they trudged home. Paikea slipped past them unnoticed. She climbed on top of the largest whale. Something mysterious happened. The whale began to move. It struggled into the ocean and began to swim away. Paikea rode the whale, so far into the ocean that she almost died. When she awoke in her hospital bed after being rescued, her grandfather had changed. He had realized that girls could be leaders. Paikea was celebrated as the whale rider.

"I want to be Paikea," said Kata. "I want to ride a whale."

"What would that mean?" I asked.

"I need to learn to stick-fight," she answered. "That would get me started like it did Paikea."

"So what stops you?" I asked, meeting her gaze.

"I don't know," she answered.

"So do it," I said. "Find someone to teach you stick-fighting and see what happens." We explored the reasons why she should avoid stick-fighting. None were compelling. She left with a commitment to become Paikea, and to ride her whale.

Two months later she returned with a radically different story. Everything had turned around. She was surrounded by men in multiple roles—work, sparring, dating. She said that stick-fighting had jump-started her energy. She felt empowered and alive again. She had found a teacher of a rare form of Filipino stick-fighting usually taught only to police and soldiers. Few women took up this art. It required intense concentration to avoid being struck in the head. After taking up stick-fighting, she had been inspired to finish the last class she needed for her graduate degree. She put her house up for sale so that she could move into a part of town where she felt more ordinary. She no longer felt depressed. She felt invigorated and ready to meet the challenges of her life. Kata had become Paikea. She was living the story, and the story was living through her.

Kata would have qualified for major depressive disorder. She met the DSM-IV criteria for the diagnosis and would have been offered medication in almost all psychiatry or primary care offices. Instead, I asked her about good movies and encouraged her to "follow her bliss," in the words of Joseph Campbell. What is remarkable is that she did so. The Paikea story was so inspiring to her that just remembering it when she started to falter was enough to keep her on her path. My telling her what to do wouldn't have served that purpose. If I'd said, "You need to exercise. Take up a martial art," would she have done it? I don't think so. Her identification with the character in the story and the knowledge of the triumph of that character provided her with the inspiration to "take arms against a sea of troubles, and by opposing end them," as Hamlet said.

Kata continued to live the Paikea character. She was becoming a woman who could be a powerful leader in the world of men. When I asked her about dating anxiety, she laughed and smiled at me coquettishly, saying, "Oh, I'm not afraid to date anymore. If they're not nice, or they give me lip, or try anything fresh, I'll just grab my stick and off them."

I knew she was joking, but what was important in that statement was her newfound lack of intimidation. Stick-fighting had made her feel like an equal in the world of men. She was someone to be taken seriously because she could defend herself against any of them. Perhaps it also helped her release some of her anger toward her former fiancé.

Kata identified with Paikea's story. I still don't know exactly why, but I am not important. I am not Kata. I do not live her life or her story. She does. And this story made all the difference. My job was merely to ask the right questions.

Finally, a word about my method. *Coyote Wisdom* is not a book about Native American stories, but about how I use stories to help achieve healing. While my work is informed by my Native American heritage and my understanding of Native American healing practices, I borrow and adapt stories freely from a variety of other cultures, including modern American culture. What is crucial is my choice of a story that will speak to the particular individual with whom I am working. This explains my sometimes use of popular movies and movie characters, not just traditional stories. My motto is to use whatever will work.

It is essential to understand that the storied (or narrative) path to healing is an uncertain one. In my previous books, I have presented stories of amazing healing and miraculous transformation. This doesn't mean that I instinctively know how to accomplish this with any given person. What I can do is to offer people stories that may stimulate and inspire transformation, which must be picked up by a surrounding community. People rarely transform on their own but instead do so in relation to others who support that transformation. Shared stories create healing communities, which is the purpose of ceremony and ritual. Unlike modern scientists who pretend to have crystal clarity, we narrative scientists of healing are stumbling through a forest of stories in which the mysteries of life of each tree remain elusive but are somehow revealed to us through the fruit of these trees.

When I lecture or do workshops, people typically want me to tell them what techniques work best with which particular illnesses. I am forced to explain that to me, the assumption behind this question is contrary to the essence of both Native American medicine and narrative medicine. We can't know how to heal until we hear a person's story. The diagnosis is one marker of the journey he or she has traveled. That particular road sign, however, doesn't tell us anything about how the person traveled to get to that point. To understand what will work for that person, we need to hear his or her story, to discover what problems the illness has solved and what values their quest pursues. How we do this is what this book is about.

1

Creation Stories

reation stories are ubiquitous in life. Our families tell us stories of
our birth. At family gatherings and holidays across the world, families love to tell memorable, hilarious, and embarrassing stories of
our childhood. At business meetings, on airplanes, and at parties, we
tell stories about how we got to be where we are today. We have the
short version for acquaintances, the long version for our closest friends,
and the cleaned-up version for first dates and potential in-laws.

Cultures also tell stories about their own creation, and people tell
stories about how they got sick and how they got well. The story about
how an illness arose is particularly powerful and has multiple versions.
In Western society, the doctor's version is called the diagnosis, and it is
a compelling story to which all members of society pay homage. A person's own story about how he or she got sick may or may not parallel
the official medical story, and this seems like the logical place to begin
a book about the healing power of stories.

Thus we begin with the idea that everyone needs a creation story,
just as much as cultures need stories about their origins. And all people
require a story about the appearance of their illness, whether or not that
story matches the medical version. The power of the creation story lies
in its predictions. The medical diagnostic story predicts what treat-

ments will work and what the results of those treatments will be. Similarly, the sick person's story about the birth of his or her illness predicts the likelihood of healing or cure and contains clues as to what treatments will work and what treatments will not work.

I begin with creation stories, just as medical care begins with diagnosis. I want to draw out the person's own illness-creation story, and then, over time, as I shall show in subsequent chapters, I try to influence that story so that the chance for healing and cure increases. As many Native healers have told me, the limits to healing and curing are a great mystery, known only to the Divine; we are required to do our best to strive for wellness in every way possible, knowing that healing is always possible, but cure is up to the Divine.

Creation stories are also important because the final story about how you or I got well must be compatible with the story about how we got sick, or the treatment will never work. In my studies of remarkable healings, I found that every person had a plausible story (to them) for how their illness occurred and how they got well.[1] Invariably, the wellness story was logically consistent with the "how I got sick" story, even if neither story made sense in terms of my biological understanding of sickness and disease. In addition, everyone in their immediate, closest circle of family, friends, and acquaintances also believed these stories of how the person got sick and got well, buffering the person from larger groups who might challenge or question either story.

Communities of believers are powerful and are created and maintained through shared stories. Recently I met a small group of people who had experienced miracle-level healings with a particular vitamin product. Others I knew had tried the same product and had succumbed anyway to their disease. I suspected that, helpful as it was, the vitamin product was not the actual healing agent. When I looked closer, I found that the phenomenon mirrored what I had observed among those healed by Native medicine people. In both cases, the people had a plausible theory to explain their healing (the product or Spirit), they isolated themselves in a tight fellowship group (in the case of the vitamin product, a group of fellow product consumers within an enthusiastic multi-level marketing pyramid structure), and everyone around them believed with fervor in the power of the product (or Spirit) to heal them, thereby reinforcing the stories. The vitamin users who were healed loudly proclaimed testimonials about the product; they had absolute faith in it.

Their involvement with marketing the product and with others who marketed the product had forced an intense, present-centered mindfulness upon them. They had no time to be bothered by the past or worry about the future—the immediate needs of marketing the product and giving testimonials about it consumed every waking moment. I had to be happy about their healing. Some people in their group had recovered from documented lupus, metastatic cancer, and other serious illnesses. Naturally, since I didn't share their absolute faith in the product, I worried about what would happen to any of them if their complete committed involvement with the product faltered, but I realized that could happen to any of us. We can all have crises of faith and lose our way.

Their culture, created and maintained through shared stories about the product, had a creation story—the story about the genius who formulated the product and his trials and tribulations in getting it out to the public. The story included his persecution by the Food and Drug Administration and by medical authorities. The stories shared by this community informed its members about how to perceive themselves and their environment, including how to view people who didn't use the product and those who were outright skeptical of it.

I found these followers of the vitamin product fascinating for their collective creation of a subculture through telling stories and sharing an understanding of the meaning of those stories. How did this shared culture and understanding translate into physiological healing? What are the biological principles behind this transformation of the vitamin product into an agent for healing and curing? The followers of the product would never ask these questions, of such interest to me. Such questions lie outside their worldview. They would have never imagined that their social network and the beliefs that it sustained and nurtured could have brought out the biological activity of healing, related in part to their complete and total faith in the vitamin product. Their faith in the product appeared to prevent them from creating alternate stories that would take the power of healing away from the product and give it back to the community.

In my studies of extraordinary healing, I didn't encounter a single person who had healed in isolation. Perhaps such people exist, but I could never have found them if they existed in that much isolation. The philosopher Ervin Laszlo believes that communities of people are connected by fields of energy.[2] He provides an explanation within the realm of contemporary physics for Jesus's statement that "I am there whenever two or more are gathered in my name." People create systems that generate an energy field, which feeds back to make the people within the system more connected to each other and more coherent in their thoughts and feelings. Ancient tradition teaches us that when two or more people gather to pray and worship, over time their prayers become more powerful. Modern research shows greater energy-field strength when more people are praying together, with increased coherence among their brain wave patterns. These energy fields are generated by the relationships formed through the telling of shared stories. Powerful healing is created through the telling and retelling of shared stories that build the energy field connecting the people involved, as has happened within Native American communities throughout the ages. When the same people do ceremony together week after week for years, great healing power is created. This process can also happen outside of church or ceremony.

The sociologist Erving Goffman wrote that language allows us to create any story or explanatory framework through our conversations.[3] He compared this to the freedom of a playwright to first create a stage and then to people it with characters of his or her choosing. Goffman asserted, "talk . . . embeds, insets and intermingles." This line of thinking would imply that the talk about the product created, in a very real sense, its healing power, which increased in strength the closer one got to the source of that dialogue—the inner sanctum around its "creator." Without the story of how the product was created, accompanied by the heartfelt testimonials about its use and effectiveness, the product would fail to have anywhere near the healing power that it demonstrated in the collection of stories told about it.

In Ervin Laszlo's systems philosophy, these physical conversations affect and become embedded within a larger energy field (the quantum waveform), which, in turn, feeds back to "in-form" the people creating the conversation about a more comprehensive version that includes everyone's ideas and contributions. The field contains the entire conversation, while each individual holds only a small part of it. Rupert Sheldrake called this energy field the *morphogenic field*, arguing that it contains ideas that become accessible to everyone.[4] What this means is that our explanatory stories, our creation stories, really do feed back to create us. They become larger than we are, even develop biological effects. Imagine that the followers of the vitamin product, through their constant living of the story about the miracle of the product and their ongoing conversations about the product, embed this information about the product into an energy field that informs their community about how to be even more effective in service to the vitamin product. Membership in the community makes one an "actor" on a stage in which the product works phenomenally well. The more central you are as an actor in that "play" about the product, the more powerful it will be for you.

Peripheral characters may not get nearly the benefit that comes to true believers. This means that the power of any substance (even a conventional pharmaceutical drug) is not separable from the stories told about the substance—stories about where and how it was created, accompanied by testimonials, told perhaps in the language of science, perhaps in the language of television commercials. Biological activity is inseparable from stories about how useful something is in practice. This makes perfect sense if biology and consciousness are inseparable. The creation stories and the biological effect inform one other, building progressively greater power.

Erving Goffman would further say that the followers of the product accomplished a creative act through their interaction, in which they produced a frame (like a stage) to contain and support their continued dialogue.[5] Participating together within the frame makes people more attuned in purpose and understanding.

In writing about creation stories, I am inviting you to imagine people coming together to create something—a community, a church, a product, a business, or health and healing. These people forge a shared story that describes how their activity began. All cultures have creation stories about how they came into being: the Book of Genesis, the Bhagavad Gita, the Native American creation stories that follow. The early Christians told the stories of the birth of Jesus, his teachings, his healings, and his Crucifixion and Ascension. Communities have founding fathers and mothers. Cities may even be named for their symbolic forebearers, as in Washington, DC (named for George Washington); Prince Rupert, BC; and San Francisco (after St. Francis), to list a few. Churches tell stories about how their faith was created. Marriott Hotels places a book inside guest rooms with the history of the Marriott brothers and their efforts to build a hotel chain.

The radical departure from conventional thinking is to imagine that these creation stories are contained as information within a field of energy mutually generated by the people involved in the activity. This helps these people to be coherent with one another in their pursuit of the activity. Some of the information contained in the field is inspirational to bodily healing, as with "The Product." The more strongly we participate in the activity (church, business, school—all of which are also systems or wholes greater than the sum of their parts), the more we are influenced by this energy field that helps reorganize our thoughts to be consistent with the goals of the activity and coherent with others participating in the activity. This is what builds power. On the most mundane level, this wisdom for how to participate is contained in the stories we tell each other, notably our creation stories.

I tell creation stories to inspire a person to discover the creation story for her own illness (and to eventually modify it so that getting well is not so hard to image). At a minimum, I am enrolling her in a system that consists of the two of us, in which I hold an intention for her wellness and healing. The more the person interacts with me, the more she is drawn into the energy field that we are creating, one in which healing becomes more possible. The stories we share provide social structure that contains this less palpable energy field. Our relationship is the stage and we are the actors. The larger we make our community of believers (participants in the story, actors in the play), the fuller our field of energy becomes with information about healing. The sharing of the story of how healing is created builds that energy and passes it back to us.

I love the Hopi creation story.[6] Since this is not a book about Native American stories, but about how I use stories for healing, I will tell the story here as I told it to Kathryn, a thirty-year-old woman with lupus. My goal was to elicit a story from Kathryn about the creation of her lupus that would also contain logical options for healing that disease.

Stories do their best work upon us when we step out of our ordinary minds. In ancient and indigenous cultures, ritual marked the telling of stories, informing everyone it was time to enter an altered state of consciousness. Our ancestors were facile at transitions of consciousness, but we moderns often need assistance. Methods for helping people enter altered states are covered in books on hypnosis, meditation, visualization, and guided imagery. I liberally use all of these techniques.

To really *hear* a story and to absorb its fullness, we need to be relaxed. Our mind must be still. The brain circuits that make lists, plan our day, remember all of our errands—the executive planner—becomes inactive during states of prayer and meditation. This circuit passes from the dorsolateral prefrontal cortex to the ventral striatum, the globus pallidum, the thalamus, and then back to the frontal cortex.[7] When this circuit is quiet, the right temporal lobe becomes more active. My research has shown that an area in the right temporal lobe actually recognizes prayer, even when the individual consciously does not. That area is very close to the area that recognizes language. We can conclude that listening resembles praying, with similar brain states accompanying each.

My goal is to help the person enter this quiet, prayerful state in order to really listen to the story. I offer a multitude of suggestions to help people move into a relaxed state of increased susceptibility to learning. I begin by focusing upon breathing, with suggestions to relax more and more with each exhalation. With each breath in, we bring in life-giving oxygen to spread throughout our bodies. With each breath out, we let go of tension, so that we can slip deeper and deeper, down into our inner world, through the gateway to the spirit world. As we let go of physical tension, we can begin to empty our minds so that we can hear the story without the usual background chatter. I often remind people of how they approach a movie, about how they forget their problems, their identity, their stress, so that they can become fully engaged in the movie. I invite them to do the same with my story, to let go of all other considerations and to get lost in the story I am about to tell and the images that will be stimulated by that story.

Having accomplished this preliminary goal with Kathryn, I began my story.

✳

"Once upon a time, Kathryn, you were well. You remember that time, though it seems like a long time ago. The birth of your lupus was tumultuous, just like the Hopi story of the birth of the world, when the bellowing fire of the volcanoes and the roaring of the earth masses caused a huge tidal wave, and the winds began to laugh. Before you knew it, volcanoes were erupting in your knees and ankles. Pain roared in your hip joints. A huge tidal wave rolled over your kidneys, throwing them into failure. The wind blew across your face, scouring a terrible rash.

"This creation was nature at her worst. The power of that display was awesome, but the effects upon your life were devastating. Overnight, you were on an entirely different planet. Overnight, your life had changed. But just as nature created the Earth out of this turmoil, perhaps something good came from the creation of your lupus, something that you might come to understand during the course of this story. Perhaps a part of you will begin figuring this out, so she can tell us later how good has come from this illness.

"In the creation of the lupus, you encountered angry nature. There were flashes of lightning and roaring of thunder, as Earth was being born, like a new baby, crying and demanding. It must have been very much the same inside your body—flashes of lightning inside your joints, a roaring of thunder inside your kidneys. All of your cells were crying and demanding attention. And perhaps they still have needs to communicate to you. Perhaps they are already preparing messages to deliver about what they need to smooth over and soothe the disruptions of this illness.

"Like all births everywhere, creation flowed like a giant faucet of lava; much the same way your lupus was birthed.

"Abreast of this noise and commotion was the loud voice of Taiowa, the god of creation, who disciplined the winds, modulating their tonalities and shaping their sounds. He funneled the noises of the wind into a powerful symphony of sounds. In the same way, a part of you may already be at work on healing your lupus. This part of you may have stepped forward quite early in the illness to prevent it from getting any worse than it did. This part of you may already be battling with the forces of lupus to sedate and shape them into more manageable forces for your benefit. I call this part of each of us the inner healer, but you might call it something else.

"Just as Taiowa brought forth the forces of creation, like a work horse to its labors, your inner healer may also be harnessing and taming the powers that made lupus.

"In creation, the currents of dark lava started to congeal. Taiowa needed a helper, a supervisor, to bring things to order. Perhaps so does your inner healer.

"Taiowa made a nephew, Sotuknang, to help him make the First World, to shape the water currents and to tame the forces he had unleashed. Your inner healer needs an immune system to calm the lupus and channel its energies toward healing. Perhaps you can think of your immune system as Sotuknang, nephew to your inner healer.

"Sotuknang was to be a companion to this world to come, but also a cocreator in his own right. Sotuknang used his Creator-given power to will into a being a force, an energy, to give help. He called her Woman Spirit, or Spider Woman, and together they shaped the bubbling hot, fuming mass called Earth and created the waters to cool it from the heat of creation. In your body this energy might be the chi, the life force, or the weblike energies of healing, the meridians. In the body, the chi weaves the energy into a healing pattern, just as Spider Woman wove the earth together. And maybe you have ways of cooling off your own inflammation. We need to wonder together about how to cool down the heat from the creation of your lupus.

"'Now,' said Taiowa. 'We have the Earth, and we have the waters to cool it. I have made the air, to coordinate the two, and formed this first world which is good, but no one is present to witness its marvels.' So Spider Woman and Sotuknang created twin brothers to look after the First World, to protect and inhabit it. That way no one would be alone and no one could fight about who was first. The Earth birthed them and sustained them. In the same way, the chief of your immune system created the diversity of cells to help you—leukocytes, lymphocytes, dendritic cells, natural killer cells, monocytes, and more. Perhaps your cytokines are like Spider Woman, changing the temperature from one that supports inflammation to one that puts out the fires. I'm wondering how you will do that, but I know that you will, know that the wise healers within your body can now come forth and blossom, without needing to fear those fires and the lupus.

"But who are your twins? What do they represent? Perhaps your yin and your yang, your inner male and female, the balancing of powers and forces that will make you well. Or perhaps something else. Only you will know.

"Sotuknang, Spider Woman, and the twins were created from the will of Taiowa to participate in the creation of mankind. They needed a song to actually bring about this creation, a song that the created people could not forget, a song to keep inside themselves, lest they lose the way, else they would not survive. Similarly, you need a song to sing to your immune cells—a song that reminds them of their ability to soothe themselves, to calm themselves.

"The younger of the twins wrote the song. Here is how the song begins. The other verses are locked inside you, inside each singing organ and dancing cell:

From the four corners of the universe:
From the East, for red is its color;
From the North, for white is its color;
From the West, for yellow is its color;
And from the South, for blue is its color;
  Come the spirits and the ancestors;
  Come the stones and the water;
  Come the animals and birds, the plants and the water;
  All to shape you, all to make you live.

"Perhaps, even as we speak, your inner healer is preparing a song that you can sing every day to soothe your immune system. Perhaps she'll begin to show you a ceremony that you and I can do together, or one that you will do alone every day, along with singing your song, to soothe your inflamed tissues, to cool down the fires of creation, and to make your inner world livable again.

"In our creation story, the counterclockwise motion of the sun brought forth the four colors of the races of humankind and each of its leaders and its destinies. On still nights, on summer nights when lightning flashes silently in the distance, on winter nights covered with soft snow, and in the spring and fall when the leaves of the trees whisper, you can hear the song of creation. Even though the people fought, as was prophesied, someday they will unite. Then they will remember that Taiowa is their spirit father, Sotuknang is their adoptive one, and that Spider Woman is the web that unites them all. And in the same way, the warring elements of your body can make peace with one another. The battles in your kidneys can stop, and all of your cells can sing the song of creation, of the health that you are about to create, of the wellness that is about to envelop you, of the good things that are about to come to you.

"As you sing your song, perhaps the intensity of the battle inside your body will abate somewhat, a little more each day in every way. And now I'd like you to tell me what you've seen. I'd like to know what these characters within you look like, what they sound like, how they behave. I'd like to know what your kidneys look like on the inside. I'd like to hear your creation story of your illness and learn who is inside to cool down the fires, rendering balance and harmony to your inner world."

☀

Through sacred forces barely understood, we collectively create the conditions of illness and wellness—new challenges and new solutions for our perpetual healing. When Kathryn was "awake," she told me what she had seen while I had been telling her the story. Spontaneous images came to her, accompanying corresponding parts of the story. She saw herself at the time just before onset of her lupus. She saw herself as a dutiful wife in a Christian community with an authoritarian husband. She was fulfilling her role by having babies as quickly as she could, caring for the house, cooking for her husband, doing every task that he required. While she thought she was happy, she saw volcanoes erupting inside her knees and ankles. She saw a war of anger and resentment occurring within her kidneys. She became aware of her smoldering bitterness and resentment. Lupus was her friend. Lupus gave her a break, allowed her to take a much-needed rest. Through lupus, she had found a way out of that marriage, since her husband had been unhappy with her inability to perform her wifely duties (of all kinds) because of her joint swelling, stiffness, pain, fevers, rashes, and general malaise. He had divorced her for a better model, and that's when her healing began.

Kathryn's old creation story had been rhyme and verse from the medical model. She had an autoimmune disease. It tended to afflict women of her age and characteristics. It appeared randomly to those genetically unfortunate enough to be susceptible. Cure was impossible, but it could be kept in check for a while by taking the right drugs.

Kathryn's new creation story was more compatible with healing. The conditions leading up to the lupus had already been resolved. She was divorced and had been exploring alternatives to her previous lifestyle for some time. Now she could see the lupus as a friend, rather than a tormentor. It seemed more possible now that it might leave her, since she had taken charge of the job it came to do.

Kathryn devised a song of appreciation to sing to her lupus. She began singing every day, participating in a daily personal ceremony that emerged from the images she had seen and the instructions she had been given during our journey through the creation of her illness. The creation story that I told and its accompanying images had inspired the production of her own creation story. The story provided a template for further guided imagery that we would do together.

Over several months, Kathryn proceeded as if her newly discovered creation story were true. She told her body that it did not need lupus anymore, that she had already taken care of the conditions that brought forth the illness. She gave lupus her appreciation and thanks, and at the same time invited it to leave, since its work was done. She assured it that she could continue what it had started. She cultivated more compassion for her younger self, who had gotten caught up in the world of subservience. She approached each of her children for dialogue about their experiences of their early lives, and explained herself to them. The quality of those relationships improved. Through our continued interaction, she began to construct a Christianity that did not require female servitude but was as friendly to men as it was to women. Slowly but surely, her lupus disappeared. Twenty years have passed, and it has not recurred, even as her life has become richer.

Here's another style of illness-creation story, coming from Dana, whom I met when I was consulting at a residential treatment center for eating disorders. She had come to the center with a diagnosis of anorexia after stints at several different hospitals. I didn't really get to know her until her treatment center sent her to one of my spiritual healing retreats, as a prelude to her discharge. That's when she began to teach me about anorexia. We began in the shadows of the Rincon Mountains as I led my small group of retreat attendees into the Saguaro National Monument, where we found a comfortable spot under the shade of a palo verde tree. Saguaros raised their arms around our humble beginnings as I initiated our opening ceremony. Rainbows and sunbeams shimmered at the base of the mountain as the heat of the day increased.

How did anorexia begin for Dana? I wondered. From what dreams had she and her illness sprung? Gradually I have abandoned the creation theories espoused by the various schools of psychology and have learned to ask the person with the problem how it arose. The conventional psychological story about our problems arising in early childhood no longer works for me, because it is not always confirmed by those who have the problems, who often find simpler, more parsimonious explanations when asked the right questions. I trust the person's "creation story" much more than those of the experts, since no two experts can agree anyway. I have come to see their theories as just stories, similar to those told by various cultures about the world's creation. All are interesting and valid, but perhaps none are meant to be taken too literally.

Dana was intentionally born to two upwardly striving lawyers in the suburbs of Philadelphia. She remembered a good childhood, a perpetual blur of fun and activities. I sensed a kind of distant relationship with her parents, who were too busy to give her much of their time, but she did not complain about this. She moved to California at the start of high school. There, with her parents' support, she threw herself fully into the world of horses and dressage, eventually winning a championship, but more importantly, learning how to buy, train, and sell horses for large profits, for the most part skipping the social world of high school.

Dana was proud of her accomplishments and her maturity, though I wondered if she had entered the adult horse world too soon, dating older men, getting engaged, conceiving, and miscarrying. Horse people told me that horses mature a young person quickly, and, true to form, Dana was typically the more responsible one in her relationships, often taking care of her older partner. She had traveled to Reno to almost marry an alcoholic dentist and had wisely declined at the last moment. The stories she told about her adventures in the horse world since age fourteen were amazing and entertaining, but also puzzling, in that they made me wonder where her parents were during this time. I guessed they were both at work, which her mother later confirmed, telling me that she and her husband were probably too absorbed in their work to create a real family life, thereby motivating Dana to find a sense of family with her horses and the people she met through horses.

How does anorexia arise? Where are the lava flows that congeal to form its shape, the unique forces that control its world, the rugged foothills and forested mountains of its homeland? Many young women are born to overachieving parents and are emotionally or spiritually neglected to some extent during childhood. Dana's parents certainly compensated with caretakers and activities for Dana, and only further conversations would tell us if some important ingredient for wellness was lacking. Many young women grow up quickly and skip the social world of high school for the world of adulthood without becoming anorexic.

The treatment center from which Dana had come had its own pet theories, insisting that Dana's anorexia was the result of sexual abuse in childhood. They saw the world through "sexual abuse glasses," interpreting fearful dreams as evidence of abuse, or dreams in which a man's face appears as confirmation that he was the perpetrator, confronting tearful parents who vehemently denied abusing their children. I had read in Dana's chart their report that she had been sexually abused from birth to age six. Shocked by that, I asked Dana, only to learn that there had been one questionable incident when she was six, when a female nanny *might* have inappropriately touched her. Nothing came of it, and eventually her parents decided that nothing had really happened. The treatment center therapists had latched onto this story, as it matched their theory of how anorexia develops and dictated a course of treatment, since they interpreted the fact that she did not report abuse as incontrovertible evidence of denial. Their notes about her protection of the perpetrators interpreted her "denial" as evidence that she was "still in her eating disorder," which was "speaking for her." They wrote that she refused to do the deep work, which consisted of using hypnosis, tapping therapy, and EMDR (eye-movement desensitization and reprocessing) to "get into" the memories of childhood abuse, thereby healing through "releasing" these memories.

I've never understood how recovering forgotten memory is supposed to heal people, or what it means to "release memory" that is recovered, though this is a popular theory. I think it's more common that we heal past pain through forgiveness, especially of ourselves, and by creating a future that gives the past pain meaning and purpose. Judith Hermann, in *Trauma and Recovery*, tells the amazing story of Freud's patient, Anna O., whose real name was Bernice Pappenheimer.[8] She fought Freud to acknowledge that she was really being sexually abused and that it was not her fantasy and was fired by him from therapy for continuing to assert the reality of her abuse. She had an emotional breakdown and then pulled her life together, going on to spend it establishing shelters for young women who were being sexually abused. She healed her past by creating a transformative future.

Conventional theories or stories about the causes of anorexia are varied. In the biological story, a trait-related disturbance of dopamine metabolism is thought to contribute to the vulnerability to develop anorexia, though it is not the sole cause.[9] Endocrine disturbances caused by starvation help explain why many people with anorexia cannot easily reverse the process. They enter a downward spiraling circle with malnutrition sustaining and perpetuating the desire for more weight loss and dieting. The hormones of starvation create a "high" that's difficult to abandon. The disordered thinking caused by lack of food and brain glucose interferes with the capacity for self-evaluation. The accompanying obsession, anxiety, distress, and altered appetite are exaggerated by neuropeptide alterations and further contribute to this downward spiral. The neuropeptide disturbances of anorexia are thought to be strongly entrenched, not easily corrected by improved nutrition or short-term weight normalization.*

Attempts to pinpoint a single cause for any disorder, including anorexia, are increasingly recognized as flawed. All conditions are multiply determined. Numerous different inciting events travel down pathways that become increasingly shared, until we reach a final common pathway leading to the illness. The more remote events are in the chain leading to sickness, the more idiosyncratic and unique they are to the person who suffers. This perspective certainly fits the nature of the "creation stories" that I unearth.

Another popular theory—that anorexia is caused by the media—also suffers from the single-cause limitation. In the words of one researcher, "Media effects are only part of a myriad of possible causes of anorexia nervosa, and yet are . . . central to current alarm regarding the way children learn (or don't learn) to cooperate with, and show concern for, other people."[10] The media is not so much the source of anorexia but the repository of the stories that maintain our culture. Anorexia is one aspect of that culture, existing alongside stories about

---

*The names of these molecules are probably not that important, but for those who wish to pursue this area of reading (which is fascinating), they consist of vasoactive intestinal peptide, cholecystokinin, corticotropin-releasing factor, neuropeptide Y, peptide YY, and beta-endorphin.

the importance of physical perfection and thinness, perhaps related to the fact that such a large number of American people are overweight today.

Another story about anorexia proposes that elevated tumor necrosis factor-alpha (an immune regulatory molecule or cytokine) is the primary cause, since it is known to contribute to the wasting-away seen among cancer patients. This story is based upon the findings that regulation of some of the same molecules is disturbed in both anorexia and cancer wasting.[11] Another story relates anorexia to reduced release of the neurotransmitter serotonin with enhanced release of norepinephrine.

Then there are psychological stories about the creation of anorexia. Personality factors have been proposed to contribute to anorexia, including obsessive and inhibited features intermixed with impulsivity, and a high prevalence of defined DSM-IV personality disorders.[12] Vulnerable individuals are thought to be temperamentally incapable of coping with the challenges of adolescence with anything other than repetitive, reward-seeking behavior. In a social environment that emphasizes thinness as a criterion for self-worth and success, anorexia becomes more likely. These stories are interesting, but they're constructed after the fact and don't predict in advance who will develop anorexia.

Another collection of creation stories attributes anorexia to psychological conflicts. These conflicts include attempts to be fashionably slender and avoid disturbing emotions. A variant of this story suggests that psychological and societal factors account for the decision to diet, and that hormonal and neurotransmitter disturbances lead dieting into anorexia. The problem with this story is that biological defects have not explained or predicted the biochemical findings in anorexia.[13] The problem with all of our creation myths for anorexia is that they are unable to tell us how to help an individual suffering with this problem. Despite all of our knowledge, we usually arrive at a different solution for each person, one in which the person herself must play a large role. Explaining anorexia is a bit like explaining Shiprock, the famous New Mexico landmark featured on postcards with its twin towers framed against a pink-purple sunset. Shiprock means something different to a geologist, a mountain climber, a Dineh (Navajo) shepherd, and a tourist, and none of these meanings are particularly better than the rest.

Nevertheless, inveterate storytellers that we are, we excel in constructing creation stories for anything, though their validity is hard to verify. Conditions like anorexia are more difficult to explain than the rapidly dropping water table in Arizona, a simple function of overuse by more inhabitants than the desert can sustain, with scant opportunity for replacement in an arid climate. We could just as easily construct a theory that relates anorexia to the drying up of our sacred springs.

The treatment center's story that sexual abuse causes anorexia is not supported by existing evidence, since in studies anorexics report the same amount of sexual abuse as nondiagnosed controls (so-called normal people) in completed studies. These studies identified risk factors, such as completely accepting the cultural ideal of being very thin, being isolated and having no social support, and having more negative emotions than positive ones.[14]

My favorite Shiprock story says that it is actually a primordial bird that delivered early people to safety and is now waiting in stone form to come to life again if the need arises. My favorite anorexia story is the one the person suffering tells about herself, coupled with the new ending we create that lets her climb onto that gigantic bird and fly to the land of wellness.

My task at the treatment center was to help Dana reduce her anxiety. Acupuncture contributed. Shiatsu, cranial osteopathy, Reiki, some storytelling, the occasional joke, and my calming presence seemed to work. Her anxiety progressively diminished. We worked in a treatment room that had once served as a stable for horses. Dana appreciated the irony of that. Sometimes we both imagined the sounds of horses and the smells of the barn.

We didn't talk much in our sessions; Dana seemed talked out when she came, so I didn't really know much about what else she was doing at the treatment center. What was clear was how bored Dana was with treatment, even as she gained weight and prepared to transition into their partial program, graduating from the required twelve-hour days. The treatment center owner asked me if I would accept Dana into one of my spiritual healing retreats as a completion to her self-help work, and, knowing how bored she was, and that her father had recently discovered spirituality, I agreed. It was during the retreat that I heard Dana's story about how her anorexia was created, as it unfolded during group discussion with other retreat members, after imagery exercises, ceremonies, and during our travels to visit Charles, a Cherokee healer living on the other side of Tucson. The four sacred mountain ranges of our valley surrounded the week's activities.

For years I have been leading intensive spiritual healing retreats in which we combine Native American philosophy and practice with what has appealed to me from Asian practices, as is described in *Coyote Medicine*[15] and *Coyote Healing*.[16] We aim to become more present-centered, change our mind state so that the past doesn't haunt us so much, and deepen our connection to the spiritual dimension and to the Divine. In keeping with Cherokee principles, we try to look at all aspects of our lives to find where disharmony and imbalance need to be corrected, learn to have more fun, and cultivate our faith in the possibility of healing and wellness. I use the tools of mindfulness meditation, art therapy, journaling, Native American ceremony and ritual, guided imagery, chi gong, and other approaches to energy healing.

On the first day of the retreat I told another version of the Hopi creation story I related earlier. My goal was to convey to participants that we wanted to learn about the creation of our own maladies and how we could re-create ourselves in a healthier manner. Then I told a second creation story that addressed the problems of each of the women attending the retreat. In addition to anorexia, other diseases represented included multiple myeloma and rheumatoid arthritis. We were sitting on a shaded porch, favored with the aromas of greasewood and lilac bushes.

✳

"The original people of Central California believed that the Earth was a woman with her feet to the North and her head to the South. She was the mother of everyone.

"The Sky was a man. He was the younger brother of the Earth, from whom all the people were born. At first all the people who were born traveled together, going from where they emerged to the end of the world and from there westward, Eagle leading the way. All of them spoke the same language. Then they began to separate, each of the different colors of people going different ways, until only the red people remained to follow the eagle where he flew, stopping when he stopped; sleeping all together in a big crowded pile when he slept. They followed him, single file, in a long row, all the way to a place called Nachivomisavo, north of the San Bernardino Needles, where they found that there was no room for them. They began to smell each other and found that they did not smell good, and some of them began to dislike others. This caused them to scatter to the different directions and lose their common language. They separated in the summer, when the valley was filled with heat waves and the land appeared submerged.

"This was when conflict was created from the original peace and harmony. The people began to fight and didn't like each other, which is what may have happened to parts of you, either within your body or within your family, or within other aspects of your lives, so that we might begin to wonder what parts of your life are fighting with each other, what parts of your insides are fighting with you, or what parts of your families are fighting with what other parts.

"Maybe some of you have felt betrayed, the way Wiyot, the people's chief, felt when they started fighting each other. Maybe you felt betrayed when parts of your body got agitated and started fighting each other. Maybe you felt betrayed when cancer appeared, or when your immune system began attacking your joints. Maybe when people around you started threatening to put you in the hospital for being too thin, you felt betrayed. Or maybe any number of other incidents in your lives, incidents that may return to your memory, have contributed to your own feelings of betrayal, or perhaps feelings of bitterness, resentment, anger, or other emotions that you might want to leave here in the desert, maybe putting them into our sweatlodge fire and letting them go back to the Creator.

"Wiyot separated the people when they started fighting, but death had not yet entered the world. People were quarrelling about whether or not they should have to die and leave the Earth, with some saying death was a good idea because there would eventually be too many people, while others argued that people should just change their shapes from time to time to prevent boredom. Wiyot grew weary of mediating that dispute. Perhaps each of you has felt that way from time to time about the conflict within your own bodies.

"Wiyot proposed a contest with three challenges, and each group picked a team. The first challenge would be a race around the world, with the winner being the first to get back to the starting line; the racers would have to bring something from each of the Four Directions to prove they had been there. Both sides cheated. The prodeath racers made a deal in advance with the mole nation to hide people in holes along the route, so that a fresh runner would appear at regular intervals and the exhausted runner could drop down into the hole and rest. The antideath racers found enchanted eagle feathers and tied them around their ankles to make them run faster. One team's runners popped up unexpectedly fresh. The other team's racers were faster than humanly possible.

"The Four Directions watched the race with disapproval of the cheating, grudgingly giving each of the racers a gift from their corner of the world. Each team's cheating surprisingly offset that of the other, and they arrived at the finish line at the same time for a tie. However, the keepers of the Four Directions had given the people further gifts. Those who ran with the moles were getting stiff in their joints. Those who ran with the eagle feathers were developing knots all over their body where the eagle feathers had touched them. The mole racers were becoming so stiff they couldn't move and the eagle racers were in so much pain that they couldn't sit still. Illness had just come to the people. There were not yet any medicines to give them comfort. The summer weather was still really hot.

"For the next challenge, Wiyot instructed each team to lasso an eagle and tame it sufficiently to fly one of them to the Land Where the Sun Sleeps at Night, bringing back a piece of the sun to prove they had been there. Again both teams cheated. The antideath racers sent an emissary to the East to bargain with the sun to give them a piece of its warmth and heat without having to go to where he sleeps at night. The prodeath racers starved themselves so they would be light enough to float up to where the wind could blow them to the Land Where the Sun Sleeps at Night.

"At the start of the race, the antideath people pretended to look for an eagle. One of them caught one and even pretended to tame it, but only to draw attention away from the people going East to pick up the piece of the sun that had been left behind a barren rock. They were sure they were going to win, but that small piece of the sun turned out to be so heavy and hot that they could barely carry it. They took turns, rested often, and coated it with skins and leaves to stop the burning.

"The prodeath group was having its own problems, since the people who had starved themselves to be incredibly light could care less about letting the wind carry them to the Land Where the Sun Sleeps at Night. They were content to do nothing, having lost all their cares and worries, including the race. Hard as their compatriots encouraged them, they could see no reason to go anywhere, until the one who had caught the eagle convinced that bird to take one of them with him to the Land Where the Sun Sleeps at Night and bring back a piece of that great warmth. The eagle brought back a warm, black rock still glowing from the sun's heat. Both groups surprised everyone by arriving at the finish line at the same time. Their cheating had angered the chief of the eagle nation and the sun. The thin people were banished from ever gaining weight or caring about anything. The eagle catchers began to ooze blood from every orifice. No matter how much they begged and bartered, those higher beings wouldn't take away their misery.

"Wiyot tried to stop the cheating with a final challenge: The two teams would fight each other hand to hand, without weapons, inside a ring they could not leave. Even so, both teams found ways to cheat. The prodeath team stuck sharp claws taken from wolverines and other beasts under their fingernails, while the anti-death team put sharp stones in their mouths to cut the others. When the fighting began and the dust rose, bodies were everywhere and no one could see what was happening. Without weapons, it would have been just a wrestling match. With their hidden weapons, they really hurt each other. When the dust cleared, all were lying on the ground, too injured to move. Bones were broken, deep gashes lay open, and blood flowed onto the ground. Because the people couldn't die, they just lay there and suffered.

"Wiyot realized that the people's cheating had allowed disease and injury to enter the world. The afflicted would suffer forever, since no one could die. Wiyot told the people how hideously cruel this was. The stiff joints were getting stiffer, and the painful bumps were hurting more. The bleeding people had lost so much blood they couldn't move. The thin, float-away people were so emaciated that their brains didn't work.

"The people were so angry that they killed Wiyot, bringing death into the world. They were angry at him for telling the truth.

He stood before them, telling them that he had to go away now that he was dead. He went to the sky, and after that they called him the moon. He's still up there in the sky today. Fog, thunder, and wind were the ones to carry him away after he was dead. They became wise doctors for the people.

"When Wiyot was dying, he refused to teach any of the people what he knew. He was angry about being killed. He told the meadowlark, 'After I depart, watch for me. I will come in the evening. Watch and tell all the people that death has not ended my existence. It just changed me.' In the early evening after Wiyot died, meadowlark chirped, 'Look, Wiyot is coming.' He rose large and round upon the horizon. Then the people knew that both sides were right. People would die to make room for more people, and in dying, they would change form. Though Wiyot had died and changed form to become the moon, he remained with them. They realized that even though they would die, they would not disappear but would change form and shape, remaining just as present as before. They called these beings who died and changed form the ancestors. They developed ways to talk with the ancestors and receive their guidance.

"While Wiyot was dying, Coyote wanted to eat him. Wiyot said, 'You see that Coyote wants to eat me. When I die, there will be a great fire in the East. Send Coyote to get that fire. As soon as he goes, make a fire and burn my body. If you do not do that, Coyote will eat me.' This is how the people learned to handle dead bodies once the essence of the person leaves and is changed."

✳

After hearing this story, Dana told us that she could remember consciously choosing to be anorexic. She described thinking she had reached the top of the horse world when she won her championship and that further victories would be meaningless. She was taking Ritalin for attention deficit disorder and was introduced by one of her boyfriends to crystal methamphetamine. She liked that it made her calm and peaceful, unlike her boyfriend, who became hyperactive and stimulated. She told us that crystal meth replaced relationships for her, which had been relatively unsatisfying anyway.

She couldn't think of another worthy challenge until anorexia crossed her radar. She had learned about eating disorders during a brief modeling stint. She once tried unsuccessfully to make herself vomit. Apparently bulimia wasn't her thing. Anorexia appealed more. She had always been thin, like her parents, and food wasn't all that important to her. The idea of achieving perfection in dieting was appealing. She felt she could do this. Each day she thought of one more food to eliminate until she weighed less than one hundred pounds. At some point, anorexia became its own reward. She wore her anorexia proudly, as evidence of her perfection in dieting. Demonstrating that degree of will power was rewarding. The thinner she became, the more proud she was, and the thinner she wanted to become. At some point, the hormones of starvation became prominent, making her care even less about food. Dana taught us about that point beyond which her thinking became impaired from starvation and the hormones of starvation.

Dana had a clear understanding of the strength and meaning anorexia gave her. She said, "No matter what anyone did to me, they couldn't make me eat. No matter how much money my parents spent on treatment, they couldn't fix me." She alone had the power to change, and only if she wanted to.

Dana's new creation story for anorexia contained possibilities for healing. The story of her illness now lent itself to finding solutions. We could look for other challenges that would demonstrate her superiority in the game of life. We could challenge the value of the self-control required by anorexia. We could search for different sources of strength and meaning that would also require a full measure of Dana's extraordinary will and self-control.

By telling appropriate stories, I convey my unshakeable conviction that the listener has the potential to grow and change. Each time a person remembers that story or relives part of it, the story seems to act upon her. The more it acts upon her, the more she starts to believe its implicit message, even if she can't verbalize that message. We eat the story through our ears and it gets digested and assimilated into our bodies, a process that is sometimes called internalization. I don't know how stories do this, but maybe they enter in the same way viruses or bacteria enter the body—through an open portal. Those portals can be cuts, mouths, or minds. The brain is also a sensory organ. Just as we hunger for food, we also crave a constant diet of stories. Just as the stirring sticks that Dineh women use to make cornmeal mush were given to them by the holy people as symbols and weapons against hunger, our stories were given to us as symbols and weapons to use for healing.

Each creation story is told in the words and images unique to its language and culture. We ensure the continued creation of our culture when we tell and retell its creation stories. By telling and retelling our own creation stories (my birth, how I decided to become a doctor, how I decided to integrate the Native and the European worlds), we ensure our continued existence. Change the story, and the person telling it will change. Stories create us as much as we create them. I write for an audience, imagining their reactions as I write, including the irate medical school dean shouting from the back of the room. I imagine the student enraptured with excitement at a new way of making sense of the world, or the bored academics waiting for the lecture to end. I write for all of them as my audience and my culture. I aim to change our context through stories that bring into relief the hidden assumptions that guided our creation, and in changing those assumptions, re-create ourselves. The new version may lack the illness contained in the old version.

Each of the other participants in the retreat had her own illness creation story that arose spontaneously in imagery in response to hearing the story of Wiyot. Nicki, for example, came for help with arthritis. Nicki had always had a tendency toward stiffness and pain in her joints, but yoga, exercise, and a good diet had kept these problems in check. Her original story was one of aging—the degeneration in her joints had just caught up with her.

Through her participation in the Hopi creation story trance exercise, a new possibility began to emerge. Nicki realized that her arthritis had not really become bad until she became very depressed five years earlier. Once depressed, she stopped exercising and had let her diet slip. She felt hopeless and worthless, as if she were a burden on her two daughters and her husband. The more she sat, the more depressed she became, and the stiffer her joints became. With stiffness came pain and with pain came depression, creating a vicious cycle that led her close to the brink of suicide. Further exploration of Nicki's creation story revealed the role of the medical profession in contaminating her story. Doctors cast her in the disabled role, both mentally and physically. They prescribed medications, one after the other, all of which gave her side effects and none of which provided any true relief. With each successive failure of treatment, her arthritis became worse, as did her depression. When alternative medicine also failed her, she was at the end of her rope. Through our group interaction, Nicki revised her story to include having been "pathologized" by the medical profession. She explored the origins of her depression and discovered that work was crucial in explaining her plight. She said she desperately needed a way to stop working. Arthritis offered her the opportunity to take disability. But then the loss of worth and meaning that came with not working worsened her depression. Through her dialogues with the spirit of her depression, generated through her new story of origins, Nicki came to understand that sitting on the Earth daily was restorative. She left the retreat with newly developed skills in meditation, prayer and ceremony, and yoga. She also left with the realization that she was fine, regardless of what her joints did.

Sitting on the beach and doing chair yoga gradually led to slow, walking meditation, and eventually to a daily walk through a labyrinth that she built on her property. Her yoga progressed and led her to a local community of spiritual seekers. After months of shared yoga, prayer, and healing circles, and with some trepidation, she joined them on a trip to the Yucatan to visit a local healer. She returned radiant and transformed. Her family could accept the story that don Jorge Gonzalez had healed her. She confided to me that she knew it was the journey that had mattered, not who was waiting at the other end. Going to Mexico, seeing herself as someone who was capable, who could travel, and who had found new meaning and purpose in work had allowed her to make a leap in her progress toward wellness. "Don Jorge just put some icing on my cake," she said.

Carolyn came to the retreat with a diagnosis of multiple myeloma. Carolyn's story of origin for her disease arose from the fact that her grandfather also had multiple myeloma. Her story was confirmed by her physicians, who told her that multiple myeloma frequently skipped a generation. Carolyn's story changed through her encounters with alternative stories during the retreat. In her expanded story, myeloma became more than just a genetic entity. It was also energetic and spiritual. She saw the myeloma as part of a larger spirit of darkness that had stalked her family for years. She remembered feeling haunted by depression for as long as she could remember.

Within her family, she had learned to expect the worst. This was the stance taken by her family, especially her highly intellectual, skeptical, doubting physician father. Carolyn had adopted his intellectual style and had spent her life scoffing at romance, altruism, spirituality, generosity, charity, grace, and other similarly suspicious concepts. Myeloma had changed her entire worldview. "It's a double-edged sword," she said. "It's brought me an awareness of all that I was missing, but at the same time, it threatens my life." Her evolving story recast the disease as benevolent, but still threatening. She didn't believe that anything short of a life-threatening illness could have led her to reconsider her stance on life and become open to spirituality. Carolyn's new story allowed her to begin a dialogue with the myeloma spirit that continues two years after the retreat, since she is still living with myeloma. It has neither regressed nor progressed, but she hopes to eventually convince it to leave.

As Dana's anorexia creation story evolved, she also taught us how ineffective are externally imposed creation stories. The treatment center's creation story for anorexia required sexual abuse and childhood trauma. Successful therapy was defined as recovering memories of that abuse and trauma. Once the memories were recovered, tapping therapy and eye movement desensitization and reprocessing (EMDR) were used to "clear away" these memories. Tapping therapies are a new form of "energy psychology" in which a person recounts a memory and the therapist taps on acupuncture points around the body with the idea that this tapping clears away the trauma. The patient is told to tap on these points herself whenever she feels bad. With EMDR, the person remembers the traumatic memory and the therapist moves a finger back and forth in front of her eyes for a period of time. This procedure is repeated until the memory is no longer disturbing. A positive cognition is introduced to compete with the negative thought connected with the traumatic memory. The procedure is continued until the patient feels the positive thought to be strongly true.

Dana entertained us at one meal with a spontaneous skit about trying to find a childhood trauma to please her therapist. Dana's therapist insisted that Dana was sexually abused, or she wouldn't have developed anorexia. Dana couldn't find any sexual abuse for her to focus on, which the therapist interpreted as denial. The best she could remember was when the class gerbil died while under her care during first grade. She had brought the animal home from school for the holidays and found it dead one morning. She told us she had been sad at the time, but her parents said it was an old animal and it was all for the best, so she let it go. Nevertheless, she laughingly told us about presenting the gerbil as her trauma. She imitated her therapist's maudlin response to the gerbil, making us roar with laughter. She enacted playing along to satisfy the therapist so that she would leave her alone and stop demanding incessant hypnosis, tapping therapy, and EMDR.

The retreat continued with meditation, journaling, ritual, prayer ceremonies, and yoga. On the third night of the retreat, we sat out all night for a vision quest. On the fourth day, we visited a Cherokee healer who had specific advice for everyone. On the fifth night, we did a sweatlodge, and did another on the seventh night. Dana returned to the treatment center on the morning of the eighth day.

If Dana's creation story involved the birth of anorexia as a way to feel self-esteem, to feel successful and powerful, to feel as though she were meeting a worthy challenge, these needs had to be honored. Anorexia solved the problem of how to meet these needs. Now she needed a new way to meet those needs, perhaps another passion to replace first horses, then anorexia. I posed these questions to Dana as the retreat ended:

1. What problem(s) did she think anorexia solved? From her responses throughout the retreat, I had identified the problem of boredom, the need for a worthy challenge, the need to feel effective in the world, the need to feel personal power and independence from the demands and influence of others, the need to demonstrate high levels of self-control and to not be controlled by others, the need to be really good, virtually perfect at something. Did she agree? What other problems or needs had anorexia solved?

2. What were other possible solutions? Anorexia only appeared after she stopped her passionate involvement with horses. What other solutions could she imagine to the problems she envisioned? Possible solutions had to include worthy challenges. Dana's desired solutions seem unavailable to average people. They required superior attributes and resources. Solutions for Dana had to demonstrate to any audience her superior attributes and ability to do the impossible.

3. What were Dana's unique strengths and skills that could help her solve any problem? I recognized her tremendous will power, self-discipline, and self-control. These were skills she had clearly demonstrated. She had shown her single-mindedness and perseverance in meeting a goal. In her skits about the treatment center and her comments made to other people in the retreat, she had demonstrated keen powers of observation and insight into the lives of others, even compassion, care, and concern. Certainly she had other unique strengths and passions that I had missed. What were they?

4. What were Dana's passions? Was she still passionate about horses? Had that passed? What could replace her passion for eliminating absolutely every milligram of fat from her diet? What could compete with her passion for being thin? What could compare with the incredible high of the hormones of starvation, a high that Hildegard of Bingen demonstrated as a spiritual pursuit years before in her own anorexia?

5. Who is Dana's audience? To whom is she demonstrating her self-control, self-determination, and will power? Who is watching? To whom does it matter how thin she is? When she feels proud of being the perfect dieter, who are the people she imagines noticing that pride?

Her answers to these questions can lead to her healing.

Everyone needs a story about his or her origins. When we are sick, we need a story to tell about how we got sick. Everybody who knows us also needs a story about how we got sick, if only to reassure themselves that they can't get what we have. If they fear catching our disease, they need a story about how much stronger they are than us, so that they can believe it is impossible for them to catch our illness. Doctors use their creation stories about illness to guide treatment. In modern medicine, the story about how the illness began contains the constraints for how the illness must be treated, and these constraints are usually biological.

Some "stories of origination" are more compatible with healing than others. The biomedical story usually strips any role in healing from the person who is sick, giving all the power to the medical treatment team and their drugs or surgeries. In modern medicine, the irrational is discounted in favor of the certain and the predictable. We want therapies that work the same way every time on every patient with a specific structural anomaly (disease). We are not comfortable with diseases like fibromyalgia, in which we cannot find structural, pathological changes in organs. Nor are we comfortable with therapies that claim to work through energetic or nonmechanical means (for example, energy healing, spiritual healing, homeopathy, or acupuncture). We are uncomfortable with the unique, the individual, the idiosyncratic, and the miraculous.

Telling creation stories—invoking the idea of creation—can inspire people to reconsider their stories of how their personal illnesses began. With appropriate trance techniques, spontaneous images arise that may be incorporated into a new story, a story that we hope is more compatible with healing than the original. We aim to maximize the likelihood that clues for healing will lie implicit within the newly constructed story. For instance, Dana's new story gave her possibilities for healing that a strictly biochemical story could not provide. It gave her ways to heal from within, without external treatment, which she appeared to disdain.

What we are discussing could be called narrative medicine, or a "storied" approach to health and disease. It insists that the answers lie within each and every person who has a problem. It suggests that the proper role of the external healer is to draw out those answers, the way I do when I tell creation stories to my clients and suggest to them that these stories give them clues for the creation of their own illness, and inspire them to produce their own story for how they got sick. In a sense, the story of the illness is the diagnosis. It is a history, and implicit within history are hidden resources, talents, and answers for progress. By studying history (stories), we discover alternate, untried solutions that may lead to new futures, and we compare and contrast problem-solving strategies that succeeded, even if only partially, with strategies that did not succeed. From this awareness of differences, wisdom proceeds.

2

Stealing Fire

Creation stories tell us how things began. Once we change our view of how things began, we can start to imagine alternatives to the path we are following, perhaps even find a route toward wellness. For some people, playing with the origins of their illness is enough impetus to embark on a healing journey. For others, creation is just the beginning. Stealing fire stories—stories that inspire a person to steal back their lost health—are the stories I most often use as metaphors for a person's active efforts to reclaim wellness.

Typically, creation leaves the people cold and unadorned. Within most cultures of North America (my area of study), once created, the people must steal fire to improve their lot—to keep them warm, cook their food, or give them light in the darkness. Fire is rarely just given to the people. It must be stolen or earned. Both Navajo and California Natives steal fire. For the Cherokee, it is given, but on top of a tall tree on an island far from the shore, with no obvious way to get it. The Creator doesn't want to make it too easy. We apparently need obstacles to force us to make an active effort on our own behalf.

Alistair Cunningham, a psychologist and immunologist at the University of Toronto, has shown that one of the most important factors in surviving metastatic cancer is the active effort made by the person with cancer.[1] My own research involving women who used an alternative therapy program to shrink uterine fibroids showed that the two most important factors for success were believing that the therapy would work and working actively and diligently in the program.[2] Creation stories inspire us to believe that we can get well. Fire stories encourage us to make the effort.

The quest for fire also opens the door for heroic journeys toward new worlds of growth and development. Stealing fire arises from our dissatisfaction with the current state of affairs—the stimulus to growth and change. Fire brings us light and warmth. The emerging sun in the East is the embodiment of fire as its golden ball rises over the mountains. Fire is the element we use to create.

Here's a stealing fire story that I told Ursula, a fifty-year-old woman who had suffered a lifetime under the shadows of the bipolar cloud. We were exploring the possibility that she might "steal back her mind" from the psychiatric establishment, rebelling against their characterization of her as defective, and thereby helping her find a new way to live. The conventional psychiatric story cast her as perpetually in need of medication, marred by poor judgment and insights. Its story is patronizing and stigmatizing. I was hoping for a radical rewrite. I wanted her to create a story in which she overthrows the bonds of "mental illness" and finds her voice, a way for her to transform, to become more than she ever dreamed she could be, to retain her creative, inspirational qualities while also finding a way to avoid hospitalization and the destructive byproducts of the manic life.

Ursula had been hospitalized on a regular basis for her manic episodes. We looked carefully at what had happened before each hospitalization. During our explorations for the origins of her problems, she came to grips with what occurred during the moments just before she gave in to mania. She saw herself facing the mirror, just as Alice faced the looking glass in Lewis Carroll's Wonderland, and making the decision to step through the looking glass into the other side. Each time she became manic, she remembered making that decision. But what she really wanted to tell me about were the fantastic things she saw on the other side.

"That doesn't interest me as much as the decision you make to cross into the mirror," I said. We discussed the ways that mania worked in her life to disrupt miserable situations and force change for the better, but at great cost. I wanted to tell Ursula a story to inspire her to steal back her mind, and the following fire story seemed well suited to my purposes. It is a traditional story of the Northern California coastal people and explains how fire, daylight, and warmth came to the people.

"Once upon a time, the world was dark and cold. The animals slept huddled together at night to keep each other warm. Food was cold and eaten raw. Lots of the animals grumbled and complained. Coyote grumbled and complained more than most. She wanted something better. Each night she dreamed about a place of light and warmth. She wanted to find it in the worst possible way, but when Coyote shared her dreams with other animals, they thought she was crazy. Nevertheless, she kept wandering further and further from her home.

"Doesn't this sound something like you, Ursula? You perceive that there's a far better place for yourself. You make valiant and courageous expeditions into foreign lands, hoping we will follow, though we never do. But you keep the dream alive. Always you've kept your dream alive, and that's important, isn't it? How many people would do that?

"Coyote wandered far and wide, looking for this dream place of warmth and light, even in the cold driving rain. She asked everyone she met if they knew of such a place. For a long time (nobody could measure time yet), no one did. Then one day, she met a squirrel who had been to this mythical place.

"Careful not to come low enough on the branch to invite Coyote's ability to leap, Squirrel described a place where people created wonderful smells.

"'What do they call that?' Coyote asked. She spun around and leaped once, just to test her limits.

"'They call it cooking,' said Squirrel, climbing higher into the tree. 'They take this bright, hot, yellow ball and they do something with it and the meat starts to sizzle and smell good. I know it's wonderful because I've snuck in to eat their leftovers. They were so delicious.' (All great Coyote journeys involve food.)

"'Where is this place?' Coyote asked. This time she leaped so high that she fell down and rubbed her posterior as if she had broken something.

"Squirrel pointed up the hill. 'Keep walking in that direction over several hills until the smell hits you. Then it will lighten up and you'll see better than ever.' Coyote felt so small compared with the branch where Squirrel now sat. When she was sure at last that Squirrel would not come down, Coyote bounded off in the direction Squirrel had pointed.

"Coyote ran and ran and ran until she was tired, and then she walked. She walked and walked and walked, until she was so exhausted that she lay down upon the cold ground and slept.

"You've run just as hard as Coyote, haven't you, Ursula? You've struggled through bone-tired exhaustion, trying to find the place of joy, this place of warmth and sunshine, the way Coyote does in the story. What will happen to Coyote? What will happen to you? Will you change your story? Will Coyote change hers? Let's see.

"When Coyote awoke, she was stiff and sore and cold. But something had changed; she noticed a glow up ahead. The closer she got to that glow, the more clearly she could see. Squirrel was right! An enticing odor wafted down the hillside, making Coyote drool. Her stomach growled, turning upside down.

"Coyote crept on her belly closer and closer toward the glow. She heard low murmurs of conversation in an unknown language. The smells were so powerful she could taste them. When she stepped over a ridge, her vision cleared. She was amazed by the vibrant colors. They simply didn't exist in the darkness the rest of the world lived in. Below her was a village, ordinary in structure but not in smell or color. Animals, the likes of which she had never seen, went about ordinary activities—getting water from the spring, grooming children, waking up, and the other routine tasks of daily living. Totally unfamiliar activity was taking place in the village center. Dancing colors flickered beneath what was clearly meat. Drops of something dripped from the meat, sizzling as they hit the dancing colors. Logs disappeared in the brightness. Coyote had never seen such a thing before and didn't know what to call it. She didn't know this was fire. A sudden alertness came over the village. Coyote ducked, hoping she had not been seen, but she quickly realized she wasn't the object of their attention. Who was?

"Maybe you've had similar experiences when you've walked

through the looking glass, Ursula, experiences of amazing and wondrous phenomena that you could never even have imagined. You can relate to Coyote's discovery of fire. You've made equally amazing discoveries in your travels, haven't you?

"The animals below stood reverently as two tribal members entered a small hut. Coyote held her breath as she waited for them to return. Even the flowers near her seemed to stand at attention. Several minutes later, the two emerged, carrying something between them, and then. . . . The pain in Coyote's eyes was too great to bear. She had never seen such intense light. Immediately a wave of heat hit her face that was both exhilarating and terrifying. Holding her paws over her eyes, she gradually adjusted so that she was able to squint long enough to recognize the source of the light. The world had never been so bright. Darkness was now just a memory.

"I imagine it may be this way for you, Ursula, when you've stepped through the mirror into overwhelming bursts of color and awareness.

"For several hunger-filled days, Coyote lay upon the rocks, spying on the village, basking in the bright colors. The yellow, glowing ball hung in a cauldron in the center of the village. Periodically, the villagers placed sticks upon this globe until they burst into dancing colors. They then placed these sticks into the pile that made the meat sizzle. On a regular basis, the same tribal members picked up the cauldron and carried it to the hut, disappearing inside. When they came out, all was dark. A guard stood at the entrance to the hut for the entire night.

"Coyote shivered all night, colder now that she had the memory of warmth. The night seemed darker, too. During the night, she snuck into the village to grab cooked food, just as Squirrel had done. She had never tasted anything so flavorful. At that moment, Coyote knew that she had to have that bright, yellow ball. She had to steal it. She wanted warmth and cooked food and light for herself and her tribe.

"Maybe you've felt like that, too, Ursula. Maybe you've wanted to steal something wonderful for yourself from your journeys through the mirror.

"The next day, once she was warm, Coyote crept back into the twilight around the glowing village and then ran down the hill toward her people. She had a plan for how to steal the ball, cauldron and all. But to make it work, she would need the help of Bear, Eagle, and Wolf. The memory of warmth and light lingered as a lamp in the darkness.

"When Coyote reached her own village, she excitedly called a tribal meeting. She told everyone about the warm, yellow ball. She struggled to describe the feeling of being warm—like being deep inside a pile of huddled, furry animals, but not being crushed. She told them about cooking and the amazing smells it produced. She described the succulent experience of eating cooked food. She described the delicious recognition of color so vibrant it made her mouth water. Everyone was interested. What magic was this! They, too, wanted the bright, yellow ball. Such a thing would greatly improve their lives, and didn't they deserve it? Why should the uphill tribe hoard such a wonderful gift, one that could have only come from the Maker?

"'Let's go steal it!' Coyote exclaimed, 'and make it ours. We deserve a turn. They should have to share something so wonderful.' Her mouth watered from the memories.

"Maybe you're going to make a journey similar to Coyote's, Ursula, when you go to steal back your mind. Coyote's task of stealing fire seems like stealing your mind back from the land of mania. Just as the up-country animals were hoarding the sun, maybe the psychiatric establishment has been hiding your mind from you, convincing you that it's okay to live in the cold darkness, grateful for the little forays behind the mirror that always end in your hospitalization. Maybe you're going to change all that.

"Eagle spoke. 'Though stealing is generally wrong, for the first time I agree with Coyote that anything so wonderful should be shared by all creatures. These animals are wrong to hoard this great, yellow ball.'

"Bear agreed. 'This is clearly an injustice. I will help.'

"Wolf agreed too, and the animals began whispering together in conspiratorial tones to plan their expedition. Now that she had seen light, Coyote could barely make out her friends in the dimness.

"Several days later they were tucked away in their respective positions. Eagle was furthest downhill in the place of the buff-colored sandstone, followed by Wolf, and then Bear, who was positioned closest to Coyote and the village. Since Coyote had the gift of shape-shifting and had originated the idea to steal fire, going into the village and grabbing the hot yellow ball was her problem. Coyote stealthily crept up to the edge of the bluff across from the village and looked down. The light filled her with delight. She hid quietly behind an outcrop of black, volcanic rock. The rock was cold, and she had a plan.

"As I tell the story, Ursula, perhaps you can imagine that you are Coyote, following the journey to liberate your own sanity for yourself. You might imagine how you will steal back your mind from the institutions that have hidden it from you. You could imagine yourself on your own path of liberation, wherever it will take you, with your own plan, just as Coyote and her friends had their plan. And just as Eagle, Wolf, and Bear acted for social justice with Coyote, you can get help to act for social justice in your world.

"That evening, when the women came out to gather firewood, they found Coyote lying on the path. She looked like the choicest piece of firewood. One of the women picked her up and put Coyote into her firewood bundle. Coyote didn't like the bouncing and jostling with the other sticks, some of which were sharp and pointed, but she kept the taste of cooked meat in her mouth as a goal that kept her still and quiet and willing to take the abuse of being carried in a firewood bundle.

"As dark abruptly returned to the land, the woman dumped her firewood bundle onto the woodpile, where Coyote rolled out with all the other sticks, forced to wait patiently until all was quiet. She had learned they kept a small fire going at night and planned to use it to full advantage. Turning back into Coyote, she grabbed several of those sticks that had been jostling her and ambled over to the fire. She lit the end of these sticks, just as she had seen the strange animals do. When the flames were dancing brightly from one end, she put a burning stick on top of each lodge in the village. She waited while the smoke grew thicker and thicker.

"Someone noticed and hollered an alarm in their strange language. The guards of the big yellow ball jumped into action and left it alone as they ran for water to throw onto the burning lodges. While they were gone, Coyote raced inside and grabbed the cauldron holding the yellow ball. She struggled with its heaviness, dragging it out of the village and down the hill. Lucky for her, she had a good head start by the time the guards finished putting out all the fires and noticed that the cauldron with the big yellow ball was gone. Coyote had almost reached Bear's hiding place when the guards sounded the alarm for the warriors to grab their spears. Coyote was struggling harder and harder to make it to Bear. Her trail was easy to follow, for sparks had flown out of the bucket and had lit bushes and grass on fire all the way down the hill. Spears were landing dangerously close to Coyote's tail as she handed the cauldron to Bear and dove into a hole in the ground.

"Ursula, maybe you'll have a similar adventure in your world as you steal back your mind. You'll grab it out of the clutches of those who have been keeping it and run down your own mountainside, just as Coyote ran down hers. Maybe other spirits will help you. However it happens, you'll carry your mind to safety.

"Bear was fresh and ran fast with her massive strength. The up-country animals couldn't catch her, even with their speed and agility. Bear moved so fast that their spears always fell short. Finally Bear was so tired that a spear landed right beside her. With one last spurt of energy she reached the place where Wolf was hiding. Wolf took the cauldron and made better time than Bear because the land was less steep. Bear ducked into a cave so the up-country animals wouldn't find her. They kept running after Wolf, following the trail of sparks and fires down the hillside. Just when they thought they would catch Wolf, she passed the bucket to Eagle, who lifted it high into the sky and laboriously flew home. The up-country animals let out a collective moan. They would never catch Eagle. The big yellow ball was lost. They dejectedly turned around and began the long trudge back up the hill to their homes.

"And in your journey, Ursula, when you finally liberate your mind from the forces that have been hoarding it, it will finally be yours. You'll be free.

"The animals cheered when Eagle landed. They loved the heat and the warmth. As Wolf, Bear, and then Coyote straggled into the village, they cheered even more. Coyote taught them about cooking. For the first time in her life, Coyote was the greatest hero in the land.

"Everyone loved the big yellow ball, but no gift is perfect. The animals eventually grew tired of always being warm and in daylight. They did not have the kinds of lodges that would contain the fire and make it dark outside. Their lodges caught fire immediately. The animals grumbled that Coyote had been wrong to steal the big yellow ball. What had once been a great boon was now a curse. The brightness was overwhelming.

"Maybe you will have a similar realization in your own journey. Once you have your mind, you may realize how painful some things have been. Not having your whole mind, having mania instead, might have kept you from seeing those things. Maybe now you will realize how self-destructive those manic episodes were. You might realize that they distracted you from the pain you now feel. So you need help, too, just as Coyote did.

"Now Coyote felt as bad as she had once felt good. The animals glared at her fiercely. Light was everywhere. She began to fear for her safety. She prayed to the Creator to take this curse off her head. As if in answer to her prayers, Bear had an inspiration.

"'Eagle,' said Bear. 'Do you remember those two holes in the sky?'

"'Sure,' said Eagle. 'One in the East and one in the West.' She stretched her massive wings.

"'What would happen if I threw this big yellow ball so hard that it went through the hole in the West, went all the way around the Earth, and came out the other side in the East?' She had chosen the west so the big yellow ball would fall harmlessly into the water if she missed and not burn up anything or anyone.

"'It's worth a try,' said Eagle. 'Nobody likes the way things are.' Bear carefully prepared, flexing her muscles and building up to her entire massive strength. She coated her paw with grease and grabbed the big, burning, yellow ball from the cauldron. She cocked her arm and threw the ball so hard that the entire Earth shook. It flew through the hole in the western sky and, after a while, came out the hole in the eastern sky. To everyone's amazement, it kept going, circling around from East to West. Now everyone was happy, because it was light and warm for half the day and dark and cold the other half, but never as dark or cold as it had been before.

"And that is how the sun came to go around in the sky and why it goes from East to West instead of the other way.

"Ursula, maybe you'll find a way to achieve balance and harmony in your world, too. Your mind will discover its own important contrasts in experience, like those between light and darkness, sadness and happiness, warmth and cold, day and night. You'll discover how to balance pain and joy, just as Bear learned how to make day and night."

❉

Ursula reclaimed her mind from mania but had to struggle with the uncomfortable emotions that mania had helped her avoid. At first she was overwhelmed with the sorrow of the many lives she had created and destroyed through mania. But eventually, she came to accept what had happened in her life and found a sense of peace in the present.

To help her, I suggested that she watch *The Wizard of Oz* every day for one month. She did and discovered that Dorothy had a choice at each moment of her journey. Ursula realized that she did too. She has been off all drugs and has stayed away from hospitals for three years at the time of this writing.

Here's another stealing fire song story, one that I told Chris to inspire her healing journey. Chris was an Olympic track medalist. She was training for the next summer games and had sustained a terrible injury to her hamstring. It had been pulled completely off the bone. A series of other, almost equally serious injuries had plagued her athletic career, preventing her thus far from reaching her dream of a gold medal.

The creation story of her illness unfolded. The theme was one of pleasing others to her own detriment, of not knowing when she should stop to prevent injury, instead letting coaches and trainers push her past her limits into the land of injury. This was a recurrent theme in her love life, her family life, and her friendships—that of pleasing others to her own detriment. We needed a story about stealing back the power she had given away to everyone else. She needed to reclaim the power to follow her inner wisdom for how to train, how to manage her relationships and family life, and how to relate to friends. I was inspired to tell her the story of how Fox stole fire from the Fireflies.

☀

"Long before there was fire, the animals and trees talked with each other. Fox was clever and tried to think of a way to warm up the world.

"One day, he visited the Geese, whose cry he wished to learn how to imitate. They promised to teach him, if he would fly with them, but maybe they were just being mean. They must have known something bad would come of this, since foxes aren't made to fly. They contrived a way to attach wings to Fox but cautioned him never to open his eyes while flying. They showed him the right way to stamp his feet and tuck his ears back to take off. Fox must have looked like easy prey to those Geese. When the Geese rose in flight, Fox flew along with them to practice their cry. Sometimes he fell on his head taking off and the Geese cackled. Then he'd try to vanish inside the flock. Nevertheless, the Geese watched Fox all the time with their slit eyes. Maybe they were planning to donate Fox to a ceremonial feast, and fly him there on his on power.

"Maybe you can relate to this, Chris. Maybe it sounds like former relationships with trainers who never seemed to have your higher good at heart, who urged you to do things your body just couldn't do without injuring itself. Or lovers who thought only of themselves and not your training needs. Or family members who wanted what you could give them, even when it cost you your dreams. So you can probably relate to wanting to learn something and paying too high a price in return. This is just what was happening to Fox.

"But the Geese didn't get a chance to play their ultimate trick on Fox. On one of his flying adventures, darkness fell when they were over the Firefly village. The glare from the flickering Fireflies caused Fox to forget a cardinal rule. He opened his eyes and looked down at the ground. The downward motion of his head cost him his balance, causing him to plummet down, since his head wasn't as small or hollow as the heads of the Geese. His wings collapsed and his fall was uncontrolled, causing him to crash within the walled area of the Firefly village, where a fire constantly burned in the center. Perhaps he would get the best of the bargain with the Geese after all.

"Maybe this is something like what happened to you, Chris. You've had a succession of injuries that have thwarted your plans, but you've never actually been in this place before. You've never had an injury so serious that it gave you the opportunity to transform your entire life. But that's what you have now, the opportunity to make a major shift. Thanks to your fall, your hamstring injury, like Fox's fall from the sky, you have an opportunity to steal something even more powerful. You can steal back your power, just as Fox can now steal fire.

"Two kind Fireflies came to see the fallen Fox, who gave each one a necklace of juniper berries. Fox decided to steal some of the Fireflies' fire as the solution to his troubles. He persuaded the two Fireflies to tell him how to get over the wall to the outside. They led him to a cedar tree, which they explained would bend down upon command and catapult him over the wall if he so desired. That was the only way out. That evening, all ate mutton to their hearts' content.

"Just as Fox will soon be doing, you could be imagining your own story, how you will steal back your power. First you will need an escape route. Perhaps you will train in secret. Perhaps you will tell everyone that you are going away so that they will let you train in secret. You can be like Seabiscuit, the legendary racehorse, training in secret and protection, overcoming a terrible injury that would have stopped any other racehorse for good. Seabiscuit was a promising young horse who sustained an injury from which no expert thought he would recover—that is, no one but a crusty old trainer who believed in the horse and brought him back to health. Once recovered, Seabiscuit proceeded to become one of the first horses to win the Triple Crown.

"After everyone went to sleep, Fox found the spring where the Fireflies got water. He mixed the colored earth he found there with water to make paint. He gave himself a coat of white. The next day Fox suggested to the Fireflies that they should have a festival where everyone could dance and he would make music. He could smell the pungent odor of the fire's ashes.

"They agreed that a dance would be fun and helped gather wood to build up a bigger fire. Secretly, Fox tied a piece of red cedar bark to his tail. Then he made the first drum ever constructed. He beat it vigorously with a stick for the dancing Fireflies. Gradually, he moved closer to the roaring fire, distracting the Fireflies with the rapid beat of his drum.

"Fox pretended to tire from the hard work of beating the drum. He gave it to some Fireflies who were aching to make music. Fox thrust his tail into the fire, lit the bark, and exclaimed, 'It's too warm for me here. I must find a cooler place.' His tail felt a lot heavier.

"Fox ran straight to the cedar tree, calling, 'Bend down, cedar tree, bend down!' His butt was getting hot.

"The cedar tree complied, and Fox caught hold. The tree carried him far over the wall. On and on he ran, Fireflies in pursuit. The pain of the growing heat brought tears to his eyes.

"Now maybe you can imagine the chaos that has reigned around you, Chris, like that dance of the Fireflies. Your trainers, your lover, your friends want to keep your fire for themselves. You are going to steal some and escape to your own refuge, to your own secret meadow where you can train in private, in seclusion and secrecy, where no one can bother you, and you don't have to do anything to please anyone else. You can just please yourself.

"Sparks flew from the burning bark tied to Fox's tail and ignited brush and wood on either side of his path. He appeared to be running through a gauntlet of flame. Fox finally tired and gave the burning bark to Hawk, who carried it to Brown Crane, who flew far southward, scattering sparks everywhere. This is how fire spread over the Earth. Flames flickered from every mountaintop and valley.

"Just like Fox, you need a team, Chris. You need your Hawk and your Brown Crane. You need a trainer who will listen to you about your limits. You need a business manager who can take care of everything during the next four months, so that all you have to do is train. You need to stop worrying about everything else. You need to exert your superhuman effort on your own behalf. That's what you can learn from Fox."

Chris did succeed. She learned to trust her instincts and found a new trainer. She asked her boyfriend to take a break from their relationship so that she could devote all her attention to training. She focused on her strengths and assets and knowing her limits, and she succeeded. She won her gold medal.

The metaphor of stealing fire is meant to instigate change in the conditions that produced an illness, to create an environment in which the illness withers away and disappears. Through the inspiration of stories (like those of Coyote and Fox and the testimonials we hear from people who have healed), we decipher the secret code of transformation.

The stories we tell ourselves about our illnesses and our lives contain hidden clues for how to change the outcomes of these conditions. One story that prevents creative change is the self-blame story. This story says, "It's my fault that I'm sick. I'm being punished for something I did. God is angry with me. I made myself sick, and now I'm a failure because I can't get well." Living the self-blame story is like getting lost in a snowstorm.

In a storied approach to illness, we recognize illness as a quest inspired by the confluence of larger forces, such as the forces that affected the characters in *The Lord of the Rings*. Frodo Baggins and his friends were caught in forces working for the destruction of Middle Earth that had been set loose thousands of years earlier. Individuals are reluctantly caught up in larger events that call them to be a hero. Frodo made that choice during the council of elves, humans, dwarves, and hobbits in *The Fellowship of the Ring*, when he ends their internal bickering by offering to take the ring to Mount Doom himself to destroy it. Frodo's only other choice was to give up and let the greed fomented by the ring destroy the collaborators.

The belief in self-blame is part of a story of passivity, of giving in to external events. The hero, on the other hand, prevails against obstacles in the quest for healing—the illness being one of them. Self-doubt is an inevitable part of any heroic journey, including a successful journey to steal fire. We eliminate blame through our storied understanding of how little actual control we have over our lives, and by knowing that much of who we are and how we react is created by other circumstances (families, cultures, larger forces at work in the world). Our genetic code, for example, is the result of all who have come before us.

Who should we blame for the genetic susceptibilities we may carry?

Our ancestors gave us our temperament and our ways of expressing emotions. They gave us physiological proclivities, which can work to our advantage or detriment. No one disputes the importance of molecular genetics for health and disease. Less recognized is "psychological genetics." Through the stories passed down within our families, we learn who we are. Family stories give us our sense of values, our sense of meaning and purpose. Psychological genetics determines the expression of molecular genetics.

Members of the Pima tribe of central Arizona are famous for their high incidence of diabetes. Is it surprising that the first case of Pima diabetes was reported in the 1930s? It had not been encountered before. As Phoenix and the Valley of the Sun expanded during the early part of the twentieth century, the traditional homeland of the Pima was needed for hotels, golf courses, government buildings, and housing developments. The Pima were pushed onto smaller and smaller parcels of land. Hunting and gathering became impossible, as the population of the valley expanded far beyond what wild game and native plants would tolerate. Plants brought from the East took over, upsetting the delicate balance of the desert. Laws prohibited the Pima from venturing outside their postage-stamp boundaries to hunt and gather. Their agricultural lands disappeared, as did some of the plants they tended. (Only in the last twenty years has the Tucson-based Native Seeds Project succeeded in recovering and reintroducing some of these seeds.) All that remained was for the people to accept government commodities and to sit in their small, boxlike houses. An active lifestyle had transformed within twenty years to a sedentary one, with a diet virtually guaranteed to produce diabetes.

Something similar occurred in North Dakota to the Hidatsu people who lived along the Missouri River. One day in the 1950s, the Army Corps of Engineers finished a dam and flooded the land around the river. They neglected to tell the local inhabitants. Some came home from trips or outings to find their homes underwater. A separate site away from the river had been arranged for these people, but it was not their home. Diabetes appeared for the first time.

What if displacement and disillusionment, hopelessness and despair create a psychological genetics that influences biological breakdown? What if the proper location for the study of health and disease is not within people (where we see the physiological effects of disharmony and imbalance), but rather in the environment—in the multiple connections an individual has with everything around him? What if a disturbance in the connection to the land leads to disease? It certainly disrupted the people's sense of groundedness, purpose, and meaning.

When the Pima became surrounded by Phoenix and when the lands of the Hidatsu were flooded, the people could no longer hunt and fish and gather nuts and berries and raise crops. Their relationship to the land that fed them was forever transformed. Hunting for wild game and foraging for food in downtown Phoenix generally lands you in jail or the mental hospital. What were the choices? Take the government food. Eat what they give you, which was lard, sugar, white flour—the cheapest stuff that no one wanted to buy. With loss of land came loss of activity. Hunting and gathering requires the expenditure of energy. Receiving an assistance check doesn't. Native people had no more reason to be active. What was the point? Sedentary life became the norm. When Native people understand this, they can rebel against diabetes in an entirely different way. It will become part of colonialism and therefore something to be opposed and rejected.

When Native peoples were moved to reservations, it was to the worst land, the land no one could cultivate, the land no one wanted. Growing food was not sufficiently easy to sustain a traditional diet. The government then provided cast-off food that no one else wanted. Probably 90 percent of people would contract diabetes if they became sedentary and ate government commodities. Diabetes is the result of the psychological genetics of the invading culture interacting with the molecular genetics of a conquered people. What worked well for life in the desert before Anglo-Europeans appeared is not naturally selected for a diet of lard, fry bread, and fast food. Psychological genetics shapes what we eat, while molecular genetics reacts to that diet in predictable ways.

Who do you blame for diabetes if you are Pima? Do you blame yourself? After all, your family raised you to eat a certain diet. You were trained to have specific tastes similar to the rest of your family, who probably had diabetes. You learned to nurture yourself with high-fat and high-sugar treats. Was this your parents' fault? Was it the fault of the conquering culture who gave its waste foodstuffs to Indians, who could no longer live traditionally or grow indigenous foods? Many of the reservation relocations were designed to kill the Indian. This was why the Lakota were given the Badlands of South Dakota. It was thought nothing could grow there and they would die. So whose fault is it when Indians get diabetes?

In treating the Native peoples as they did, the whites were simply acting within their psychological genetics, carrying out the logical extensions and actions of the beliefs they learned from their parents and other ancestors. They learned that Indians were animals, to be slaughtered like the buffalo. Who taught these beliefs? The Catholic church, for one. Christianity saw people of other religions as less than human. So can we blame Christianity for Native American diabetes?

From a storied approach to understanding illness, we see that the search for blame is absurd. No one really controls his or her own destiny or life. We are caught in the tides of multiple interacting cultures and stories. Cultural currents shape and determine us in the same way that rivers carve serpentine shapes in the land. We have precious little free will with which to make our own choices. A free choice is a rare event, celebrated in heaven with trumpet fanfare. A free choice is what heroes have to struggle to make. We are heroic when we make a choice within the time given us and in concert with the many forces moving upon the face of the world.

We live within our culture and through participation as cells in this body called the Earth. Within the Native American worldview, if one is sick, the entire community is sick. The sick person is expressing an illness for the larger group, as large a group as we can imagine. Sickness points to a disturbance within the family, community, village, and society. Responsibility diffuses into ever-larger spheres of influence. Remember the adage: Think globally, act locally. We work with whatever the illness presents, even as we remember that the individual's suffering is part of a "global" problem.

Genetic mutations are not accidents. All have design and destiny. Not all are compatible with present conditions. Not all insure survival in today's world. But nature must be this way. Nature must experiment to be ready to adapt to changing conditions. Some of these experiments are more successful than others.

We humans affect our genetics by how we live. We can live in harmony with genetics or in adversity. Patients who live in harmony tend to live longer, even if they have genetic diseases. The violinist Niccolo

Paganini (1782–1840) was rumored to have sold his soul to the devil in exchange for his prowess on the violin. Paganini had Marfan's syndrome, a connective tissue disease in which the joints and connective tissue become excessively flexible. Unfortunately, the connective tissue of the heart also becomes excessively flexible. The muscles become too lax, the heart cannot contract, and the person eventually dies of heart failure. But Paganini's fingers moved in ways that no other violinist's ever moved.

What happened to his life span? He lived twice as long as most people with Marfan's syndrome. Paganini had a tall, lanky body with underdeveloped muscles, unusually long extremities, and hypermobile joints. He played with a twisted stance but had a spectacular bowing technique and awesome mastery of the fingerboard. Since Bernard-Jean Antonin Marfan described the syndrome in 1896, musical historians have come to believe that this condition explained both Paganini's virtuosity and his unusual appearance. Most sufferers succumb to the condition in their late thirties. Did Paganini live to the age of fifty-eight because his disease was mild? He could bend his fingers backwards to touch his wrist without discomfort, which argues against a mild case. I believe he lived longer than most because he made the most of his affliction. His satisfaction and his adaptation to his condition may have created a friendship with the disease that allowed him to live longer than others with the same severity of disease. He faced the obstacle of his illness with courage and determination, and his body responded with increased longevity and health.

Blame becomes meaningless as we reflect upon our interrelatedness with all other beings (*mitakuye oyasin* in Lakota). Our health is a reflection of all our relationships. How can we blame anyone for illness when that illness is the natural outcome of relations with our genetic code, relations with the invisible beings, the *minne watu* (microorganisms), relations with our family, and relations with our culture? We are caught in a cultural sea like a fly on a spider's web. Rarely do we act by individual choice alone.

A common Native saying resembles a Zen koan: "Every thought is a prayer and every prayer is answered." What is remarkable is that every person thinks different and often conflicting thoughts. So how are mutually incompatible prayers negotiated? Stories and guided imagery practices become important in facilitating the process, which goes against our modern cultural training in North America and Europe. Understanding an illness means understanding the story within which the sick person is being created. What is crucial to understand is that even illnesses are relational. While the structural changes of organs occur within individuals, giving rise to the "treat the individual" assumptions of modern medicine, the conditions that nurture and maintain illnesses are relational and are manifested among people. These conditions arise out of harmony and imbalance in multiple relationships. Through hearing the story, we come to understand these factors.

Donna provides another example of the power of the stealing fire story. Donna had spent years visiting different doctors and trying different treatments for fibromyalgia and chronic fatigue syndrome. I suspected Donna could thrive if she empowered herself to find internal solutions for her problems. I hoped to inspire her to stop going from doctor to doctor and to rely on the spiritual strength that she had been cultivating throughout her illness. Though a devout Catholic before her illness, her beliefs had transformed during the illness into her own brand of Catholicism, a kind of feminist, populist theology. I believed that within this theology and the group of friends who worshiped with her was a previously untapped power to heal.

My rule of thumb is simple—if multiple treatments have failed to solve the problem, then we need to consider the context or stage upon which the problem operates. We must look at the problem as its own entity with its own relationships. How does it find meaning and purpose? How does its quest for meaning and purpose interact with Donna's? How has it helped her? How has it hurt her? How does it relate to the other people in her life, and how do its relationships with them change her relationships with them?

The story I was inspired to tell Donna was the Choctaw version of how fire came to the people.

❋

"The Choctaw say that when the people first came up out of the ground, they were encased in cocoons, their eyes closed, their limbs folded tightly to their bodies. This was true of all people— the bird people, the animal people, the insect people, and the human people. The Great Spirit took pity on them and sent down someone to unfold their limbs, dry them off, and open their eyes. But the opened eyes saw nothing, because the world was dark—no sun, no moon, not even stars. People moved around by touch. If they found something that didn't eat them first, they ate it raw, for they had no cook fires. Battles among creatures could be sharp and fierce.

"Perhaps this kind of blindness is familiar to you, Donna. You've been blind about how to help yourself. You've felt constrained and wrapped in a cocoon when it came to healing yourself, just like the new people coming forth upon the earth.

"The people poured forth from the darkness to meet in a great powwow, with the animal and bird people taking the lead and the human people hanging back. The animal and bird people decided that life was too cold and miserable. A solution must be found! Someone spoke from the dark, 'I have heard that the people in the East have fire.'

"This caused a stir of wonder: 'What could fire be?' There was a general discussion, and it was decided that if, as rumor had it, fire was warm and gave light, they should have it, too. A clamorous roar threatened to erupt into violence as those gathered argued over who should control fire.

"Another voice said, 'The people of the East are too greedy to share with us.' So it was decided that the bird and animal people should steal what they needed, even if force were required!

"Perhaps this feels familiar to you, too, Donna. Maybe it feels like someone else always has your fire. Maybe that's why you've been searching so hard to find the doctor who will fix you. You've been looking for that doctor in the East who has your fire. But maybe you can take it for yourself.

"But who should have the honor of stealing fire? Grandmother Spider volunteered, 'I can do it! Let me try!' Her voice could barely be heard over the clamor.

"At the same time, Opossum began to speak. 'I, Opossum, am a great chief of the animal people. I will go to the East and since I am a great hunter, I will take the fire and hide it in the bushy hair on my tail.' It was well known that Opossum had the furriest tail of all the animals, so he was selected to travel the underground trails to the East.

"When Opossum arrived in the East, he soon found the beautiful red fire, jealously guarded by its people. Opossum got closer and closer until he was able to pick up a small piece of burning wood. He stuck it in the hair of his tail, which promptly began to smoke, then flame. The stench was terrible. The people of the East said, 'Look, that Opossum has stolen our fire!' They took it and put it back where it came from and drove Opossum away. Poor Opossum! Every bit of hair had burned from his tail, and to this day, opossums have no hair at all on their tails.

"Donna, maybe these powerful animals will remind you of the powerful physicians who are always telling you what to do, but never seem to get it right.

"Once again, the powwow sought a volunteer. Grandmother Spider again said, 'Let me go! I can do it!' But this time, to her dismay, a bird was elected, Buzzard.

"Buzzard was very proud. 'I can succeed where Opossum has failed. I will fly to the East on my great wings, and hide the stolen fire in the beautiful long feathers on my head.' The birds and animals still did not understand the nature of fire. Buzzard flew to the East on his powerful wings, swooped past those defending the fire, picked up a small piece of burning ember, and hid it in his head feathers. Buzzard's head began to smoke and flame! The faster he flew, he brighter it burned.

"The people of the East said, 'Look! Buzzard has stolen the fire!' And they took it from him and put it back where it came from. Buzzard fell to the ground.

"Buzzard's head was now bare of feathers, red and blistered. To this day, buzzards have naked, red heads. Everyone felt sorry for Buzzard.

"Next the powwow sent Crow to look over the situation, for Crow was clever. Crow was pure white and had the sweetest singing voice of all the birds. But he took so long standing over the fire, trying to find the perfect piece to steal, that the smoke turned his white feathers black. When he tried to sing, he found the smoke had turned his beautiful voice into a harsh 'Caw! Caw!' He was reduced to sitting beside the rushing spring and breathing the cooling mist to relieve his suffering.

"The Council said, 'Opossum has failed. Buzzard and Crow

have failed. Who shall we send? If only we had a great sorceress!'

"Tiny Grandmother Spider shouted with all her might, 'LET ME TRY IT! PLEASE!' Though they thought Grandmother Spider had little chance of success, they agreed she should have her turn. Grandmother Spider looked the way she looks now, with a small torso suspended by two sets of legs that turn in opposite directions. She walked on all of her wonderful legs toward a stream, where she found clay. With those legs, she made a tiny clay container and a lid that fit perfectly, with a little notch for air in the corner of the lid. She put the container on her back, spun a web all the way to the East, and walked on tiptoe until she came to the fire. She was too small for the people from the East to notice. She took a tiny piece of fire, put it in the container, and covered it with the lid. She walked back on tiptoe along the web until she came to the people. Since they couldn't see any fire, they said, 'Grandmother Spider has failed.'

"'Oh no,' she said, 'I have the fire!' She lifted the pot from her back, and the lid from the pot, and the fire flamed up into its friend, the air.

"Maybe in your own life, Donna, you can find a way to be like Grandmother Spider, the one voted least likely to succeed. You can rely upon your own talents and resources to save the day. We could wonder what those resources might be. We might decide that your spirituality would qualify, that it provides you with a kind of vessel or container, just like Grandmother Spider's clay pot.

"All the bird and animal people began to discuss who would get this wonderful warmth. Bear said, 'I'll take it!' Then he burned his paws on it and decided fire was not for animals, for look what happened to Opossum!

"The birds wanted no part of it, as Buzzard and Crow were still nursing their wounds. The insects thought it was pretty, but they too stayed far away.

"A small voice said, 'We will take it, if Grandmother Spider will help us.' The timid human people, whom none of the animals or birds thought much of, were volunteering!

"So Grandmother Spider taught the human people how to feed the fire wood to keep it from dying, how to keep the fire safe in a circle of stones so it couldn't escape and hurt them or their homes. While she was at it, she taught the humans about pottery made of clay and fire, and about weaving and spinning, at which Grandmother Spider was an expert.

"Maybe this can be you, Donna, listening to your inner wisdom about how to heal yourself. This can be you, making a pact with the spiritual wisdom within, represented by Grandmother Spider. Maybe then you can be well.

"The Choctaw remember Grandmother Spider. They make a beautiful design to decorate their homes, a picture of Grandmother Spider, two sets of legs up, two down, with a fire symbol on her back. This is so their children never forget to honor Grandmother Spider."

The week after the story, Donna was inspired to write her own healing ceremony to be enacted by her spiritual community. We worked upon this for several weeks, and she invited twenty-seven friends to the ceremony. She was immediately disappointed, for she didn't have a miracle cure. The effect was more subtle than that but turned out to be farther reaching. Without even noticing, she stopped searching for external solutions. Before, she had run after every new theory and every new treatment. Now, though she still felt pain and fatigue, she was more calm and peaceful about it. Her group of friends committed to a monthly ceremony for healing. Donna stopped seeing me but also stopped seeing all of her other doctors. In her own small way, like Grandmother Spider, she held her fire within.

One year later, Donna came again to see me. Though she didn't think she was better, several of her friends had written to me about the dramatic shift she had undergone. They felt that she was much more substantially present as a friend now. They appreciated how much less anxious she was and how much less she talked about her pain and her illness. They suspected she was better, although Donna did not agree when asked. They offered that she was more involved in life than she had been in years—through her theological studies, her volunteer work, and her work for the local diocese. I could see this myself in Donna, in how differently she presented now than she had one year ago.

It's worth closing the chapter with a less-than-complete success, because that's sometimes the best we get, and it still makes a difference.

I suspected that Donna's community would continue to slowly transform her, but that perhaps she would never know the true extent to which she was being transformed.

Stories like Donna's remind us that we are engaged in a dialogic process. We cannot control the outcome of that process. This new storytelling or narrative medicine (inspired by indigenous healers) aims to expand beyond the role of fixing people. I no longer say that I treat people or do therapy. I say that I engage in dialogue. That dialogue can take many forms (ceremonial, imagistic, energetic, physical), but the beauty of dialogue is that all parties are involved in cocreating the content and moving the process along, albeit toward an uncertain result. I could "cop out" and say that Donna just didn't want to get well badly enough, but how could I ever know that? And wouldn't I just be expressing my arrogance or annoyance that the dialogue didn't produce the outcome that would put me in the best light? Therefore, I prefer to avoid blaming invisible entities like "want" or "will." I prefer to say that we can't control the direction or the outcome of the dialogue; we can only influence with our individual voices and wait and see—what I continue to do with Donna's community.

The famous song says, "I left my heart in San Francisco." Sometimes it does seem as if we are continually losing things—happiness, people, health, traits, money, and so on. Some Native American elders teach that any time we make a difficult decision, a part of us goes the opposite way, following the path of the choice we did not make. Stealing fire stories may inspire us to consider reclaiming these lost attributes. Can we go back and find some important trait or quality that has gone missing? The idea inspires a multitude of visualized journeys and imagery experiences, and stealing fire stories provide an excellent template for such guided experiences. While creation stories help us to consider the birth of an illness or a problem, stories about stealing fire spur us to think about how we can reclaim what seems to have been lost. Sometimes a rebellious spirit is needed to get well. Stealing fire nourishes that attitude as well.

We can allow fire to represent many things to us, including our soul's heat, our passions, and our connections to spiritual beings. We can think of stealing fire as embodying ourselves with spirit. Stealing fire can also represent reclaiming our power, but this empowerment can only occur within the context of the larger community within which we are operating. The empowerment of the individual requires the empowerment of the community. Without its support, the individual cannot get fire.

Above all, the idea behind the stealing fire story is that we must make the journey. It's not enough to know how something was created. We must make the effort that stealing fire implies. We have to labor in the mines, cross Middle Earth, sneak into the camp of the Fireflies, and fight our way out. In short, to harness the healing power of a stealing fire story, we have to do the work.

The Sufi mystic Rumi said,

"[K]nowing depends on the time spent looking!"[3]

3

Stories of Transformation

A miracle of stories is their ability to convey knowledge that we don't know we need in a manner we can easily incorporate, without ever knowing what we are learning or even that we are learning. Stories teach us how to do things that are otherwise impossible to learn. Nonstoried information resembles a list of seemingly disconnected facts, while storied information presents a coherent package that's easy to remember.

Creation stories inspire us to consider our own origins and the origins of our illnesses and other problems. Stealing fire stories provide a metaphor for becoming powerful and taking back what is rightfully ours. Other themes of transformation exist, however, and that is the topic of this chapter. Ultimately, the best way to help people learn how to change is through stories of transformation. By hearing stories about other people's transformations, we learn how to engineer our own.

Stories are so much richer than lists of facts. Culturally embedded stories carry implicit information that cannot be memorized. We learn principles for how to do things for which a rigid set of rules cannot be articulated. As we listen to other people's stories or testimonials, we perform an amazing process in which we imagine emulating or imitating these other people, but with changes that allow their stories to apply to our own lives. This process is implicit in human language itself, in both the telling and the hearing of stories, and is inherent in our uniquely human capacity to emulate and imitate, to use words to signify things we cannot see, and to use grammar to talk about things that have happened in the past or that we imagine will someday happen. Stories inspire us to believe that we can transform, which is half the battle.

No one has complete power over his or her life. We are all positioned in relationships and kinship networks. Transformation necessarily changes those around us, or they will force us back into our old ways. We tell stories to influence the others in our lives to allow us to change and to change with us. In the Chinese legend of Mulan, the captain of the soldiers, the emperor, and Mulan's parents all change profoundly as a result of her transformation from recalcitrant teenager to courageous savior of China. Dorothy's journey in *The Wizard of Oz* allowed the Scarecrow to believe in his intelligence, the Lion to believe in his courage, the Tin Man to believe in the power of his heart, and Dorothy to believe in her ability to meet a challenge. In addition to those changes, she liberated whole swaths of Oz. Change is never isolated.

Some of the world's best stories are about transformation. We revel in heroes and the changes that come over them as they pursue their destiny. We compare ourselves to these heroes, and through that comparison decide how to make ourselves more like the hero we admire. We emulate the hero, or at least our perception of the hero that comes through the story we hear about his life.

The hero is usually the main character of the story, just as we are the main character of our lives. Heroic stories are about change. The hero is presented with a challenge. Sometimes she refuses it, only to be confronted later by its necessity. Heroes often sense the difficulty of what is presented and would rather stay home in the "comfort of the hobbit." Nevertheless, the call to adventure persists, and finally the hero accepts. Then a struggle begins, sometimes with the outer world, sometimes entirely within the self, though usually with both. During this struggle the hero confronts obstacles, tries and fails several times, retreats to a place of reevaluation and learning (often called "the dark night of the soul"), develops resources and helpers, and finally takes the leap of faith to try again, this time emerging victorious. Then she must teach what she has learned. This is the healing journey. People go through these steps to find wellness.

The ancient Chinese legend of Mulan provides a powerful example of transformation to empowerment. Mulan is faced with a problem. Each family is called upon by the emperor to provide one male to the army. Her family has only one male, her father. Despite her father's advanced age and injury in the last war, the law demands that he go again. If that weren't enough, his honor, pride, and duty would never allow him to refuse. Mulan considers going in his place. She struggles with this decision, for a woman to impersonate a man in China is punishable by death. Impulsively and bravely, she grabs her father's armor and rides away to report for duty. Then she encounters a series of obstacles. She must learn to act like a man; she must learn to fight, even to climb a tall pole with her bare hands. She finds resources and allies—a strength she didn't know she had and even pride in herself.

Difficult as it is, Mulan figures out how to be "one of the guys." She rides into battle as bravely as the rest. The enemy appears. The Mongolian hordes are massed on the ramparts of the snow-covered land, ready to ride down upon her small band of soldiers. The tension mounts as the order is given to charge. Terror reigns as the Mongols ride down toward the badly outnumbered soldiers. Mulan sees one chance. She grabs a rocket and fires it at a glacier, which breaks off and thunders over the enemy as an avalanche ensues. Mulan is wounded by an arrow to the shoulder as the Mongol chief's horse goes down in the advancing wall of snow. The soldiers cheer Mulan for saving the day, but then, in tending to her wound, they discover that she is a girl. The political advisor wants her immediately executed, which the captain cannot do, because she has saved his life as well as the lives of the men. The most his conscience can bear is to banish her.

Imagine the sadness and despair of the soldiers picking up their gear to begin the march back to Beijing, completely ignoring Mulan, who is left shivering at the side of the mountain pass. Instantly she has transformed from hero to villain, despised by the entire army despite having saved their lives. She is shamefacedly making her way home when she discovers that the Mongols are not all dead. She sees their leader and several survivors making their way to the capitol, clearly bent upon killing the emperor. Mulan resolves to follow them, regardless of the personal risks or how scorned she has been. Duty demands that she warn the emperor.

When she arrives in Beijing, no one will listen to her. The captain and the soldiers ignore her as if she doesn't exist. Frustrated, she runs ahead to the palace, where the Mongolian leader appears on the balcony with the emperor held at swordpoint. Now they believe her. But what can they do now?

Again, Mulan comes to the rescue. Quickly and ironically, she thinks to dress the soldiers as concubines, presenting them coquettishly to the guards at the gate, who let them pass. Once inside, they race to where the emperor is captive, and Mulan confronts the Mongol chief. Through sheer force of wit and not a small amount of luck, she saves the life of the emperor and triumphs over the Mongol chief. The crowds watching below cheer and celebrate, and all of China is indebted to Mulan.

Mulan provides the essence of the hero's journey. She takes up the challenge, struggles to meet it, and triumphs, changing herself and China in the process. This is transformation at its finest, and this is what we want to achieve for ourselves, our relatives, and our clients. Mulan's story informs us about one way to do this. What is so remarkable is how trite the insights of the story would be without the story. A string of "facts" distilled from this story would be unhelpful and definitely not inspirational or transformational. The flow of the story teaches and inspires so much more than its apparent facts or conclusions. It invites us to begin an internal scan to discover how we are similar to or different from Mulan. We automatically incorporate Mulan's example into our resource list of possible ways to solve problems, even though she lived long ago.

Typically, people are reluctant to transform. Were we not, chaos would rule our lives. Change must be important to be worthwhile, for the consequences can be severe. In *The Wizard of Oz,* Dorothy doesn't ask to become the sworn enemy of the Wicked Witch of the West. A tornado brings her from Kansas to Oz, landing her on top of the witch's sister and forcing her to join the battle. The only advice comes from the Munchkins, who tell her to follow the yellow brick road. She reaches the Wizard of Oz, who has little to offer except to tell her and her friends to look within to find their hidden talents and resources, and to take action to defeat the witch. Armed with the understanding that they will find what they need, they continue to the witch's castle, where the final confrontation occurs.

Faced with the sudden onset of an illness, so many of us feel like Dorothy, standing by the house that now seems so out of place, that landed where it didn't belong, a dead witch's feet sticking out from underneath. We feel completely clueless about what to do next.

The beauty of *The Wizard of Oz* is the timeless message that whatever you need is already inside of you, that you already have the qualities for which you search and the answers that you need. The journey only makes this apparent. This is also the essence of the wisdom of indigenous healers from around the world. One Cree healer from northern Saskatchewan told me, "Knowledge is unimportant. We can give that to anyone. What matters is wisdom, which must be earned." He said this in response to a critic who claimed that my lecture on Native American healing was giving away knowledge that should be held in secret by pure-blooded Indians. Another healer at the same meeting told me that the only secret of Native American healing is "You are the healer." How you become your own healer can be explained only through story. No pithy eight-step algorithms exist or can ever exist.

What inspired Dorothy to throw water on the witch who was taunting the scarecrow with the threat of fire? Where did she get the inspiration and the motivation to act? The answer cannot be articulated. It can be absorbed only by listening to the story.

Many other stories can initiate change, including the Russian story of the Firebird and its Native American equivalents. Through such stories, we begin the shared exploration of the talents and abilities that have become obscured by the person's illness. The person begins to identify with these stories of overcoming adversity.

Here is a story that inspired a young Native American woman to leave an abusive relationship. Police and social workers had begged Jackie to leave her boyfriend, to press charges, to enter a shelter—but to no avail. Jackie kept appearing at the emergency room with unexplained bruises and injuries that she wouldn't discuss. The ER called me for a consult to determine whether she was sufficiently sane to release. Jackie and I made a good connection, since she was Cree and I had once visited her hometown of La Ronge, in Saskatchewan. We even knew a few of the same people. Based upon that preliminary trust, she agreed to stay in the hospital for several days on the medical floor.

On the second day of her stay, I told Jackie a story about transformation, a North American version of the culturally ubiquitous "bird on fire but cannot die" story. I use this genre of story to inspire people who are broken and traumatized to undertake a healing journey in which they become heroes of their own adventures. It is violent in parts, but so are their lives. The story is about escaping violence and breaking through abuse into transformation.

☀

"Our story begins in a village not unlike other villages on Earth at that time, and not unlike small villages in your home of Saskatchewan as they existed hundreds of years ago, built along the Churchill River as it flows to Hudson Bay. Our hero is the only girl, as you were in your family; the middle child in a large family. Her family had passed through three mothers, two of whom had mysteriously died. Our hero's mother was the most recent death, after which her father took another wife from a nearby village.

"Our hero is called Spotted Fawn, or Fawn for short. Her name conveyed the state of nature around her when she was born— innocent and safe. Convention gave children names in accordance with what was in the environment at the time they were born. The Deer nation was well represented during that gentle spring.

"Spotted Fawn had sadly been alone since age seven, when her mother died, just as your mother died when you were still rather young. Spotted Fawn's new mother was pregnant. Fawn's brothers were rough and mean-spirited, forever teasing and tormenting her. Her father was the meanest of all, spending his time scheming to conquer neighboring villages in his quest to become the most powerful chief ever known. He encouraged his sons to be cruel and to fight among themselves, lest any of them decided to form a coalition to do away with him—which is what he had done to his own father.

"Maybe this reminds you of your own childhood, Jackie. You told me that your father was alcoholic and could never be trusted. Sometimes he was nice, but he could also be violent and abusive, especially after your mother died. There was no one to really take care of you then. Maybe you can identify with Fawn. Maybe she will remind you of your past and of other situations in which you have found yourself trapped.

"Our story opens with Fawn feeling humiliated and uncomfortable as she sat at the edge of her father's dwelling place. His name was Makes Others' Blood Run, or Blood for short. She had come inside to eat and to catch the gossip of the day about what her brothers were doing so she could avoid them. They treated her the way they were treated, despite her being the only girl, becoming increasingly violent with her, even breaking her arm last summer, which the village healer had set remarkably well.

"That morning her father was in a reasonable mood, so she could relax and eat. Her brothers barged in and out, missing her presence in the shadows of the lodge. They were planning a hunt, mercifully unaware of her as they boasted and teased.

"Fawn had been partially adopted by the village herbalist and midwife. The village healer also looked after her. That evening, she wanted to go into the sweatlodge with the healer to ask counsel from her spirit mother. She was tired of the constant battling and wanted to leave her father's village before he married her to some cruel neighboring chief in exchange for a pledge of loyalty and some trinkets. Escape was no small feat. Anyone who fled from her father was hunted down and killed as an example that everyone and everything belonged to him.

"Fawn left the lodge and quietly walked down the path to the healer's dwelling. Her father had placed him well beyond the confines of the village so that his lodge was protected only by his own magic. The healer preferred his isolation and had built a sweat lodge nearby, where hot springs ran.

"She crept along the path, well out of sight, until she saw the healer's lodge. She ran furtively but urgently from the shadows and slipped beyond the door covering. 'Uncle,' she said. 'I came for a sweat bath. I need to talk to my mother.' Soaring Gull quietly nodded and bade her sit upon furs covering the floor of the lodge. He sang and offered tobacco to the spirits.

"Gull made his way to the door opening, glancing in all directions to be sure none of her brothers could be seen, and then motioned for her to follow him quickly. They ran across the clearing to the sweatlodge, where he held open the door flap for her to go inside. He had already heated the stones. Using long antlers, he carried them from the fire to the pit in the center of the lodge that was waiting to receive them. Fawn threw sage on each stone as it toppled into its place. When all had been brought, he set a container of water inside, slid under the door covering, and rearranged the hides to achieve total darkness. He threw water onto the hot stones, letting the steam rise in torrents, and the lodge became very hot. His songs and the shaking of his rattle filled the quiet of the forest. When he stopped singing, he opened the doorway to vent some heat.

"When Fawn was ready, he closed the opening and threw more water on the stones. Heat rose again as he sang. Upon finishing, he invited Fawn to pray. She prayed to the Creator and to the spirit of her mother for help in getting away from her father. She prayed for kindness, and befitting her nature, also prayed for her father and her brothers. Maybe you have made similar prayers.

"During the third round, the spirit of her mother came, telling her to watch for a sign, a flaming bird to show the way. There would be challenges, but none she couldn't meet. Perhaps your mother would say the same.

"Unfortunately, Fawn ran into her brothers on the way home, and they beat her unconscious. Gull found her lying beside the trail as he made his way back to the main village. Hazy clouds partially covered the face of the moon. Gull carried Fawn to the midwife's dwelling, where they examined her wounds. They carefully bandaged her and put her to bed. 'What are we going to do?' Gull asked, once they had doctored Fawn. 'If her brothers continue this abuse, they will kill her.'

"'I don't know,' replied Rising River, the midwife, 'but we will prevail. We must persist.'

"Time passed and Fawn mended. The healer and the herbalist prepared potions to speed things along. They assisted Fawn in exercising her limbs and mending her wounds, just as healers here in the hospital and elsewhere have helped you mend your broken parts and soothe your bruises, aches, and pains. 'She can't take much more of this,' they unanimously concluded. The wind howled outside.

"Perhaps you can relate to Fawn's predicament. Maybe you've been abused the way she was. Maybe you've been beaten or had some of your bones broken. Maybe you've been in terrible danger, or are even now. Maybe you sit at the same moment in time of your life, at the same pinnacle where two roads converge, one toward death, one toward a different life of safety and comfort.

"When Fawn did heal sufficiently to venture out of River's lodge, her brothers barely acknowledged her beyond a few snickers. Her father appeared to care less, his love having withered up and died on the vine long ago. No one remarked upon her absence, inspiring her to think escape was possible. She carefully snuck from place to place, surrounding herself with other people whenever possible. When her brothers noticed her, it was with long leers.

"A month passed before they caught her again. This time they dragged her down to the burial ground, a place so sacred that no one went there. The two oldest brothers stood guard while her middle brothers beat her senseless and tied her to a burial platform, putting her next to an unnamed ancestor's bones. Who would have thought to look for her there? Luck or the spirits were on her side, because that same day, the healer was performing a ceremony in the graveyard for a departed relative. He heard moans from deep inside the burial ground and had the courage to search, as few would have done. Far from where anyone but a healer would have dared to venture, he found her and untied her from the burial platform. Judging her to be alive, he stashed her in a small cave until evening, when he and the midwife carried her back to River's lodge.

"That sounds similar to what happened to you this time, Jackie. Like Fawn, you were almost unconscious when you arrived here; at least you were pretty loopy.

"'We've got to do something to save her life,' Gull declared.

"'I have an idea,' River exclaimed.

"'What?'

"'We'll teach her to be a fool!'

"'What!'

"'That's right. Even these cutthroats would leave a fool alone. We'll tell her father that the brothers went too far and addled her brain. We'll tell them she's no longer all there. We'll teach her how to play the part, and she'll be safe until we can get her out of here.' They finished resolving the details of the plot. The mountaintops were still mottled with snow.

"As Fawn returned to awareness and strength, River and Gull gradually outlined their idea. Though Fawn initially resented it, she slowly warmed to the idea. Hours were spent teaching her how to talk like a fool, walk like a fool, and behave as though addled. Finally, the day came for her debut. River walked her into the chief's lodge, to show him what the brothers had done to his only daughter. Fawn was so nervous she couldn't have talked if she'd wanted to. Fawn's father surprised her with genuine regret. 'Those assholes,' he exclaimed. 'Now I'll never be able to marry her off. They just cost me one good village.'

"To everyone's relief, the brothers left Fawn alone. She soon discovered the joys of being a fool. People ignored her. She could sit beside the cooking fires and hear the most interesting gossip. No one held his tongue before her, since no one credited her with the gift of understanding. Her special place became the side of the cooking fires, where she played with the dogs and fed them, and otherwise enjoyed the warmth, food, and gossip. She learned more about her brothers' plots against her father than she could have ever imagined.

"One day, as she was scratching behind a black-and-white dog's ear, she heard an amazing tale. She was inside her father's dwelling place, being ignored as usual. Her father was ranting and raving at her age-closest brother for being incompetent as a guard. His job had been to guard her father's orchards and berry bushes. The fruits of these favored plants were for her father's consumption only. Fruit and berries had disappeared overnight, and her brother had been found asleep on the ground. She was intrigued at his claims that spirits were to blame for his failure. None other but a spirit or a sorcerer could have put him to sleep! The next brother up the age ladder volunteered to take guard duty from this second fool in the family.

"More fruit disappeared the next night and this brother was also discovered asleep on the job. Her father beat him silly while he cried for mercy, claiming he had been bewitched. Fawn's curiosity grew as yet another brother was found asleep the next morning. She vowed to sneak into the berry patch that evening to see for herself what power was at work. She stole a sharp knife from the kitchen to keep herself awake. If she started falling asleep, she planned to poke herself with the point of the blade. That night, while her two oldest brothers boasted and bragged at their guard post, she snuck around the pond behind them and climbed to the top of one of the surrounding trees. She settled herself comfortably in the branches and waited for spirits to appear. Each time she started to doze off, she prodded herself with the point of the knife.

"In the darkest hours of the night, she saw a fiery light coming toward her. The desire for sleep overwhelmed her. Her brothers had fallen asleep below. She had to poke herself with the knife so hard that it drew blood, but she stayed awake. An amazing bird was flying straight toward her, his wings blazing with fire. His face was that of a handsome young man, and he had arms and hands instead of talons. He gazed upon her as he ate fruit beside the very tree upon which she sat. After a long stare, he flew to other trees and bushes, sampling whatever he desired.

"His fiery wings drew spirals as he flew away. Fawn climbed down and slipped away, hours before her sleeping brothers would be found. The face of the flaming bird was etched upon her mind. This was the sign foretold by her mother in the sweatlodge. She wanted to see this man-bird again. Who was he? How could he be so handsome and compelling? What kind of spell was this?

"The next morning she sat at her usual spot, petting the dogs, while her father berated and humiliated her brothers. To her surprise, one of the dogs spoke. 'He's in a particularly foul mood today, isn't he,' said the black-and-white.

"A homely brown mutt answered, 'And all because of some berries. I can't see what he sees in that stuff anyway.'

"She listened in amazement while the dogs conversed before her. Finally she had enough. 'Don't you guys ever talk about anything except food?' They looked at her strangely.

"'Are you talking to us?' said the yellow dog.

"'Who else is chattering away in front of me?' she asked.

"'It's not common for people to hear us,' said the black-and-white. 'You must have seen the Firebird who's eating all the chief's berries.'

"'How do you know about him!' she exclaimed.

"'All the animals know about the Firebird,' he said, flashing his teeth as if smiling. 'We know other marvelous things too. The last person who saw the Firebird was the old healer who left. He could talk to us also.'

"'Where did the healer go?' she asked. 'I thought my father killed him.'

"'No,' said the brown dog. 'He went up north. I know some foxes who visit him from time to time. He feeds them well.'

"From that moment on, Fawn could hear all the animals talking—the birds, the dogs, the insects. Over time, she learned where the former healer had gone and vowed to go there, too.

"Seeing the Firebird marked Fawn's transformation. I wonder what will mark yours, Jackie. Maybe it has already happened, and I just don't know it. Maybe you have met or will soon meet your Firebird, who will inspire you to seek a different reality, another story for your life, a story different from the one that brought you and me together."

"Unfortunately, Fawn's brothers were ready for some mean fun at her expense, even if she was a fool. One day, the oldest brother tied her hands and pulled her on a rope behind him. 'Let's go hunting,' he said. 'You'll be the bait.' What did he have in mind?

"The black-and-white dog was following along. 'A lion has come down from the mountains,' he told Fawn. 'Your brothers are tracking him. They're going to tie you to a tree with meat hanging from you and hope that the lion will attack you. They'll get the lion and you'll be dead at the same time, and in a way that your father can't pin on them.'

"'Why do they do this?' she asked.

"'It's what they do,' the dog answered. 'But don't worry. We've been talking to this mountain lion about you. He's not hungry and he's willing to pretend to attack you and then take you to the shaman's house up north. That is what you want, isn't it?'

"'Of course,' she replied.

"'Then scream and pretend to be eaten,' the dog said, 'while the mountain lion cuts away your ropes and runs off with you. Don't worry. He knows that old grandfather, the shaman, rather well. They do ceremony together under the full moon.'

"True to the dog's word, her brothers dragged her into a clearing and tied her hands to a tree limb. One of them tied pieces of meat to a rope and attached the ropes to different parts of her clothing. When she smelled like raw meat, he backed off. 'Happy hunting,' he sneered.

"She waited anxiously for the lion to appear. Silence overtook the clearing until she heard a scratching sound behind her. The shadows of evening fell across her feet. The lion quietly announced himself. 'The dogs tell me you can talk to us,' he said.

"'Yes,' she replied.

"'Then I'll untie you. Scream like I'm eating you, and then run after me. You can feed me that meat on the rope later.'

"She did as the lion directed and was soon running through the brush behind him. Whenever they stopped to rest, she gave him meat on a rope. Eventually, they came upon a lodge hidden in the middle of the forest. 'This is it,' said the lion. 'This is the shaman's lodge.' A gentle mist was turning into rain.

"She knocked on the door and the old man answered. 'The lion told me you were coming,' he said. 'So you can talk to them, too,' he mused, ushering her in. 'You've seen the Firebird, and you're young enough to fall in love with him. Tell me,' he said, as he bade her sit upon skins in the center of his dwelling place, 'are you compelled to find this bird again?'

"'Yes,' she said. 'He's all I can think about, day and night.'

"'Then you must stay with me for a while so that I can teach you what to do. After that, I will send you with a friend of mine to find the Firebird.' She agreed, and her apprenticeship began. The lodge sat below mountains white with snow, and tall evergreens surrounded their dwelling. The friend turned out to be a coyote who knew where the Firebird lived and often visited there.

"Maybe this is what we're doing together, Jackie. Maybe this is your apprenticeship. Maybe you're finding something else at which to direct your passion. I don't know what your Firebird will be, but it will be something that makes it worth leaving your situation. It will be all you can think about day and night. It will be your obsession, your passion. When you find it, you won't be able to turn away from it. You won't be able to live with things the way they have been. I'm looking forward to hearing about your Firebird, about what will drive your passion to change, whether it will be another human being or a cause or something else.

"'Oh, Coyote,' Fawn implored, 'will you take me to the Firebird?'

"'Yes,' he said, 'and I am proud to help you, also.'

"Together, she and the old healer and Coyote hatched a plan to liberate the Firebird. Coyote said that the Firebird was under a spell cast by an evil medicine man who had taken over the village just north of them. He had turned the people into strange animals and mixed up their body parts so that some had wolverine paws, bird beaks, pig tails, dog legs, and on and on. He ruled the area with an iron fist. It was rumored that he had gained his power through a spell in which his heart had turned to stone—a green crystal kept in a secret pouch, guarded so well that even if you knew where to look, it would be impossible to steal. 'Break that crystal and you break his spell,' said Coyote.

"I've heard that people who are ruled by alcohol are like that. Their hearts turn to stone, maybe even an evil green color. Maybe that's happened to the men in your life—the alcohol and drugs have turned their hearts to stone. The alcohol and the drug spirits have put an evil spell upon them. When that happens, there comes a point at which they stop being fully human—when the alcohol has claimed them irreversibly. I wonder if that has happened to anyone you have known.

"Coyote actually *wanted* to help, which was uncharacteristic for him. He vowed to bring his bow and arrows and to do whatever it took to break the spell. Perhaps he thought food would be involved, or perhaps he was truly altruistic. No one will ever know but Coyote and his descendents.

"Even so, Jackie, for reasons that you can't understand, people around you want to help, just as Coyote wanted to help Fawn. Are you wondering what their motivation is for wanting to help? What's my motivation? Am I a Coyote, just here for the food? Or maybe I just want to do what's right.

"For weeks, the old healer instructed Fawn in how to survive in the Far North and how to weather the evil medicine man's cold glare. 'You must play the fool,' he said. 'Play it better than you have ever played it, for not only is he evil, he is also extremely observant. Don't let him catch you in a mistake. You will find the Firebird and figure out how to set him free. But to keep him free, you must destroy the crystal heart. Only then will the spell be broken.'

"The bright, cold day of departure came. Snow covered the land and smoke from the heating fire hung in the air as if frozen in place. The snow crunched when stepped on. Coyote and Fawn got ready to go. Fawn walked upon snowshoes, while Coyote bounded through the drifts. The wind grew colder as the day grew longer. The weak sun was a red orb on the western horizon. As the sun disappeared, Coyote showed Fawn the entrance to one of his hidey-holes—the perfect place to pass the cold night. Bundled warmly, Fawn snuggled up to Coyote, and they snored away the darkness. The sun was stirring as they left the hole, frost forming on their faces with each breath. Onward they trudged.

"After days of this, they found a hedgerow that was surprisingly green in the midst of the cold winter. 'This is the beginning of the enchantment,' said Coyote. Mist hung like a wall to mark the boundary from cold to warm. 'Inside these walls, it is always summer. The evil medicine man stole the heat from the rest of the land, where it is now always winter. I know the way through the labyrinth, so you must follow me carefully.' Coyote crawled through a hole in the hedge and they were inside. Fawn followed Coyote as he ran and turned and dodged and turned back again. It was a mystifying sequence of directions, but suddenly the maze opened onto a lush, green field, and there was the Firebird, inside a wooden cage.

"Fawn fearlessly ran over to him. 'How did you get in here?' she asked. "'Don't touch the cage,' the Firebird said. 'It's a magical trap. You won't be able to open it.' Fawn was undaunted, continuing to explore how to open the trap. She found a small latch that was easily released! But before the Firebird could fly away, she grabbed his foot and held on tightly. 'You must return when I call,' she said. 'You must help me to undo this spell. I will not let you go until you promise.'

"Grudgingly the Firebird promised and then rose above Fawn and Coyote, his wings catching fire from the light of the sun. Soon he soared out of sight, beyond the bounds of the sky. 'We must go inside the village,' Fawn said. 'I must play the fool and you must not be seen. Together we can succeed.'

"It will be the same way for you, Jackie. Once you find your passion and your mission, nothing will stop you. Just like Fawn, you'll find your resources and your allies and you'll overthrow the reign of terror that alcoholism has held upon your life. Maybe I'll be your ally, or maybe it will be someone else, but who it is won't matter as much as how wonderful it will feel to be liberated, to cast off the spell, to rise above the misery that you've felt during your life.

"Fawn staggered toward the first dwelling she saw in the distance, singing a silly song. She practiced maintaining a glazed, stupid look. As she neared the dwelling, she was met by two of the most ridiculous creatures she could ever have imagined. Holding spears, they stood upright in pigs' bodies. Their arms ended in sharp claws and their legs were thick and padded like bears'. Their tails swung like those of lions. Their mouths had rows of fangs, like stories she had heard of vicious fish, and their eyes were blood red. 'Halt,' one yelled, poking her with the end of its spear. She played even more stupid, despite the hue and cry they were raising. The hoopla heralded the arrival of the wickedest looking man she had ever seen—worse than her father and apparently far cleverer. He stared at Fawn while she mustered her internal strength to show no response. 'What should we do with her?' asked one of the pig-things, while Fawn continued to babble mindlessly.

"'Keep her,' said the evil medicine man. 'I let you guys eat our last fool, and it hasn't been the same since. We need some comic relief. Keep her, and don't you dare eat her.' The pig-things grumbled but reluctantly obeyed. Fawn soon had free run of the village.

"That's a strategy that some people use before escaping or overthrowing their captors, Jackie. You could do that, too—pretend to be stupid or sweet and nice or totally obedient until it's time to make your move, just as Fawn is doing.

"Fawn performed well in her role as fool and made friends with a funny-looking, rabbitlike critter who tended the evil shaman's roses and other gardens. She helped this creature with his work, which no one else had ever done. She worked hard to keep her fool guise operating when she was with him. Her ruse worked, and he talked freely with her, telling her about the magical tree on the other side of the hedge, where the medicine man's heart was placed. She learned that a monstrous creature guarded the tree, a beast made by the evil shaman just for that purpose. Taller than a bear with sharp tusks to skewer a person, it breathed fire, could jump from limb to limb in the tree, and had sharp claws to tear a person to shreds. Only under the watchful eye of this ferocious creature did the evil medicine man feel safe enough to sleep. The stone heart was hidden in the top of the tree, locked in a magical container. Digesting this information, Fawn and Coyote began to formulate a plan. They would act at the new moon.

"On the appointed night, Fawn and Coyote crept to the hedge where the monster lived. They snuck through the hole the rabbit-like creature used to feed the monster and reconnoitered the grounds. Just as the rabbit had described, a large pond filled the perimeter of the garden. Fawn quietly cut several reeds to use as breathing tubes. Coyote prepared his arrows and readied himself to whiz back to the hedge. Then they made their move, shouting and throwing rocks at the monster to get its attention. Its roar was unbelievably loud. Waiting the requisite time for the alarm to be heard, Fawn jumped into the pond with her breathing reeds. Coyote dashed into the hedge. The guards ran into the garden looking for the intruder. The monster stopped bellowing. Eventually, they gave up and went back to snoozing.

"Fawn emerged from the water, as Coyote did from the shadows. Again they threw rocks at the monster to elicit its hideous screeches. Again they dove for cover when the guards came. After five cycles of this, the evil shaman appeared, very angry. 'If you can't find this intruder, I'm going to feed you to this monster,' he threatened. The guards sheepishly promised to look harder. They went all around the garden, sticking their spears into hedges and looking up into trees, but still they found nothing.

"On the sixth, seventh, eighth, and ninth cycles, the evil medicine man continued to return, hollering at the guards almost as loud as his monster had. On the tenth try, he stuck spears into the pond, barely missing Fawn. He cursed everything in the garden. The twelfth time, he turned the monster into stone, muttering that he would finally get a good night's sleep.

"When she was sure that everyone had left, Fawn sprang out of the pond and climbed up the stone monster to the first bough of the tree. Grabbing that bough, she swung into the tree and climbed from branch to branch, heading for the highest point. At one point, she made the mistake of looking down and was paralyzed with sudden fright, hanging onto the trunk of the tree in a cold sweat. She imagined the voice of the Firebird telling her that only she could finish this job, and that she would have to get over her fear or all would be lost. She willed her breathing to slow down and forced herself to look up, never down. Finally she continued her climb. Coyote stood at the ready on the ground, arrow drawn and ready to fire.

"I'm sure you can imagine that you might feel this scared, too, if you were to take action or to run away. But Fawn had courage. She fixed her gaze on her goal and never looked down or backwards.

"Fawn was swaying back and forth at the top of the tree. With great fear and trepidation, she took the carved container holding the stone heart. She could feel its evil beat inside. Grabbing the box, she threw it to the ground, where it shattered and a snake crawled out. Coyote swiftly put an arrow through the snake's head and it shriveled up, revealing the beating, green, heart-shaped crystal. Seemingly from nowhere, the Firebird appeared and plucked her off the tree to carry her quickly to the ground. Coyote was frozen, mesmerized by the beating stone. Fawn heard the ruckus of the evil medicine man and his animal entourage coming. 'Someone has my heart,' he shouted. 'Catch them; hurry.' She could feel the pain and anguish in his voice. She had to smash the heart before the evil medicine man got there.

"She picked up the cold greenness of the beating crystal and threw it as hard as she could at the stone guardian frozen by the edge of the pond. Just as she let go, the medicine man burst into the garden. 'Get her,' he yelled. He was running toward her as the crystal shattered against the stone. He faltered in midstep, clutching his chest. As the shards fell to the ground, so did he. Life ebbed out of him as the light in the crystal faded. Finally he was still. After a silent pause that seemed to last forever, the animal monstrosities cheered, even as some of them began to transform back into human beings. The Firebird landed, also becoming fully human. He walked toward Fawn, and, taking hold of her, kissed her in a long embrace. The evil medicine man had melted. The animal caricatures all turned back into people. The temperature normalized. Fawn knew that she would never go back to her father and brothers again.

"Fawn became the hero of her journey. She broke the spell, killed the evil medicine man, and returned the people to their true state. She found her true love and stayed with him. Life was good.

"Jackie, can you imagine feeling as good about yourself and your life as Fawn did at that moment of success? Maybe you can imagine how triumphant you would feel if you kicked all the influences of alcohol out of your life. Maybe you'll find your one true love, or something equally important. I'm really looking forward to finding out."

☀

The next evening I arranged for one of the local healers who often came to the hospital to perform a sweat lodge ceremony for Jackie. I attended, along with several nurses from the hospital and some friends that Jackie invited. Steven Bearcat performed his usual powerful ritual and we prayed for Jackie's highest good. Jackie prayed intensely for protection and the courage to take care of herself. Did I imagine seeing the spirit of her mother hovering in the steam above the stones?

A month later, Jackie called me for help arranging shelter. She had discovered she was pregnant and was inspired to prevent her child from being terrorized by alcohol and violence. We made the arrangements and some local shelter folks met Jackie at the grocery store. They helped her get a restraining order against her boyfriend and to press charges against him for domestic violence. Jackie told me that she couldn't stop thinking about the story I had told her. She wanted to be as brave as Fawn. She said she told herself the story whenever she was tempted to falter or cave in. The story and her repetitions of it, coupled with her own Firebird passion (for her unborn child) had facilitated an act that no number of well-meaning counselors, doctors, and police could catalyze through their rational discourse and cajoling. Herein lies the power of story to induce and sustain personal transformation.

Both Fawn and Mulan would acknowledge that we lack complete power over our lives. We are all positioned in relationships and kinship networks. Transformation necessarily changes those around us or they will force us back into our old ways. Stories of transformation carry the wisdom of change.

Stories contain humanity's best hopes. Like a mountain spring, stories originate at the source of our creativity and, through our reflection upon them, become the vehicle for our further communication with that source. Telling our story, organizing and expressing the parade of images from within—in short, storytelling—unlocks the internal maker of stories who resides within all of us. This is clearly what happened for Jackie. Story helped more than any amount of urging, coercing, and demanding by social workers, nurses, doctors, and police. Through internalizing the message of the story (which is different for each listener), she was able to extricate herself from her destructive situation, a powerful transformation in itself.

4

Stories of Connectivity

We are sufficiently impressed by stories of unusual meetings, destiny, chance, and happenstance that we tell such stories repeatedly. Our frequent repetition of these stories expresses our surprise at improbable events and reinforces a sense of synchronicity, of connectivity to all of life. These stories remind us of our interrelatedness. My friend, Peter, tells the story of looking for me for years, only to run into me in the lobby of a hotel in Orlando when we were both visiting Disney World. Such improbable stories inspire us with awe and wonder. They make us want to believe in magic, that anything could happen. They open our eyes, even if briefly, to the many overlapping spheres to which we belong—family, friendship networks, communities, cultures, and physical environments.

Victoria came to me with the challenge of debilitating pain. She had multiple diagnoses, ranging from chronic interstitial cystitis (a painful, inflammatory bladder disorder with no known cause) to lumbar disk disease. She had tried multiple conventional and alternative therapies, to no avail. Chiropractic made her worse, as did Reiki, acupuncture, and Rolfing. Everything she tried seemed to make her worse. Only staying home and being still offered any relief.

Victoria had been a high-powered accountant before her illness. She had been inside billion dollar deals. Defeated by pain and the accompanying inability to concentrate, she had moved from New York City to Tucson in search of a healing that had not yet manifested.

A common first step for me in finding a healing story is to probe the person's passions. Victoria was fascinated with Native American culture and spirituality. She had already visited some well-respected reservation healers, though none had been willing or able to help. She believed healing was possible, and thought she just needed to spend more time with the healers. She had business skills that she thought a tribe could use, in exchange for their acceptance of her interest in Native American healing.

Victoria was also keenly interested in the history of her ancestors. She believed there had to be a Native American relative for her to feel so drawn to these ways and to the culture. She wanted to explain why she felt so comfortable on reservations. She wondered why going there felt like coming home. She was interested in people who made sudden and total transformations and found themselves well.

I wanted to draw a remarkable story out of Victoria, one that included her unique talents and strengths. It would have to include her formidable organizational abilities and her sharp mind. I asked her to remember times when she had used her resources well and had felt empowered and whole. We made a list of these times, cataloging them for future reference. I encouraged her to be open to any images related to her passions and talents that might arise.

The anthropologist Gregory Bateson believed that change begins with the recognition of difference. A healing story generates awareness of the differences associated with times of greater health and promotes those qualities to resurface. I asked Victoria how she was different now from when she had been so healthy that illness never crossed her mind. Her first thought was how much more spiritual she had become since her illness began. She thought about the various men she had dated, married, and left. Illness had dissolved any lingering temptation to leave her husband.

Hence we were led to an awareness of the benefits of the illness, which had promoted stability in her relationship and directed her toward the spiritual. When this happens, I like to wonder whether the person could uphold these changes without the benefit of the illness. Victoria thought she could. The goal of her healing story became more complex. We wanted to find a way for her pre-illness vitality, energy, and creativity to resurface, while maintaining and nurturing the positive benefits illness had brought. This could become a path to wellness. It is important to understand that we can never go backward. A healing story takes us forward to a new place on the trail. I imagine that the pre-illness person continues as a kind of *possible person,* and that we extract the desired relationships from that possible person while leaving those not desired alone.*

What were the desired relationships for Victoria? Her relationship to work had previously given her a great sense of meaning and purpose. Even though the goal of that work now seemed hollow to her (making lots of money for other people), the importance of a "right relationship" to work, in which work enriched and enlivened her, was obvious. We needed a story to promote a return to what she would now consider meaningful work. She came to believe that her susceptibility to illness had some connection to her difficulties in romantic relationships, in which she met various men, became romantically involved, married some, and ultimately left them all. She wanted to retain the passion of romance but in a more stable, committed relationship. She perceived the illness as having helped her do that with her current husband. We needed a story that would preserve and augment her continued commitment to her marriage while celebrating the romantic, passionate self within her.

I want to emphasize how different my concept is from what psychologists call *secondary gain*, which suggests that people get sick and stay sick because the illness role rewards them in some way. Instead, I am presenting the idea or hypothesis that one aspect of illness is its ability to partially solve other problems. This does not necessarily mean that illness arises to solve the problems, but that we are so creative that we quickly figure out what problems being sick can solve. We may come to rely on the illness to accomplish tasks that we couldn't do earlier. Then a part of us will cling to the illness for fear of going back to

---

*The term *possible self* comes from psychologists Hazel Markus and Paula Nurius and refers to the multiple conceptions people have of what they might become, would like to become, or are afraid to become.[1] I wonder if these possible selves might also dwell in the possible worlds described in the parallel universe interpretation of quantum physics. See Max Tegmark's Web site for details about parallel universes (www.hep.upenn.edu/~max/multiverse.html).

our old ways and problems. To transform beyond the illness (when this is possible), we may need to reassure some parts of ourselves that we can solve former problems in other ways. Victoria needed to reassure some parts of herself that she could stay committed to her husband and follow a spiritual path without being sick. The temptation to return to the fast track, billion-dollar-deal lifestyle and its income might be enormous if she didn't examine this consciously. Healing stories that could work for her might include those in which the main character renounces wealth and fame to pursue love or spiritual development.

Victoria had been driven, compulsive, and aggressive before getting sick. She had taken advantage of the illness to help her develop a softer side and did not feel compelled to return to the world of corporate finance even if healed. She wanted to do something else. She even fantasized about becoming a healer. I wondered how she could redirect all the skills and talents that had made her so successful in business toward healing and being a healer, if that was what she wanted to be.

I looked for ideas and images that had power for her. The stronger the feelings associated with an idea, the more likely that idea can catalyze transformation. If Bateson is correct that awareness of difference lies at the heart of all knowledge, then we should ask how our various ideas and stories differ from one other. How are the resources and talents that support particular ideas different from those that support other ideas? What can we learn from looking at the effects of our beliefs upon our lives?

I needed emotionally charged images to bring a story to life for Victoria. I began with guided imagery. Victoria saw a field of blowing grass. Later we discovered that we were simultaneously seeing a faded, old farmhouse near a river. The images were compelling and powerful but had not yet formed a story. Victoria asked for a ceremony to help her make sense of the images.

I began with a simple prayer ceremony. I sang the Four Directions song as we sat outside in a secluded wash, having blown sage over both of us to cleanse and purify us. Upon finishing the song, I asked the spirits to come and assist us. I acknowledged that we little people hadn't been able to solve Victoria's problem on our own. We needed their help. I addressed the West, asking the Man in the Black Blanket and the Bear Nation to help us with courage. I asked the North—the Man in the Red Blanket and the Buffalo Nation—to help us with strength and endurance. Next, I asked the East and the Man in the Yellow Blanket, along with the Spotted Eagle Nation, to give us vision and direction, followed by the South—the Man in the White Blanket, the White Buffalo Calf Woman, and the Red-Tailed Deer Nation—to give us compassion, love, kindness, and forgiveness. Then I addressed the sky spirits—the sun, the moon, the stars, the light, and the darkness—thanking them for the protection they provide us. I addressed Mother Earth and the mole nation that dwells within her, that heals and nurtures us. Last, I acknowledged all the ancestors and the spirits who had come to help—the creepy crawlers, the winged ones, the stand-up people, the many leggeds, the two leggeds, the four leggeds, the stone people, the finned people, and so on. When I had acknowledged everyone, I asked for their help on behalf of Victoria.

Victoria's voice rang out with her heartfelt request for help. She spoke to her ancestors and to the spirits about how she had suffered with pelvic and low back pain, and about how ready she was to stop suffering. She asked for their assistance in making that so.

When she finished, I sang a doctoring song. This simple song repeats over and over that a powerful spirit is coming and it's going to doctor someone. Upon completion, I took a smoke stick and offered tobacco to the spirits, asking them to help. I placed my hand over her abdomen and prayed for the spirits to send energy through me and into Victoria. As I blew smoke toward them, the images began to come.

I saw the same field of grass, but in richer colors and detail. The farmhouse stood old and dilapidated in the foreground. A powerful, wide river ran nearby. Oaks and sycamores grew near the bank; the plains rolled westward. I saw an old couple rocking on the front porch. I received a very clear message that Victoria needed to go there.

When we finished, to my surprise, Victoria had seen the same images without my having said anything to her. Independently, we saw the same images of her ancestral farm situated near the confluence of two rivers. Victoria knew exactly where she needed to go. She knew immediately that she needed to recover the story of her ancestors, particularly her grandmother and great-grandmother.

Now we were constructing a story, not a traditional story or myth, but the story of Victoria's ancestors. A new story was emerging with the help of the spirits in our ceremonies—one in which Victoria returns to her ancestral land to pray for it and for her female ancestors who suffered so greatly with more children than they could handle or support. We were forging a story that could lead to healing—a story of asking for forgiveness from the land, finding it, and letting its fertility spread forth again, upon those who wished to receive it. The story involved transgenerational healing.

Very soon we learned that Victoria's great-grandmother and her grandmother had both been hospitalized in the state mental hospital for "defective heredity." We learned that Victoria's grandmother had been so poor after being abandoned by her husband that she had to burn her furniture to keep her children warm. This was interpreted by the mental health experts of the time as confirmatory evidence of defective heredity.

Victoria came to believe that she would be well when she visited this place. She flew to Oklahoma and found herself in the laundromat of a small reservation town, asking for directions. People knew the farm, even knew its most recent inhabitants, though now it stood empty. She followed their directions and drove there, discovering that the farm and land looked just like our vision. As she followed the directions to recover the story of her female ancestors and to bring to light their plight and their suffering, the pain in her bladder and her back began to lessen. Her consumption of pain medication decreased, and other therapies that hadn't helped before started to provide comfort.

We entered a problem-solving phase in which we recognized that the life she led before her painful condition began could not continue. She could not go back to the work she once did. She had to move on. She wanted to pursue healing as a potential career, perhaps by creating interfaces between Anglo-European culture and Native American healing. She needed to transform her relationship so that both she and her husband were looking in the same direction. We began to imagine alternative stories about a future life that felt more compatible with bodily health.

Synchronicity describes the intense connectivity that Victoria and I experienced during her ceremonies. We had the same visions. We saw the same spirits. These stories seemingly express our surprise at improbable events but actually reinforce our awareness of the intricate web of connections in which we are embedded.

I want to use this concept of synchronicity and connectivity to further our understanding of the hero and his or her journey. The naïve idea of the hero in contemporary culture is that his or her success springs from an inherent trait that was present at birth. This view of the hero denies the hard work and the important relationships that go into the journey. The hero may have dual attributes, be simultaneously mortal and immortal, fragile and invincible. In the world of the spirit, we all are sacred, immortal, invulnerable, and imbued with divine power. We are both ordinary people with our foibles and heroes who can do anything. We live multiple roles. We have a role at our job and a collection of stories to accompany it. We have a role at home and corresponding stories. We have other roles within our communities—spiritual, social, sporting, to name a few. In each of those roles, we have our flaws, which make us interesting. Super beings without weaknesses or flaws are boring. Similarly, heroic stories would be boring if not for flaws and weaknesses within the hero.

The seemingly random events upon which a plot evolves are not random or chance but are integral to the story and part of the field of resources upon which we draw. Synchronicity is at work even in the selection of the hero, who is often reluctant, and the youngest, neglected, least likely character in the family. The hero-to-be would often prefer to stay home and have a nice lunch. (In Russian fairy tales, this type of hero may be the youngest brother or the simpleton or fool.) Nevertheless, the hero has an inherently good heart, is honest, and is willing to make mistakes. He is kind and perseveres once the adventure begins, and is willing to take advice (a characteristic that represents openness to secret, spiritual, mysterious help). This openness and innocence makes the hero susceptible to luck or synchronicity. Seemingly slight twists of fate take him to one place instead of another, producing a dramatic shift in outcome. Without the hero's openness to being connected, none of this could happen.

The landscape in which the hero moves (like the dreamer) is not inert. It is a living landscape in which the hero and the other helpers and obstacles are embedded. The willingness to be a part of the living landscape is important, for our embeddedness and entanglement with others who are similarly embedded is itself the source of synchronicity, connectedness, and destiny. The landscape maintains an often secret collaboration with us and the adventure.

Frodo and Bilbo Baggins from *The Lord of the Rings* are examples of reluctant heroes who rise to their destiny. The Shire, where they live, is an enclosure in a larger world in which strange forces are afoot. Gandalf is the emissary of the secret world of the mysteries. In the Shire, the hobbits present a "collective value" (not to mention comic relief). Within the Shire, we find ordinary life—eating, drinking, and laughing, all within comfortable homes. Like Frodo and Bilbo, how many of us have planned our lives based upon comfort, family, food, and the ordinary vicissitudes of life? How many of us have felt a larger destiny brooding around and about us that threatens to disrupt our picture of ordinary life?

Synchronicity or coherence occurs because everything is related on all levels. The philosopher Ervin Laszlo relies upon stories of physics to give us clues from which to examine our psychological and social worlds.[2] The phenomenon known as *interference* is one way to measure connectedness. Those of us who studied high school physics will remember that interference patterns are produced when we simultaneously drop two pebbles into different spots in a pond. The patterns are formed as the waves ripple toward one other and the troughs of one wave cancel the peaks of the other wave. The result is a net effect of zero, assuming that the pebbles hit the water with equal weight and force. Two troughs or two crests double one another's effects.

We also learned in high school that light behaves both as particles and as waves. Its particles are called photons. Waves of light interfere with each other, but only if they are emitted from the same source, even if they arrive on Earth fifty thousand years apart. We know that they are coupled because of the interference patterns they produce. Pebbles thrown into a pond are coupled because the same agent threw them at the same time. Light waves from a star are coupled because they came from the same source. Interesting, when a wave interacts with a wave from a different source, it becomes uncoupled from its origin. We then say that the *coherence* it had with other waves from the same origin is disrupted. When coherence is disrupted, the interference patterns we saw previously disappear.

Coherence represents an intrinsic relationship among particles (or people!) arising from the same source. Coherent particles (and people) communicate at speeds faster than light. The physicist Richard Feynman called the phenomenon of coherence the "central mystery" of physics. When people experience coherence, we call it synchronicity or connectedness. Coherence arises out of our connectedness with one other. It happens because we are all embedded in the same world, coming from the same source, and maintaining symmetry with each other.

When Victoria and I had the same experiences while silently contemplating during the ceremony, when we received the same physical description, and when Victoria then used those images to find the actual physical location of her ancestors' farm between two rivers in Oklahoma, we were experiencing connectedness. Victoria received information about her female ancestors that was confirmed by hospital records. Psychic insights, telepathic experiences, and the sudden urge to walk across a room and subsequently avoid disaster are further examples of connectedness.

We tell stories about these events, such as the stories I still hear people tell about waking up on the morning of September 11, 2001, and deciding, for seemingly silly reasons, not to go to work. Or consider one woman's story that a handsome Italian man offered to buy her coffee at Starbucks, where she stopped for coffee every morning before going into the World Trade Center. It was against her nature to let herself be "picked up," even by a handsome Italian, but at the moment she felt giddy, like a teenager. She let him buy her coffee and was sitting at the table flirting with him when the first airplane hit the building. When she looked back for him during the shock of that scene, he was gone without a trace. She searched for him as she moved away from the towers. The plane had hit her floor.

Philosophy tends to follow physics, so let us review some of the experiments that demonstrate coherence (or synchronicity) on the particle level, for those substantiate our claims for coherence on our level, that of the human being.

In the early nineteenth century, Thomas Young performed what is perhaps the earliest of these experiments.[3] Young studied light passing through two slits in a surface. He placed a screen behind this surface to receive the light penetrating the slits. Because light behaves like a wave, the light waves coming through the two slits interfered with one other, producing characteristic patterns on the screen onto which the light was shining. (Remember this is the same phenomenon as the waves produced by pebbles in a pond.) When the peak or crest of a light wave hit the trough or bottom of another light wave, the two waves canceled each other out, and an area of darkness was projected onto the screen. Two crests arriving together doubled the brightness, and this also appeared on the screen. Young discovered that even when the light was so weak that only one photon (particle of light) could be emitted at a time, the wave-interference pattern remained. He concluded that this could occur only if the particles were actually waves, for how could one particle pass through both slits? Yet it did. This became the great mystery of the time. How can light be both particulate and wavelike? How can one particle of light maintain the nature of the wave?

In 1984, John Wheeler devised a related experiment.[4] Photons (particles of light) were emitted one at a time and made to travel from an emitting gun to a detector that clicked when they arrived. Wheeler inserted a half-silvered mirror along the path of the photons. This split the beam, giving rise to the possibility that half of the photons would pass through the mirror and half be deflected. Wheeler confirmed this by placing a counter at right angles to the beam hitting the mirror. The counter-detectors now registered an equal number of photons. When a second mirror was placed further down the path of the undeflected photons, an amazing change took place. Suddenly only one of the counters clicked. The other stopped counting and was silent. Amazingly, now all of the photons arrived at the same destination—quite a violation of what we expect from the rules of ordinary life. For example, imagine that I have a machine that fires tennis balls for someone to hit back to me, and I put up a barrier that sends half of the tennis balls to another player. If I then try to deflect half of the tennis balls that are going to the second player (downstream from my first deflector), how would I ever explain the fact that my second deflector now makes all of the tennis balls go to the first tennis player? Yet that is what happens in the world of quantum physics.

In 1991, researcher Leonard Mandel took an interesting new direction.[5] He generated two beams of laser light and allowed them to interact and form the typical interference pattern we saw in high school. When he attached detectors that allowed the path of the light to be determined, this interference disappeared. Surprisingly, it disappeared whether or not the detectors were turned on! Thus, merely attaching a measuring device to tell us with certainty what path a photon takes is sufficient to disconnect its relatedness to the other photons coming from its source. The very possibility of such "which-path" detection destroyed the wave nature (or superposed) state of the photons. How do the photons know that we have attached a measuring device, when we haven't even turned it on?

To understand how this might work in ordinary life, assume we have two batting cages where youngsters with baseball bats receive a constant stream of balls to hit from a machine. Assume that the balls come out of the machine at regular intervals, alternating between the first batter and the second batter. We decide we want a way to measure which ball from the machine will go to which batter. We set up a device to keep track of the balls that go into the machine and how they come out. Suddenly, without our even turning on the device to track the path of the balls—just because we set up the device to make the measurement—the balls suddenly lose their regularity of output and start flying out in seemingly random order at the batters.

Similarly, in experiments at the University of Konstanz in 1998, Durr and colleagues produced puzzling interference patterns through the diffraction of a beam of cold atoms by standing waves of light.[6] When they made no attempt to detect which path the atoms were taking, the interference patterns were distinct, with sharp contrasts. When they encoded information within the atoms so that they could know with certainty which path the atoms would take, this interference pattern vanished. Again, this means that we don't have to make the measurement for the interference pattern to vanish. We simply need to make it possible to make the measurement. That is enough. The counting instrument need not actually be used; it is enough to label the atoms so that it can be used! On the level of ordinary life, this represents yet another example of the batting cage phenomenon just described.

To fully understand the significance of these experiments, we need to return to 1935, when Albert Einstein and his colleagues, Podolsky and Rosen, proposed that Heisenberg's uncertainty principle could be beat.[7] Heisenberg had argued that knowing everything about one aspect of a particle meant knowing nothing about the other aspects. He argued that complete certainty is impossible. Einstein resisted this explanation and proposed an experiment to refute it. He suggested taking two particles that are connected (electrons with opposite spins, for instance), separating them at a great distance, and then measuring different aspects of each completely. Since the measurement can be made faster than energy can reach the other of the two electrons, we can know two parameters completely.

When the experiment was over, to everyone's surprise, the particle not measured "knew" instantly that the other particle had been measured and adjusted itself accordingly. If the particles had been spinning "up" originally, when the spin of the first particle was determined (by a procedure that reverses the direction of the spin), the second particle adjusted itself by also reversing its spin, thereby maintaining their connected, complementary relationship. The second particle manifested different energy states depending upon what was measured about the first particle. The measurement on the first particle actually produced a new state on the second particle. Somehow, the second particle "knew" when the first particle was measured and knew what the result was, for it assumed its new state accordingly. Even more impressive, this knowledge about the first particle passed to the second particle instantaneously (much faster than the speed of light) and through physical barriers that no known energy can traverse. This refutation of Einstein's claim provides some of the best evidence for connectivity. If particles can be that connected (and the experiment has been replicated over distances of up to 41 kilometers), why not people?

In the 1960s, the Aharanov-Bohm experiments showed that the interference pattern produced by a beam of charged particles could be produced or altered by the presence of a constant magnetic field in a region from which the particles are excluded.[8] (One of the experimenters, David Bohm, went on to write a series of books on the implications of quantum physics for how we see the everyday world and our lives within it.[9]) The researchers fired particles through slits at a target, which produced an interference pattern. Lines emerged where the waves canceled each other. Charged particles produce similar interference patterns when fired at a target. The presence of a magnetic field changes that pattern. But in this experiment, the magnetic field was in a distant location and was shielded in such a way that it could not physically affect the experiment. So how did turning on the magnetic field change the pattern?

The significance of the Aharanov-Bohm effect was that it demonstrated that the presence of a magnetic field in a place where no known energy could reach the particles changed the results of the experiment anyway. This seems to involve action at a distance, also called *nonlocal action,* meaning that no physical explanation exists. The explanation is coherence—what we call synchronicity on the level of ordinary human beings.

These experiments resulted in the elaboration of the concept of *nonseparability,* which states that wholes cannot be dissected. They still behave as wholes, even though we imagine that their parts exist in isolation. To my view, this phenomenon helps explain the actions of twins who seem to know what the other is doing instantaneously. Twins must maintain some degree of nonseparability, perhaps more or less in accordance with how emotionally close they remain over the course of life.

These studies from physics force us to endorse holism, meaning that connectivity prevents us from explaining ourselves as merely the isolated sum of our parts. Stories show the ways that holism occurs in human affairs. Stories contain the "interference patterns" for human systems, in the way that mathematics contains the interference patterns for physical systems (such as electromagnetic fields). Stories represent a kind of human mathematics.

At first, coherence was assumed to happen only at the level of the particles of physics, but then, in 1999, Nadeau showed that coherence occurred at the macroscopic level of the whole universe.[10] Currently accepted theory holds that the universe originated in a vast explosion of prespace, creating a fireball of staggering heat and density. In the first few milliseconds, it synthesized all the matter now found in space-time. Particle-antiparticle pairs collided with and annihilated each other, resulting in survival of only about one-billionth of the originally created particles, which is the matter content of the universe we now observe. After about two hundred thousand years, these particles cooled off enough to form the galaxies, solar systems, and stars we now recognize. Studies of the cosmic background radiation reveal clues to this process. A critical number exists, above which the universe expands forever and below which it collapses back upon itself. The value of this number is exactly the critical value, rendering the universe flat—neither expanding limitlessly nor contracting upon itself. Only if all parts of the universe are cooperating can such fine-tuning be maintained. Thus, coherence must occur also at the level of the whole universe. The probability of the universe being as it is due merely to random processes and chance, without cooperative, connected fine-tuning, was calculated as a percentage with 126 zeroes to the right of the decimal point, too small a number for a human to begin to comprehend.

What does coherence or connectivity mean for us? Since we consistently find that the same phenomena occur at every level of scale, with microscopic processes mirroring astronomical processes, we could conclude that the stories told by indigenous healers, medicine people, shamans, and quantum physicists are accurate and that connectivity does exist at our level (that of animal or human interaction, society, and family).

The mathematician Ralph Abraham at the University of California at Santa Cruz has startling movies of Mexican jumping beans that confirm connectivity among insects.[11] Using NASA's computer and a laser array, he rigged a measuring system that would record the height jumped by each of ten thousand Mexican jumping beans. The jumps, of course, are caused by insects inside the beans who are trying to get out. The height of each jump was assigned a color by the computer, which then displayed the patterns produced by the jumpers as colors on a screen. The movies of these patterns showed amazing geometric designs, with sharp demarcations that could well be the plan for an Aztec city. The insects cohered with their neighbors and jumped to the same heights. In short, they were connected!

What does this mean for social interaction and relationships? It suggests that we are much less autonomous than we had imagined. It means that we experience coherence. It means that we do what is necessary to preserve symmetry with others who originate from the same source (family members, community members), just like the particles of light, the spinning electrons, and the Mexican jumping beans. It means that we sometimes radically change directions to maintain symmetry when others from the same source change. It means that connectivity or synchronicity is a powerful explanatory concept in human behavior.

As a youth, I was thrilled by the writings of Hermann Hesse. I loved the romantic ideal of the solitary hero, self-determined, answering to no one. However, through my studies of people in various states of health, disease, and transformation between the two, I have realized that we are inextricably embedded in a world of interconnections. Solitary is an illusion, as is self-determination. I answer to everyone and everyone answers to me. There is no individual apart from the milieu in which the individual dwells. This milieu includes the geological world as well as the human world. The indigenous healers that I study would add that it also includes the spirit world.

My only clues as to why I do much of what I do lie in the stories that I tell. My manufactured explanations for my behavior fall flat. I am tired of glib explanations for current events based upon childhood trauma, poor upbringing, castration anxiety, bad parenting, or mercury amalgams. Many therapists and doctors make a living providing others with explanations (interpretations) of their behavior. But are these real? The Native Hawaiians said that the mind is useful only for making up a story after the fact to explain what happened. Trust your gut, they said, not your mind. We participate in the formation of intricate patterns, just like the Mexican jumping beans, *without anyone actually directing us or telling us how to do it or what pattern to make*. It just happens.

I suspect Laszlo would agree that it is a momentous act, akin to "stopping the world" in Yaqui terms, to initiate an act that leads to pattern shift. This could correspond to Kuhn's paradigm shifts, in which suddenly everyone sees the world differently. Kuhn described brilliantly the switch from the romantic paradigm to the modern paradigm.[12] Whitman gave way to Hemingway. Allusions to nature gave way to the metaphor of the machine. Classical mechanics and hydraulics were used to explain everything. For Freud, the romantic notion of the soul was replaced by that of the id, coupled with a hydraulic explanation appealing to modern man about pressures forcing the id skyward (toward the ego) under constraints from the superego (presumably representing the maximum allowable pipe size for the conduits from the deep mind to the surface mind).

We are entering a new paradigm, the paradigm of systems science and of story. Since the interconnected world is too complex to allow us to make simple lists of rules, we are forced to tell stories that contain explanations for how to do things that defy list-making efforts. The best we can do to describe our experiences of being entangled and inseparable from others is to tell stories about our "amazing" experiences that demonstrate that the modern point of view is wrong. These stories of coherence and connection are only amazing because we all grew up believing the modern paradigm, that we are separate individuals, that independent variables exist, that physical boundaries between things demonstrate that they are not connected.

Coherence and connectivity can explain what happens in family therapy. The presence of the "therapist" (or anyone else, for that matter—a new dog, a foreign exchange student) can initiate a change in pattern. The therapist can observe aspects of the pattern and can even comment on the pattern, but unless the family invites him or her in, or unless a family member takes up singing the therapist's song, then failure is inevitable. Change occurs when a new pattern is initiated.

Years ago, I realized that I didn't need to know what happened during "therapy." It was enough to sit with a family or a group and hold a positive intent for their highest good. I learned to trust the wisdom of families to do what's best for them, with my role being only to provide a small perturbation—just a little nudge. This concept of trusting the system and the coherence of its members allows me to let them be responsible for change without my needing to worry too much about it. In keeping with the finding that the measurement doesn't even have to be made, that just hooking up the device is sufficient, I think some therapy succeeds because of the possibility of measurement—an external observer exists, even if he doesn't have a clue what he's seeing (which is the way I feel sometimes).

Thus, using stories represents *holism,* defined as an understanding of a certain kind of complex system best sought at the level of principles governing the behavior of the whole system, not at the level of the structure and behavior of its component parts. These principles governing whole-system behavior are found in the stories systems tell about themselves or that members tell about living within the system. *Reductionism,* the opposite of holism, encompasses the belief that an understanding of a complex system is best sought at the level of the structure and behavior of its component parts. This approach has dominated medicine and psychology throughout the twentieth century, leading us to lose track of whole systems or even human beings in our work to solve human problems.

The fantastic observations of coherence leave us with awe and wonder at the nature of the universe. Only through story can we speak about the unspeakable. Through story, we can explore these concepts. Jorge Luis Borges comes to mind as the master of the genre, especially his story of the dreamer realizing he is being dreamed and that the dreamer is about to awaken.[13] His book, *Labyrinth,* contains a number of intoxicating stories informing us about the entanglement of reality—that we cannot escape being irrevocably caught up in everything else. We cannot escape entanglement.

Tina came to me in the midst of a complete panic attack. She was an unscheduled drop-in at our Center for Health and Healing at Beth

Israel Medical Center in New York City, where I worked from 2000 to 2002. Tina met all the diagnostic criteria for full-blown panic disorder. Within the half hour allotted to us, I could do little more than listen to her, ask the questions necessary to make the diagnosis, and recommend a medication to keep her symptoms under control until we could start working together to find nondrug approaches to her problem. I chose to give her two drugs commonly used for panic disorder, clonazepam and imipramine.

I began seeing Tina every day during the height of her crisis. I learned that she had once weighed 500 pounds and had undergone weight-loss surgery. She had dropped to 220 pounds. As the pounds rolled away, Tina became more emotional and symptomatic, common in surgically mediated weight loss. Prior to her surgery, she had dabbled in a variety of religions, most extensively Zen Buddhism and the Native American spirituality of Wallace Black Elk. She had actually attended one of his workshops in which he treated a man diagnosed with colon cancer, who had a nonexcisable tumor the size of a grapefruit. Black Elk worked with the man in ceremony and in private talks after the workshop. The tumor shrank to the size of a lemon and was excisable. The doctors removed the tumor and the man lived.

Tina had been at some of these healings. She told me she believed in the power of joining mind, body, and spirit, but for the last two years, she had lost her faith. This experience of losing faith (connectedness) for people makes me whimsically think about what particles might "feel" when the measuring device is placed in the studies previously described. Suddenly, they're alone, on their own, isolated. Tina had lost her coherence. She had not even touched the sacred pipe that Wallace had blessed for her in over two years. She had forgotten the power of ceremony and the comfort of spirits talking to her.

I suggested we do a pipe ceremony together. I arranged a time to come to her house after clinic hours, as I was not supposed to burn sage and tobacco at the Center for Health and Healing. We placed both of our sacred pipes on the altar Tina had recently created. As I sang the Lakota Four Directions song, she began to remember the words and sang along. We prayed together for the spirits to heal her and for her life to change. She wanted back onto the Good Red Road, as we call it, from North to South, the road that we walk from strength and courage to kindness, love, and compassion, the road where we find healing.

We smoked the pipe in the manner taught to the people by the White Buffalo Calf Woman, singing the pipe loading song first, then offering tobacco to all the directions, then honoring all our relations, and letting the smoke carry our prayers skyward across the Milky Road to the Lodge of the Creator.

Tina felt much relieved after the ceremony. During that ceremony, I heard a voice telling me to instruct her to pray with her pipe every day for one hundred consecutive days. She should walk down the path along the red sandstone cliffs to the river, sing the sacred songs, pray, and smoke her pipe each day. If she did this, her suffering would be relieved.

Tina made a commitment to do so, and shortly thereafter, no longer needed the medication. Her panic symptoms resolved as she used the traditional spiritual teachings. By singing the songs and repeating the prayers and the ceremony, Tina was able again to tap into the story told by Wallace and multiple teachers and healers before him, a story about how the White Buffalo Calf Woman brought the pipe to the people, about the power of prayer, and about how prayers would be immediately answered if the proper procedure was followed. In doing ceremony again, Tina was recovering the experience of connectivity that Wallace gave her when he taught her the ceremonies and gave her a pipe to use. By retelling Tina the Lakota sacred stories that Wallace had previously told her, I restored her place in the spider web of connections, linked for her to Wallace Black Elk. By being the one present, on the scene at the time, I stood in for him in a way, and thus was able to help her recover the sense of connectedness with nature that he had shown her.

Tina had lost her story as she lost weight. Being heavy had made her feel spiritual. Her return to prayer and ceremony brought back her sense of being connected. She remembered forgotten skills for coping with anxiety. She remembered the importance she had previously placed upon spiritual transcendence. After I reminded Tina of the power and meaning of the cultural stories that she had learned from Wallace, these stories and their segue into prayer served as change agents for her panic disorder, which fell below the point of diagnosis with her daily enactment of the stories through the ceremonies.

Ruth, a depressed young mother, gives us another example. Ruth presented with a profound lack of energy to motivate her life. She was expert at turning suggestions into impossibilities. She drained the energy of her therapists, seeming to engage in a contest of "You can't help me."

My answer was, "No, I can't. I'm just a mere human. Not at all the stature of someone who should and could help you." I challenged Ruth to look to a higher source for help with her problems.

Ruth held an affinity for the Native American worldview, even though she was raised Jewish. She felt more comfortable praying to nature or Mother Earth than to a male Yahweh, as the Greatest Power was presented to her as a child. We went outside. We were alone in the desert outside of Tucson. The rugged Catalina Mountains blazed in the late afternoon sun, the shadows changing every five minutes as the sun headed west. We began with a song to invite the spirits to come look at us. The heat of the sun was still intense. We had climbed down into the wash, where I sang and drummed. I prayed, and then Ruth began to speak honestly to the spirits gathered. Sunset would come in another couple of hours. Her conversation was more deeply real than any she had held with me. Her frustrations in her marriage emerged. She spoke of past incest with an Orthodox father. Because she was not speaking to me, but to the spirits, she could speak more openly and honestly. She was communing with nature. She was connected.

She prayed for the first time since childhood and felt deeply moved. She left with a sense that the source for solution of her problems was always with her, inseparable from her, not dependent upon me as a therapist or even as a healer.

Later we scheduled a sweat lodge ceremony for her further spiritual development and purification. We entered the small, wood-framed, blanket-enshrouded structure, perfectly dark inside. My newly acquired teenage helper brought the hot stones into the lodge and placed them in the central pit. We put water on the stones to make steam and followed the prescribed traditional ritual of song and prayer. Within this context Ruth further contacted the source of her own energy.

Ruth became her own therapist. She took long hikes and communed with nature. She learned how to do her own personal ceremonies whenever she felt low or stressed. Her depression shrank so small that it could be put into the cage with her son's pet mouse.

What was Ruth's story, and what changed it? Having grown up in an Orthodox family, Ruth's presenting story gave doctors, fathers, and rabbis all the power. Not only did they get all the power, they also got all the anger. The women in Ruth's Orthodox Jewish family were furious at the privileged men. They fumed inside and discussed subtle but nasty ways to get back at the men. Ruth was enacting that story in her relationship with doctors. She passively came to see them (almost always men), presenting her story and demanding that they fix her. She rarely complied fully with what she was told to do and returned with a "see, it didn't work, so screw you" attitude. To her credit, she let me challenge her with another story in which she was the powerful, central character. In this story, God was a woman—Mother Nature. Men weren't involved. She took to this new story and constructed an alternative path for herself in which she didn't have to stuff her anger at men (including male doctors) and could be her own healer. Ruth's transformation pivoted around the concept of self-determination versus being pushed around by others (particularly male experts and authority figures).

So why are stories of connectivity and synchronicity important in healing? Since we are connected but live in a culture that continually asserts that we are separate, these stories remind us of intrinsic knowledge that we all have but forget. Feeling connected allows us to access greater resources. Stories of being connected, getting connected, feeling coherent, experiencing synchronistic events, all bring us into the mind-set of connectedness. We realize we are not as isolated or alone as we thought. The modern enemy is isolation. I believe that as people become more alone and lose their sense of embeddedness in community, distress and illness proliferate.

We need other people; stories are the glue that binds us together in communities. Within these communities, we experience connectivity and tell stories that further reinforce our experience and sense of connection with one other. And from this connectedness comes stories that heal.

5

Stories That Heal

S tories soothe us and heal us. Stories put children to sleep, can stop chemotherapy patients from vomiting, and lift our spirits from depression. Stories help people with eating disorders and a hatred of their own bodies to feel better. For every patient, there's a healing story. Just the way we speak about illness or wellness determines a lot about what those things are.

Where do healing stories originate? Who makes them? How do we know that a particular story is right for us? We do sense wisdom within us. This wisdom knows more about healing than the part of our mind that deals with ordinary life. Our healing stories carry the wisdom of our ancestors, just as this wisdom is stored in our DNA. Telling the ancestral stories, the cultural myths and legends, is like speaking the ancestral language, because these stories contain the blueprints for healing that our cultures and tribes have followed since antiquity.

Healing stories point the way toward the higher power and the hidden wisdom that we possess. When creative people say they tap into this power, I think of their having tapped into a main water line to drink what flows within. Great stories, especially those from the oral tradition, make ancient and hidden wisdom accessible to our working brain, the part of us that makes decisions and figures things out.

Healing stories contain the information that tells us how to use this wisdom—what to do with it.

Creating a healing story relies upon the storyteller's art. Healing requires a hero and a transformation and compels us to listen. How do I pick a healing story for a particular person? First, I need to get some sense of their own creation story for their illness. Then I try to find a story with which the person will identify and that will suggest an alternate ending for his or her own story. The story should reveal how the person can use his or her hidden talents and resources to arrive at a new and more desirable outcome. An interactive component is necessary as we construct a shared story to which we both contribute. In the stories I will discuss in this chapter, I will attempt to demonstrate this process. We will see how a healing story grew out of my interactions with Maureen, a sixteen-year-old woman labeled with anorexia. The story that we developed allowed Maureen to tap into hidden resources and wisdom that eventually helped her transform and overcome her symptoms.

Maureen was attending an exclusive private school in Switzerland. She was referred to me by another sixteen-year-old, who had come to me to learn ceremony. He told her that I would listen without judging her. Since she could go anywhere in the world, she decided to check me out.

Maureen clearly expected the usual clinical interview, which I didn't do. I have watched typical rapid-fire psychiatric interviews (and even did them to pass my psychiatry boards), but they are aggressive and dehumanizing. The Griffiths, University of Mississippi psychologists, wrote that one of the dialectics of human interaction ranges from tranquillity to threat.[1] I prefer tranquillity to threat. In tranquillity mode, we contemplate each other's stories. We listen with open minds and hearts. In threat mode, we fire rapid questions at another with the purpose of classifying and processing them. We evoke defensiveness, shame, and anger.

I started by asking Maureen to tell me the story of how she thought she developed anorexia.

"I thought you were going to tell me why I have it and how to cure it."

"No," I said. "I wish I could, but I can't. You're a unique human being, and I couldn't begin to guess why anorexia has you and what you're going to do about it. But I know that together we will find clues about how you are going to get from where you are now, caught in its tendrils, to where you want to be, which is what interests me."

Maureen told the first version of her story of anorexia. The first version of an illness story is highly edited for the audience. Maureen didn't know me. She wanted me to like her. She wanted to please me, to tell me a version of the story that would fascinate me. She started her storytelling by probing my fascination. She watched my responses to learn how to structure an appropriate story for our context. It's like market research. We tell the story we think others want to hear. This is most dramatic on first dates, where we tell highly edited stories about ourselves that even our families might not recognize. During the first telling of the story, I try to show an even acceptance. Since I don't have a pet theory of anorexia, I'm not going to jump on one detail over the others. I simply want to start the healing process, which will involve telling and retelling this story numerous times, with frequent revisions.

Maureen's story bore some resemblances to the story of Dana, from chapter 1. Maureen knew she was very intelligent. She could get better than perfect (more than 100 percent of possible points in a class) in any subject of her choosing. Teachers doted on her, wanting her to take up their particular subject for her life work. Her romantic relationships were more problematic. She tended to feel used more as a tutor than a girlfriend. She thought boys were put off by her intellect. In a highly competitive academic environment in which she was on top, potential boyfriends were intimidated. She had thought of dating women, and had tried it several times, but found that it really wasn't "her thing."

Maureen saw her parents three times a year—for Christmas, for two weeks in the summer, and at spring break. Her parents were married but may as well not have been. They had homes in multiple countries, and her father and mother were rarely together in the same house at the same time. Maureen knew, though no one discussed it, that both parents had other lovers. She suspected they stayed together because the economic and legal implications of divorce were massive, and they got along well enough, liked one another from a distance, and didn't interfere with one another. Nor did they interfere with her. Whatever she wanted she could have, though her story evoked a sense of loneliness within me, a longing for family and belonging.

Maureen had attended boarding school since age six and had been cared for primarily by nannies before that. Her mother had a complicated social calendar, and her father spent most of his time doing business, conducting one or another international trade, merger, or acquisition. She had dabbled in religion, and believed there was a god, but wasn't sure which religion to follow. She felt restricted by the rules each religion manifested and was sure she didn't want to "swallow something whole." She wanted to pick and choose what fit for her. Her parents were no help. They had no deep convictions and attended whatever church or ceremony was socially, politically, or economically correct at the moment, without letting it affect them one way or another. She felt that both of her parents lived to be noticed—her father by making more money than any other human on the planet (a goal he had not yet achieved) and her mother by attending more parties and social events than any other human on the planet (a goal that Maureen felt her mother was close to achieving).

Maureen had read about anorexia on the Internet and thought it sounded like a worthy challenge. Her mother perpetually strived to be thinner and more beautiful. Her mother sometimes criticized Maureen for being too heavy (which she wasn't, in my judgment, even for the celebrity world they inhabited), so Maureen thought she would play with anorexia for a while.

Maureen found anorexia satisfying. As she became thinner, she received more praise from her environment. Apparently, in her culture, losing weight was uniformly celebrated. She couldn't remember when she crossed the line from praise to concern, because it was a subtle transition, but she remembered enjoying the concern perhaps even more than the praise. Like Dana from chapter 1, Maureen loved the idea that her thinness marked her as a woman with tremendous will power. No one could accuse her of not having discipline of steel. This was more visible than academic success: she wore her awards as part of her body.

Since her grades had not suffered, she couldn't see what was the big deal. (Later, we learned that she knew that her intellect had deteriorated, though she still had the Swiss equivalent of A in all of her subjects.) She just wanted people to leave her alone and let her do her thing—that is, to be anorexic.

"Then why are you here with me?" I asked.

"Because they won't leave me alone. They keep pestering me to get treatment."

"So what would your goal be?"

"For people to leave me alone."

"So what if we worked on that goal?"

"What do you mean?"

"I mean that we figure out the minimum necessary for people to leave you alone, and we do that and cut some deals with people so that they will leave you alone."

"OK," she said. "How do we do that?"

"We find out what is the minimum weight at which everyone will agree to shut up if you reach and maintain that weight. Then we write contracts with everyone that they will not mention weight or food to you so long as you are at or above that weight."

"We can do that?" she asked, amazed.

"Sure we can," I said. "After all, your weight should really be your business, shouldn't it?"

"Absolutely," she said.

"Call everyone tonight," I said, "and get a weight from them. Then you and I will strategize how to achieve that number."

"Don't you want to know about abuse?" she asked me, suspicious now. "Every therapist always asks me who sexually abused me."

"OK," I said. "I'll take the bait. Who sexually abused you?"

"No one," she said.

"OK," I said. "Fine."

"Aren't you going to tell me that I'm in denial and protecting my abusers?"

"Why would I tell you that?"

"Because the other therapists did."

"How would I know that you're in denial? Where is it anyway? I thought the Nile was in Egypt, and we're sitting here in Arizona." That stupid joke worked as it usually does, and Maureen smiled and relaxed. "What I am curious about," I said, "is your passions. What passionately interests you in your life? What fascinates you?"

"Do you mean besides losing weight and eating no fat and virtually no calories?"

"I mean besides that. I'm looking for another passionate interest that perhaps isn't as well developed."

Maureen looked sheepishly at the floor. "I love physics," she said.

"Why are you looking embarrassed?" I asked.

" 'Cause my mom says girls aren't supposed to like physics. We're supposed to ride hunters and jumpers, and be into modeling, and go to parties, and snare the richest guy on the planet, at least a count or a duke."

"But physics is great," I said. "It's probably the most happening field in the world right now." That led Maureen to an impassioned talk about CERN (the European Organization for Nuclear Research in Geneva, Switzerland), where major research was taking place on anti-matter, parallel universes, cosmic foam, geons, and more. Now we were following her passion. I could clearly see what inspired and excited her. At the same time, I was developing hypotheses to test later about what kept her from following that passion. Just as I had thought Dana needed to replace anorexia with a different passion, I thought that Maureen could potentially replace anorexia with physics, unless something else emerged as more appropriate. Maureen had come alive in talking about the quantum universe. To paraphrase detective stories, "follow the passion to find the healing story."

Next we pursued the idea of differences. I asked Maureen what was different about how her body felt when she was absorbed in doing or reading about physics. What she described resembled a meditative state, in which she was so absorbed that she lost all track of her identity. She was fully engaged and felt as if she were one with what she was studying.

"How is that different from when you're around a boy that you think is cute?" I asked her.

"Then I feel so uncomfortable," she said. "I'm so aware of my body. Am I thin enough? Am I cute enough? How's my makeup? What does he think of me? Am I being too flirtatious? Am I being too shy? My mind is so full I can hardly talk."

"And how does that feel in your body?"

"I feel a tension in my shoulders. My stomach is all tied up in knots. I feel butterflies, sometimes even nausea. I get all restless like I just want to run."

"And is there a way that anorexia helps with that?"

"Oh, yes. At this weight, boys don't take me seriously as a potential girlfriend. I'm too thin. They're afraid they might break me. And also, you get such an incredible high from not eating. It's like everything in the world is connected. It's like how I feel doing physics. It's just wonderful. I don't feel any pain. I just feel great."

"That's the hormones of starvation," I told her.

"What?"

"The body is kind to starving animals and people. It produces these marvelous hormones that make them feel great, so they won't suffer when they die. I've heard about this from so many others, including people who ran out of food in the wilderness. I'm sure it's wonderful. And it makes sense that it feels like doing physics, because these same hormones are generated when you are following your passion. I'm interested in your finding other ways beside anorexia to feel this way. Then you will have more choices. When anorexia is your only alternative for feeling good, it's hardly possible to choose another path." This made sense to Maureen, and we continued to explore how she felt in her body in different states of mind. We used hypnosis and guided imagery to help her more fully understand the experience of being embodied in different emotional states.

Next we created an alternate story. Using the various tools in my kit, we forged a story in which Maureen could maintain a weight that would keep people from harassing her, and in which she would have an alternate passion besides fat-gram counting—namely, physics. Through hypnosis, it had also become clear that this new version of Maureen needed to address the "boy" piece of her story and the fact that she felt she had "no home." Even though she had a dozen homes, Maureen felt like a homeless person. She wasn't grounded. There was no one place to which she could return over and over, where she could leave her things and come back to find them again. Her dorm room at school was not a home. Wherever her parents chose to spend holidays with her was not a home. She wanted a home. And she wanted to feel more comfortable around boys.

As crazy as it might sound, we stumbled upon a solution in the form of a Disney character, Kim Possible. Kim goes to high school by day and fights evil in her spare time. She's also a cheerleader and gets good grades and is, of course, a genius. And Kim has no boy problems. Maureen was really excited by the Kim character, because physics was part of Kim's genius. The Kim Possible character introduced the idea of an athleticism that was appealing to Maureen. That jarred my memory of Kata, the woman who had been so inspired by the movie *Whale Rider*, who overcame her fear of men when she learned Filipino stick-fighting. I told Maureen her story and it sparked an interest in her, too. Kim Possible was great at martial arts.

Kim Possible also paralleled Maureen's "homelessness," since you rarely see the Disney character's parents. They don't really play a part in the show. Her only family seems to be her trusty male sidekick, Ron Stoppable, who, interestingly, is less competent than she is. Kim also has her cheerleader friends. Maureen began to brainstorm about how she could be part of a martial arts–physics community. She realized she could find a home in what she did, rather than where she lived.

Now we were immersed in conjuring an alternative story for Maureen—one in which she fashioned herself along the lines of Kim Possible. She'd pursue physics, she'd keep her weight above the cutoff for harassment, she'd take up a martial art, and she'd beat up boys on a regular basis, maybe adopting just one as a trusty sidekick. I jokingly suggested that her "Dr. Evil" could be anorexia. In other words, we could make anorexia the evil genius that the Kim Possible character always defeats.

We tested this story through a number of guided-imagery hypnosis sessions, in which I threw different challenges at her and her new character learned to handle them. Finally, we looked at the problems Maureen's new story could solve. Martial arts and physics would provide great endorphins. She could cultivate a home, she could expect boys to be less competent than she is, and she could accept this (as Kim does Ron Stoppable). We negotiated a contract with the school and with her parents for an acceptable weight (which she had already reached). I helped with some physics contacts at CERN, and we created a plan with the school for her to work at CERN on weekends in a high-energy particle physics lab, so long as her weight was above the magic boundary line.

Two weeks later, Maureen left Arizona happier than she had come. She had a new identity, a new story that appealed to her. I have continued to get e-mail from her. She keeps her weight just above the cutoff point. That's her current challenge and she always meets it, flirting with how barely she can meet it, but she does. And her target weight is high enough that she has menstrual periods, so that keeps her out of the anorexia league. She's taken up Shotokan karate and loves that, along with her work at CERN. She hasn't found a boyfriend yet, but that doesn't seem as important to her as it once did. She's less anxious around boys because she spars with them regularly in karate class. She figures one will find her when the time is right.

I'm looking forward to seeing Maureen next summer. Perhaps we will improve on her story a bit, or perhaps it is good enough. She is the judge of that. We externalized anorexia when I talked about it as something that had taken hold of her, instead of a part of her character. Through story and hypnosis, I was able to model ways in which she could see it as separate from her. We became certain of its otherness when we playfully turned it into the Dr. Evil character, whom Kim Possible battles. Anorexia is a perfect villain because it lurks in the shadows, waiting to take over a person when she is weak or vulnerable.

A healing story that personifies a problem or illness and moves it outside of a person is more likely to succeed than a story that localizes the illness or problem within the person as a diagnosis, flaw, genetic defect, or character trait. By recognizing that the problem is separate and has its own identity, we can more readily confront it. Successful healing is not as likely to happen when anorexia is so entwined with the person's self-concept that she and the people around her cannot see her without seeing an anorexic person.

Culture provides us with the landscape in which the hero's journey unfolds. Culture provides the symbols, metaphors, roles, and supporting characters. Kim Possible was a character derived from Maureen's culture. I could never have guessed that this character would work for her, though I have watched the show with my son. When working with younger people, it becomes very important to be familiar with popular culture and facile with its symbols and images. Of course, this happens without effort for those of us with children or grandchildren, for we study their worlds and their icons, trying to find topics for dialogue. Popular culture will change with each generation, but it remains the shaping force for our young people and must be grasped if we are to encourage healing stories to emerge from them.

Maureen demonstrated how only the strongest of wills could achieve anorexia. It requires a focus of concentration and a level of self-sacrifice that borders on the saintly. In the Middle Ages, near-death fasting was one way that nuns showed their fierce devotion to God. Hildegard of Bingen, now popular for her spiritual music, was one of those figures. Therefore, I see the anorexic person as a hero from the beginning, since I'm quite sure that I don't have the strength or will power or attention to detail that she possesses.

For Dana from chapter 1, anorexia solved the problems of lack of meaning and attention in her life. For Maureen, it solved the problem of being noticed as exceptional in a world of exceptional people. Are the qualities that we associate with "the anorexic personality" brought forth by living the role? These qualities include a demand for perfection, an insistence on success at whatever they attempt, and a kind of compulsive attention to detail. The life stories of anorexics cannot be broken down into simple, neat, causative categories. They defy that, for each story is separate and unique. The commonalities we find relate to the common landscape upon which the story is enacted and the similar audiences for whom it is played.

The healing story of the fight against anorexia is a struggle for freedom, a rebellion against slavery and oppression, a search for freedom. Maureen found that. Her anti-anorexia story fit her imagination and desires. Just as there are many stories about the struggle for freedom fought by different people and different cultures, each person's healing story will be different. Our interaction helped Maureen connect with a possible self who resembled Kim Possible. Perhaps she had secretly wanted to be Kim Possible for some time. She and the Kim character shared so many resources and talents. In some ways, she had already absorbed a "Kim self" as a kind of shadow reality, someone she wanted to be but couldn't yet visualize how to become. My story and my interaction with her created a pathway from present day Maureen to an imaginable Kim Possible–Maureen combination. The Kim self had the resources to transcend the problems of the Maureen self.

Tom's story provides another example of the healing power of story. Tom sat with me in a Houston hotel room. I had seen him numerous times before. He had originally come to me with a diagnosis of schizophrenia. When I first saw Tom, he could barely communicate. Through a combination of story, prayer, ceremony and ritual, hypnosis, imagery, and a very small dose of medication, Tom learned how to communicate, returned to junior college and eventually graduated, was producing art for sale in two galleries, and had a part-time job as a barista in a Starbuck's. Despite his amazing successes, he was unhappy because he still didn't have a girlfriend.

Tom came from an unusual background. When he was still quite young, his father had been arrested for growing marijuana. The entire family went on the run. They fled to Mexico and made every effort to become invisible, for the law was after them. Tom's father was actually arrested soon after he came back to the United States to bring Tom to see me. I continued to work with Tom during the entire time in which Tom's father was in prison—a long five years. It was during this time that Tom made his amazing strides forward.

"Why don't you have a girlfriend?" I asked him.

"Because I'm invisible," he replied. "No one can see me."

"Why is that?" I asked.

"Because I'm afraid of being seen."

"What would happen if you're seen?"

"I don't know, but it's terrifying."

"I guess no one can date you if they can't see you." Tom nodded. "Maybe I could tell you a story and then we could do some imagery about being seen," I said. Tom agreed. I started telling him a story about stealing summer that I thought would inspire him. My idea was to suggest to him that he imagine he could steal back his visibility, in full color and vibrancy, just like summer.

❋

"Once upon a time," I began, "a long time ago, there lived a young man of about your age. He lived in a family the way you do, probably not too different from your family. He was the oldest son and likely felt responsible for the other children, just as you sometimes do. But there was one twist. This was a long time ago, when the world was always cold and summer was not known.

"Maybe you used to feel as if the world was in perpetual winter. That's why I picked this story, because I think you can relate to that feeling, the feeling of being frozen, of everything being so cold that you can hardly move. I remember when it used to take you three hours to get into the car because the world felt so cold for you. But now things are much better, much warmer, and we can wonder how it got this way for the world as a whole.

"Our hero hunted, like other young men his age. He brought home his share of game to feed the family. But he dreamed of something better. Sometimes his hands grew so cold that he couldn't even pull back his bowstring. Sometimes the cold made his hands ache and burn, even inside his muskrat mittens. The old men of the village told stories about a magical place where the colors were vibrant and varied and where you could walk outside without heavy clothing. Our hero, Eagle Boy, dismissed these tales as the prattle of old men. He had no time for such nonsense. However, he kept quiet and didn't disagree with them, for that was not his way.

"It reminds me a bit of how everyone used to think of you— that you'd always be frozen in winter, that you'd never thaw, but you did. Maybe you didn't believe summer was possible for you, either, just as Eagle Boy thought that the old men were being silly.

"One day he was out hunting, drawing back his arrow on a big buck deer, even though it was so cold he could barely grasp the bow string. 'Stop,' said the deer, 'and I will tell you something so magical it will be worth sparing my life.'

"Eagle Boy stopped, for how often do you meet a talking deer? Surely it was magical. The deer told him an amazing story about what he had seen on the top of the Mountain that Touches the Sky. 'There,' said the deer, 'you can see into the sky, and you can make out some of those amazing colors that the old men talked about. I have heard that the grass is green and warm,' said the deer. 'I am so tired of eating frozen grass. I long for something warm. Please go find this thing they call summer.'

"That's like what happened to you, Tom. When you lived in the perpetual winter of being almost mute, of being so frozen that it took three hours to get into the car, something stopped you and got your attention. Maybe it was those sweat lodges that we did. After your father was caught, you lived in fear of what would happen to him, how long his sentence would be, but you were no longer on the run. There was no reason to hide anymore. We started our work together right around the time your dad was caught. We couldn't have done that work in the frozen climate of your being on the run. We needed a thawing of that way of life, which I think you helped to find.

"Eagle Boy listened to the deer's stories about summer until he was so cold he had to start moving again. For the next month, he kept his own counsel about the deer's story and what he would do with it. Over time, he decided to go to the Mountain that Touches the Sky to see for himself. Without telling anyone, Eagle Boy quietly collected supplies for his journey. He didn't want anyone to see what he was doing. He didn't want to be ridiculed if his journey turned out to be fruitless. One morning, he gathered his supplies and quietly left the village on the trail to the North. He walked and walked and walked, sleeping in caves and fox dens, as he journeyed further and further from his village. After many days, he came to the tallest mountain he had ever seen, so tall he couldn't see the top. This had to be the Mountain that Touches the Sky. No other mountains came close to being so tall.

"Tom, some of your trips to see me on the Greyhound bus must have seemed as arduous and as difficult as Eagle Boy's journey to the mountain. You certainly persevered, the way he did, for it was never an easy trip for you. The distances were great, but you kept coming back, year after year, to see me, because you wanted to.

"Eagle Boy began the steep, arduous climb. Several times he almost slid down. Like you, only the most ferocious tenacity kept him from falling or sliding off the mountain. When he reached the top, he could see through the sky. Maybe it was thinner there than usual, or maybe he was just closer than anyone had ever been. On the other side of the sky, he could see hints of the colors foretold by the deer. He knew he had to get a better look. He jumped and jumped but could barely touch the sky. He needed something more, so he decided to shoot arrows into the sky. The first two bounced off, but the third one pierced the sky. Now he had an entranceway. He tied a sinew to the next arrow and fired again. Now he could pull himself up to the sky on the sinew. Using his obsidian knife, he cut a bigger hole, large enough for him to crawl through. Finally he was on the other side of the sky.

"You had to work just as hard to get to the other side of your frozenness, Tom. Just as Eagle Boy broke through the sky, I can imagine you triumphantly breaking through the barriers that keep you from achieving these final few things, especially the relationship that you so much want. Being in love must be like discovering summer, right? That's probably why so many weddings take place in June.

"To Eagle Boy's eyes, the colors of summer were amazing. He

had never before seen a green so bright—only the dark green of the snow-covered pine trees. He had never seen flowers of such splendid colors. He had never seen so many different colored birds flying about. Before he could decide what to do, he heard someone coming. Quickly he hid behind a bush. Two sky people walked by, talking about whatever sky people talk about. Eagle Boy decided he should hide and gather more information. For days he hid and watched the sky people at work. He studied what they did, how they tended their plants, how they cared for their birds. When he was sure of himself, he cut a really big hole in the sky and watched the summer start to pour down. It was falling toward the Earth. Bright colored birds flew through the hole and down into the world. Warmth poured out of the sky. Eagle Boy was ecstatic to imagine how excited his relatives would be when summer finally reached the earth. They would be so thrilled by the colors and the birds and the warmth. The thought of what the sky people might do to him paled in comparison with the joy he felt at what he had provided for his family and friends.

"That's how you'll feel, isn't it, when these last few obstacles are lifted, when you've reached your goal. Every time you've reached a goal that no one believed you could ever reach, you've felt really good, full of joy, just the way Eagle Boy felt.

"When the sky people noticed what was happening, much of summer had already drained out. They started looking for the hole. Eagle Boy knew he had to keep them off the path until the egress of summer was irreversible. He started throwing rocks to divert their search. When they got too close, he showed himself and began to run. The sky people went after him, forgetting to look for the hole. Eagle Boy ran long and hard, but eventually they caught him.

"'What are we going to do with him?' the sky people asked. It was getting cold up there.

"'We should just kill him,' one of them said.

"At this point, Eagle Boy was probably just as scared as you get sometimes, Tom.

"'It's too late,' Eagle Boy said. 'Too much of summer has escaped. You can't keep it forever. Now you have to share it.' But no one could agree on how to share summer. They argued back and forth until the spirits intervened. Thunder shook the sky.

"'Stop fighting,' Thunder said. "You have to share. The earth people will get summer for three full months. Then they have three months to give it back to the sky people, who get to keep it for three months, and then have three months to give it back to the earth people.' Everyone agreed that was fair and that was how it was going to be.

"Eagle Boy returned to the hole in the sky and climbed down onto the mountain, which was already growing warmer. When he returned to Earth, he was a hero. Everyone cheered his role in bringing summer to the Earth.

"Tom, you are a hero, too. You've made an amazing journey, just like Eagle Boy, only you had to reclaim your mind. When we met, you had lost your mind. I didn't know where it was, and neither did you. You did what was required to find it again and now life is much better for you. What remains for you to complete is rather small.

"It's time for you to become visible, the way Eagle Boy showed himself to the sky people. You can trust that the thunder spirits will help you, and that it's okay to be seen, because you're warm enough now and won't ever go back to being so cold. Your life is too vibrant and warm to revert to the frigid world you once lived in. You're already visible to the sky people. You've stolen back your mind, and there's nothing they can do about it. Now it's up to you to claim the things that you still lack, the way Eagle Boy claimed summer."

✳

At the end of the story, I asked Tom to go a little deeper into himself, to allow his inner wisdom a bit more latitude. I suggested that he begin to allow an image of his fear to form, to be open to understanding this fear and where it comes from. Tom saw that he was born to a family on the run. Reflecting back upon the time when his parents were living in Mexico in flight from the warrant for his father's arrest, Tom realized how important it had been for everyone in his family to be invisible. Being seen meant being caught and brought back to Texas for trial. He was born into a family of secrets, a family in hiding. How could he help but perceive that his role was to hide, to avoid being seen?

Tom realized that his fear of being seen was now pointless. His father had already been caught and had spent five years in prison. He wouldn't be arrested again for that crime and hadn't committed any others. Hiding didn't matter anymore. The worst that everyone had feared had already happened and hadn't even been that catastrophic. No one had died.

When we had finished the imagery, Tom opened his eyes with a commitment to learn to be comfortable being visible. I suggested a daily ceremony in which he would make yellow prayer ties for vision, burn sage, and offer tobacco to the spirits. Then he would announce to the world at large that he wanted to be a visible part of it, and that he wished to be found by the woman looking for him. I taught him a song to sing as part of that ceremony. He committed to doing that ceremony daily and to leaving yellow prayer ties all around his city on trees, bushes, shrubs, and other natural objects. After six months of this Tom's fear disappeared, and his girlfriend found him.

The next story demonstrates a different kind of healing power, one that helped a woman with cancer who feared death to die peacefully. Her doctors had insisted on another round of chemotherapy, though she was clearly teetering on the edge of life and death. She was anxious and agitated. Her family was upset and wanted something done. Medication wasn't a viable option, considering her delicate physiology. Nausea was severely interfering with the quality of her life.

I encouraged Nan to pay attention to how her breath affected her chest and abdomen, to the movement of air through her sinuses, without thinking that she had to change her breathing in any way. Simply paying attention to the ongoing process of breathing makes us more conscious, focuses attention on how shallow or deep the breath is, and allows us to construct mantras to accompany the breath. We can feel the power of the breath to dislodge tension in the body, especially in the neck and shoulders, but also in the chest and abdomen. Little by little, relaxation becomes a reality, as real as the sky outside and the clouds passing by. Even the sound of the intravenous pumps beeping and the hustle and bustle of efficient nurses can become a part of the meditation, since this is what is happening in the present. In each moment, the noise of the hospital is just so much background that can be appreciated and incorporated into breathing.

Nan was beginning to relax, to release the tension generated by the high stress environment of the chemotherapy ward. Seeing her increasing relaxation, I encouraged her to continue to breathe out tension with each exhalation. I encouraged her to accept the sensations in her stomach, to welcome them into her body. These are just sensations, and only one part of the brain defines them as nausea. I told Nan about the time the disciples were out on the Sea of Galilee, frightened by a sudden storm with large swells and whitecaps, when Jesus appeared, walking on the water. He asked them why they were frightened, and they said they feared the wind and the waves would capsize them. Jesus responded that they need not be afraid. When that didn't comfort them, Jesus stopped the wind and the waves.

I compared the lake to Nan's stomach and the wind and the waves to the chemotherapy. The cells are frightened and sending urgent messages to the brain, I said, but the brain, like Jesus, can hear these messages and tell the stomach that the wind and waves are not harmful, that conditions are safe. Knowing that, we can ignore the storm. Knowing that, we can let the healing power of Jesus calm the wind and the waves. Knowing that, her brain could allow the sensations to exist and could shut down the alarm button from the stomach. Whatever was happening could be allowed to happen, could even be welcomed into the body. Mindfulness teaches us to examine sensations carefully, not as nausea, for example, but as sheer sensation. Focusing on the breath becomes the technology that facilitates this, that allows a slow and steady adjustment to the stomach's messages as harmless.

After helping her to relax and to feel less nauseated, I said, "I want to tell you a story. It is sad but important.

"Being in the present moment does not mean your body will not die. Your body may die, and you may not even notice. You are not this body. You are the ocean and not the wave, rolling onto the shore.

"While you are suffering through this chemotherapy, I want you to remember that you are not the body who suffers. That body is a wave. That suffering is a wave. It peaks, crests, and then rushes toward the shore. When it reaches the shore, it is gone. The nausea, too, will pass. You may live another fifty years, but eventually your body will pass. You could choose to remember that you are not this body. You do not need this body. It is merely the vehicle through which you negotiate this physical reality of time and space.

"You are feeling uncomfortable for many good reasons. Current body conditions are not favorable. You feel you are on the right course. You need this medicine. How can your body accommodate this medicine? We need to help it find a way.

"In a way, it is like being out in the cold. We cannot deny that we feel cold when we are cold. We cannot deny feeling nauseated when we feel this way. We cannot deny pain when it is present. But consciousness is like a searchlight. What is illuminated can eclipse all else. What is caught in shadow does not go away. Rather it loses its prominence. Consciousness can rotate again like the lighthouse beam and catch the unpleasant in its light. Or we can linger on other matters.

"Let's allow the searchlight of consciousness to rotate, like a lighthouse on Martha's Vineyard. Your body is nauseated, yes. But there are other experiences to consider. There are other possibilities for this present moment. Your body will take care of itself. The nausea is not dangerous. The discomfort you feel is not an alarm. You know what is happening; you are having chemotherapy. There are other places to explore, other states of mind to visit.

"What about Hans Christian Andersen's story of *The Little Match Girl*? Her situation was more desperate than yours. But her story holds magical words, just as your story does, though it is very different. You might wonder, why would I tell you such a sad story? Surely I have sufficient experience to find a happy story. What does this story of a little girl, of the misty lights of a cold, snow-covered city, hold for you and me?

"For the moment, we have only the concept of freedom, freedom from pain, freedom from discomfort. But if you squint your eyes ever so slightly, you can gain access to that long-ago day, with its fresh scent of falling snow (for fresh snow does have an ever-so-unique smell, one that only those who have lived in winter climes will know), its cries of seagulls still active despite the cold, its veiled sun, its North Sea port . . ."

✳

"We begin late on a bitterly cold New Year's Eve in a French city. Influenced by the falling snows, a little girl wanders the uncharted avenues of a winter city, a bundle of matches for sale clutched in her apron. Since the death of her mother, the immensity of poverty had slowly closed in on the Little Match Girl. She knows where to grab quick warmth, knows when to run from the *gendarmes*, knows how to sell matches to gentlemen wishing to light their cigars. She also knows how poverty and cold create a spell that binds the soul into slumbering time.

"This particular evening, the Little Match Girl is wandering through the freezing cobblestone streets barefoot and bareheaded. Earlier in the evening she had a scarf, she had shoes, she had a dream of gold received for matches rendered. Through a series of mishaps, her shoes and scarf were gone. But even in the intoxicating cold, she enjoyed the beauty of the snow falling, perhaps as you can enjoy in a funny way the dripping of the medicine entering your veins. The snow continued to fall, harder and harder, like a blizzard in a Siberian winter.

"Despite her innocence and beauty, our young hero cannot go home. Not so unusual for those times, her father sent her out into the cold to sell matches to raise money for the family. Though it is New Year's Eve, the poor girl has not sold a single match. After each refusal from a gentleman hurrying home, her hope of pleasing her father faded a little more.

"Lost in the future means being paralyzed by the fear of what will happen next, including fear of death. The Little Match Girl had no such fears. She had been trying to sell penny matches all day long, but no one had bought any. She no longer even tried to smile at the hurrying gentlemen who might have needed a match. Now she was walking upon the snow with bare feet, which were red and blue with cold. She clutched her stiff apron to keep the matches from falling out. She was hungry and cold as she listened to snowy gusts of wind tinkle against passing windowpanes. You would have thought she looked absolutely miserable huddled in her oversized coat. She dreamed of holding her frozen hands to a warm stove.

"Lights shone from every window. A delicious odor of roast goose filled the streets—the city's customary New Year's Eve feast. Windows were open along every street, venting the heat from cooking, as icicles melted above the window frames. The fine smells kept anyone from forgetting the holiday mood. Not even the Little Match Girl could forget. Her blonde curly hair made ringlets around her face, but no one noticed as she passed in the shadows. Her hair was hidden by white snow. No one paid attention to her, not even the apothecary who sometimes favored her with a gumdrop. Now it's hard to remember your troubles, isn't it? Hers are so much more compelling.

"The Little Match Girl found a corner between two houses, partially sheltered from the wind. She was tired of struggling against a wind laden with ice crystals, was deafened by its whistling, and just wanted to turn her back on her troubles and her pain. She crouched there in the corner of two buildings. For a moment she had an intense awareness of the fragility of her life held only by the ebbing warmth of her thin body, while she kneeled and drew her feet up beneath her. They were warmer if she sat on them. She was almost frozen, like the earth beneath her. She dared not go home for fear her father would beat her. She dreamed of less lonely times, when her mother still lived. She had her reasons, as we all sometimes do, to turn away from the discomfort of her present situation. The city loomed at the entranceway to her hideaway; people still scurried by, though no one noticed her.

"In desperation, she thought to light one brilliant match. She pulled one out and struck it. She watched with lowered eyes, fascinated as a moth by the flame, by the promise of warmth and brightness in the cold night. She tried to speak but her lips were too cold.

"She imagined a big fire, blazing warm and beautiful in the fireplace. The floor was covered with thick carpeting so that her feet could never be cold. Her mother sat on the couch, smiling at her as she played with dolls before the fire. Everyone was well groomed.

"But then the flame went out. The match had burned down to her fingers, but they were too numb for her to notice. Perhaps the wind had finally snuffed it out.

"The girl grabbed a new match. She brought it up from the depths of her frozen apron, for a moment afraid to light it, afraid that her father would beat her for burning the product she was to sell. Then, refusing to wait any longer, she struck the match on the hard, cold sidewalk. Immediately a flame flared, sparkled, and burned brightly, despite the icy blasts of the wind. Where the match's light fell on the rough brick wall of her corner, a shimmering came, transparent like gauze. She could see through the gauze into a room. A table was spread with snowy cloth and pretty china. Children's laughter came from the next room. A woman was playing beautiful music on a piano—Christmas music. She wore a long, elegantly cut dress, the kind ladies wear to the theater in the evening.

"The match died and the girl struck another. Before her eyes appeared a beautiful meal on a table. Each place was filled with a vibrant, smiling face. Her mother sat at the head of the table. Her father was nowhere to be seen. The match fought a long and painful battle with the wind, finally fading. Now, your present moment is her present moment, and whatever was before is now no more.

"She struck another match. In its flame she saw a beautiful bed, covered with filmy curtains and a white canopy overhead. Her mother was tucking her in, reading her a story in the voice that she still remembered, a melodious, loving tone. The match burned out, taking the scene with it. But the Little Match Girl's face had achieved luminosity.

"How many matches remained? She kept lighting them. She had to see more of this beauty. A luminous grandmother stood over her bed. Her smiling mother stood behind in the doorway, calling to her. She wanted to get out of bed and go with her mother.

"As she lit the final match, she felt her feet hit the floor and knew that nothing could hurt her any more. She was coming to her mama. Perhaps they would go downstairs to where the candles on the Christmas tree still burned. The matches were gone. The wall returned to darkness, but the Little Match Girl did not experience any interruption.

"They found the Little Match Girl in the morning. I don't know who went into her corner. Perhaps the street sweepers were pushing snow back there to make way for New Year's Day pedestrian traffic. She was smiling. She looked happy. Her face was frozen. Her hands were locked around the stubs of a match fragment. Despite miserable conditions, she had remained in her present moment, the moment of joy in her mind.

"The present moment is like that. It can be a story; it can be a memory. It doesn't have to be the symptoms of chemotherapy. It is possible to be mindful of a memory. It is possible to become so absorbed in a memory that you forget all about your present circumstances and discomforts. It's possible to become so wrapped up in a wonderful present, as the Little Match Girl did, that you rise above all pain and sorrow."

❋

Mindfulness of the present moment is sometimes the only gift to offer patients, so that the length of their life becomes unimportant. What is important is being in the present moment, which knows no time or duration, as it is perpetually present.

Nan found peace. Her nausea subsided. She rested comfortably all that night. I spent more time with her the next afternoon. She smiled and told me how much she had enjoyed my story. She died one week later. The story had contained the secret instructions she needed about how to die peacefully, which she did despite her medical treatment. Her family felt relieved by her transformation.

The Little Match Girl story activated Nan's own hidden inner wisdom about how to die, how to find peacefulness in dying, and how to transcend the suffering of her body. We can't be certain how the story did this. I can't even be certain what inspired me to tell that particular story. It helps to read widely and to have multiple stories from which to choose, but the choice of a healing story is not one that comes from an algorithm. There is no formula from which to work. Here is a situation in which the richer our experience of life and its stories, the more extensive our reading of literature and even our experience of movies and popular culture, the more able we are to respond to the unique needs of the people with whom we interact.

For years I struggled to find formulas for how to pick a story. I struggled with concepts of archetypes, Jungian types, Meyers-Briggs types, enneagram types, and homeopathic constitutions, until I realized that it is much more complex than any of these simplified typologies. It is so complex that it cannot be rationally predicted. Reason cannot aid us, except provisionally, by providing suitable templates. Once a basic template is chosen, the art of storytelling lies in the modifications we make to wrap the story around the individual to whom we are telling it.

What went through my mind before I picked *The Little Match Girl* story was how much suffering the girl's death might have entailed, but how very peaceful and painless Hans Christian Andersen made it seem. That seemed like the transition that Nan needed.

Great stories, especially those from the oral tradition, make ancient and hidden wisdom accessible to our working brain, the part of us that makes decisions and figures things out. Healing stories contain the information that tells us how to use this wisdom—what to do with it. These stories contain the images of how the unseen inner world really works. This is the wisdom that we can't understand with our minds alone. It must infiltrate us and take seed. When the seed bursts open, it becomes what it could only become within us and no one else. Stories begin the healing process; stories inspire us to believe that we can heal. Then, through our identification with and incorporation of characters in the story, we "drink in" the hidden wisdom they offer, a wisdom that cannot be articulated.

The values we pursue have structure, and particular problems prevent their achievement. Story isolates these different threads and examines them in detail, giving us insight into the greater mystery of life. Stories use the creative process to bring forth the truth of these other dimensions. This information is already inside us. The creative process awakens this inner, hidden wisdom that has been accumulating throughout our evolutionary path. Thus story reconnects us to our lost or forgotten inner self. It leads to a perception of the path that can lead to transformation. This is how we heal. This is how we overcome adversity and suffering. Whenever we participate in story—hearing or telling—we participate in an opportunity for the growth of the soul.

6

Telling Our Story

E ven as hearing a story can be healing, so can telling our story. In some African cultures, a woman healer tends the storytelling tree. Traumatized and suffering people come to the tree, place their hands upon it, and tell their story. Their suffering flows into the tree and away from them. Then they can walk away from that pain and trauma, because they have given it to the tree. The tree has taken it from them and put it back down into the Earth. The grandmother's job is to care for the tree. Her presence as audience is relatively unimportant compared with the role of the tree.

Telling our story is a creative act of community formation. When we speak, relationships form. Telling is an act of relating. Connections are created. Responses are expected. A community arises, made up of us and our audience. The audience is never passive. We expect the audience to react—to encourage us, to sigh with us, to cry with us, to get angry with us. In this way, we know our story is being heard. Hearing is an active process, just like telling.

People need to tell their stories, to be acknowledged, to feel part of a human community. Just telling the story is healing, for reasons we are only beginning to understand. Native Hawaiians say we form community through "talking story." In community, as in any participatory theater, roles shift, and the storyteller becomes the audience for another's story.

People, individually and collectively, use the response of the audience as feedback for community formation. The audience helps us to "self-regulate." It helps us to know how to adjust and realign ourselves with the community we are forming. In the context of a healing community, the audience tells us that others believe we can become whole again. The response of the audience, metaphorically, allows us to reset our thermostat so that we can participate more integrally in a community. I would go so far as to suggest that all communities are formed through the sharing of stories that bind the members together through their shared responses to those stories. These responses shape the stories to fit mutually accepted beliefs and values and evolve to become the stories that tell people how to belong to a particular community. Telling one's story and being heard and recognized by a community is integral to health and wellness.

On the other hand, through listening to the stories told and retold by families and communities, sometimes we can recognize the hidden assumptions implicit within the story and the contribution those assumptions make to the inability of the storytellers to see possible solutions to their problems. This is where familial and cultural diversity is helpful. Members of other families and cultures can see our hidden assumptions much more clearly than we can, because they do not share those assumptions. They grew up under a different set of assumptions and values.

People feel stuck when they have acquired "learned blinders" that stop them from seeing solutions that might be obvious to someone else. Stories can sometimes give us that "ah ha" experience that shows the potential for a new life, previously unimagined, sparkling out before us. Stories show how other characters solved problems similar to ours. When these characters are from other cultures, sometimes we are shocked at how obvious their solutions were. This, in turn, may lead us to obvious solutions for our own dilemmas, solutions that were hidden by our allegiance to what is considered acceptable or not acceptable in our own culture.

Ceremonies provide a formal structure for the sharing of stories and represent a kind of community healing process, often very effective and more appropriate for traditional or indigenous peoples than conventional psychotherapy. Most traditional people would not trust the psychotherapy format, in which the audience doesn't respond. What a strange invention of this Sigmund Freud—a method of "healing" in which one communicates to a blank screen. A traditional person would never trust such an artifice, seeing it as inhibiting the development of shared understanding. During my psychiatry training, I was confronted by a teacher who had written a paper about his inability to do psycho-analytic psychotherapy among the Lakota. He blamed his failure on the lack of emotional development of the Lakota people, without realizing that the root assumptions underlying psychoanalysis were foreign to the Native American. Not only that, but were those assumptions elab-orated, the Native American would disagree with them. My teacher could not see his own cultural assumptions but instead viewed the Lakota people as inferior and their worldview as reflective of immatu-rity (compared with his).

On the down side, support groups for particular illnesses some-times encourage stories that keep people sick and support them in see-ing themselves as ill. People who absorb these stories can come to define themselves as forever ill. A healing story needs to challenge their mem-bership in the community of sufferers.

Odessa's story provides us with an example in which challenging hid-den cultural assumptions with new stories was important. She was a twenty-two-year-old woman with a diagnosis of bulimia. She wanted to stop vomiting. I met her at a treatment center where I was consulting. We had the opportunity to meet for several sessions. I learned that she had grown up privileged in Minneapolis. She had studied acting throughout college and planned to move to Los Angeles to break into the movies. She had developed the habit of inducing vomiting to con-trol her weight to get parts. She tended to be chubby, as did all the women in her family. Her parents stressed appearance as very impor-tant. The consistent feedback from directors and casting agents was "lose weight to succeed." We talked about actresses who weren't slim. Bette Midler came to mind, along with Roseanne Barr, Oprah Winfrey, and other notables.

Rumi said, "The images we invent could change into wild beasts and tear us to pieces."[1] Our culture has invented an image of the lead-ing lady that could tear Odessa to pieces. Odessa had a family who sup-ported the cultural ideal of thin and beautiful; she rebelled by being chubby but still wanting to succeed as a leading lady. We needed a story that would bring to light the various hidden assumptions of her family culture and our modern American culture to help Odessa come to terms with her dilemma.

With young people, I tend to use elements of the popular culture to find stories to which they can relate. For Odessa, I needed a healing story that would help her change her view of her body. She felt worthless if she didn't look good. I couldn't think of an appropriate Native American story, because body image and weight are not seen as problems in that culture in the same way as in our modern culture. As I scanned my memory, the best story to fit the need was that of *Shrek*.[2] I asked Odessa if she had seen *Shrek,* and she hadn't. "So let me tell you about the movie," I said, "and you can watch it later. That will make what I told you even more powerful in your memory."

The *Shrek* story is a modification of the traditional story of the prince who fights his way past the dragon, slays the dragon, rescues the princess, brings her home, and lives happily ever after. Shrek combines this theme with an old tale from Chaucer—the tale of the Knight of Barth. In this story, a knight is banished for violating one of the queen's ladies in waiting. He has one year to journey throughout the kingdom to answer the question of what women really want. If he doesn't answer correctly, he will be killed. He is returning to the queen forlornly, without an answer, when an ugly hag confronts him on the road. She offers to tell him the answer the queen wants to hear if he will marry her. His choices are limited, so he agrees. On their wedding night, she turns into a beautiful princess. She tells him that a spell has been placed upon her. She must be beautiful half the time and ugly the rest. He has the right to choose whether he wants her beautiful by night for his eyes only or beautiful by day for the eyes of world. His answer is to choose not to choose. He tells her that the choice should be hers alone, at which point she chooses to be beautiful all the time.

Shrek plays on a variation of this theme. Shrek, the hero, is an ugly ogre. This is the essence of Odessa's conflict—thin and beautiful or chunky and ugly. We begin with her being twenty-five pounds overweight, ugly (in her mind) like the ogre. The princess in the story is beautiful by day and an ogre by night. Only the kiss of her true love will return her to her proper form. I chose this movie story because Odessa could watch it repeatedly.

"*Shrek* begins in a swamp," I told Odessa, "with an ogre who's really quite ugly, unless you're another ogre. The story casts the evil Lord Farquhar as the villain, who has taken over the Land of Make-Believe and is banishing fairy tale characters from the kingdom. They show up in Shrek's swamp, which really upsets him, for he loves his privacy. As part of that entourage, Shrek acquires an obnoxious but loyal donkey as a sidekick, who then accompanies him wherever he goes.

"Shrek, the ogre, comes to the castle to challenge Lord Farquhar to remove the fairy tale characters from his swamp. Farquhar agrees, on the condition that Shrek retrieve the Princess Fiona from a castle guarded by a dragon and bring her back to marry him, at which time he will create space for the fairy tale characters so that they can leave Shrek's swamp.

"Shrek and the donkey undertake the arduous climb to the high mountain castle to rescue Princess Fiona from the dragon. They succeed, and to Fiona's surprise, don't kiss her or even want her but plan to take her back to her 'true love.' On the long journey back, they learn that Fiona must hide at night. Little do they know, at night she transforms into something ugly, too embarrassing to reveal. She is a beautiful maiden only by day.

"Strangely for an ogre and a human, Shrek and Fiona are attracted to each other. As the story plays out, the donkey discovers that Fiona becomes an ogre by night and looks just like Shrek. She's not pretty by conventional cultural standards, only by ogre standards.

"As Fiona and Farquhar are about to be married, Shrek realizes he loves Fiona and will do anything to stop the wedding. He crashes into the church and begs Fiona not to marry Farquhar. They kiss, and the kiss turns Fiona into an ogre! So the two ogres marry and ride off into the sunset, arm in arm, happy."

Shrek is a perfect story to challenge the bulimia-promoting beliefs shared by Odessa's family and the dominant culture. In the *Shrek* story, the beautiful princess turns out to be an "ugly ogre" and lives happily ever after with another ogre. I told Odessa this story to seed her with the idea that thin is not necessarily the only way to be. She could be happy at weights other than model-thin. The *Shrek* story provided some humor for Odessa as she thought about the constant pressure to be thin. The alternative was to be Fiona. She could be a perpetual ogre.

Why did this story (and later watching the movie) comfort her? We can't ever really know for sure. She bought the movie on her way home and watched it many times. The movie helped her challenge her "hidden cultural assumption" that thin is happy. We spoke about that as well. I asked her to name five thin people who were happy, and she couldn't. I asked her to name five fat people who were happy. She couldn't. "Do you know anyone who is happy?" I asked her.

"No," she answered. "No one is happy."

"So what makes you think that being thin makes you happy?" I asked. She didn't know. But she did know that it would help her get acting parts, and unfortunately, this was true.

Odessa stopped vomiting and accepted herself as heavier than the ideal for a "leading lady." She still struggles with self-esteem but is trying to succeed as an actress anyway. She told me a moving story about the original Ziegfeld Follies, in which the dancers were Jewish and had bodies that were more plump than the New York norm. As we continued our dialogue, Odessa told me more stories about actresses with "voluptuous" bodies. She had to help me with this, because I didn't know what to tell her. I knew that the theater industry stresses being thin. I knew that overweight people get parts, though they are definitely in the minority. Overweight males are more common in the industry than overweight females. I knew that experimental theater had different rules, and that parts existed for characters for which weight didn't matter, though these were almost never leading ladies on Broadway.

What do we do when people's desires don't match those of the culture? I think we must keep talking with ourselves and the culture within us. I use hypnosis to facilitate this process. Odessa had a strong belief that her weight would always be heavier than what the entertainment industry desired. She could have chosen to change that belief and find a way to visualize herself as thinner. On the other hand, I remarked to her, she could be an agent of change for that industry. She could lead the charge to change the obsession with thinness. That could be a source of meaning and purpose. She liked that idea.

I heard from her in Los Angeles that she left bulimia in Arizona. She continues to struggle with her weight and where to position herself in an industry hostile to anything but a washboard abdomen, but she took seriously my advice about telling her own story. She has started a theater group for "voluptuously beautiful" women. Together they create plays about being "chunky in America." She sent me a videotape of one of their plays, which was hilarious. I wrote her back that if she didn't replace Nicole Kidman, at least she could be a regular on *Saturday Night Live,* since she was so funny. Time will tell.

Odessa was able to transform the hidden cultural assumptions that shaped her life into a theatrical story about her conflict with the culture. Listening to stories based upon other value systems, such as *Shrek,* led her to be able to challenge her own culture's ideas about weight by telling her own and others' stories about being heavy in Los Angeles. New movies address similar concerns. In a recent Whitney Houston movie, one of the characters says, "I like my women large." A "voluptuous" woman, as Odessa would call her, is one of the four female costars.

Through the *Shrek* story, I introduced Odessa to a postmodern world in which she could begin to recognize that each of us constructs our own images of beauty. Through this recognition, even though Odessa still lives in a world in which thin is considered necessary, she has begun to challenge this concept in her thoughts and deeds. The challenge is still complicated, because Odessa wants to succeed in a world that constructs beauty in one particular way, and I am suggesting that she can construct it any way she wishes. I believe that the real healing will happen as Odessa turns her struggles into "storytelling." The more plays her theater group produces about weight, the more she will heal through telling her story.

Creating an action or a setting through which someone can create her own story is powerful. We give people the opportunity to tell and retell their stories. Being and doing is half of the story cycle; telling and communicating is the other half. Good and interesting stories involve a change. Consider this story: The king died. The queen died. That's a story, but not interesting. A better story: The king died. Then the queen died of heartache.

Communities form and remain strong through their shared stories. As I mentioned in chapter 1, every group needs a creation story. Married couples tell the story of how they met. Parents tell children the story of their birth. In history classes all over the United States, children learn mainstream culture's version of the birth of America.

Here's an example of another woman who found a way to tell her story differently. Marianne was a sixty-year-old woman with metastatic ovarian cancer. She had completed surgery and a cycle of chemotherapy and came for a spiritual healing retreat to achieve guidance on what to do next. After an opening ceremony in which I asked the spirits and the ancestors and the keepers of the directions to bless our activities, I used hypnosis to help Marianne achieve an altered state of consciousness. This altered state is one in which the body relaxes and thinking slows down. It's an optimal state for receiving images from the inner storyteller and messages from the inner healer. (These terms are name tags for something far deeper and mysterious that I can't begin to describe.)

In my work, I use hypnosis frequently, though I often call it by another word, since stage hypnotists have corrupted the word and Christians fear it. I use it in the manner I observed medicine people using it, as a tool to help people become receptive to exploring and listening to their inner worlds. One Arikara word for this process translates as "putting them to sleep so that they dream like they're asleep, but they're really awake." Hypnosis is the language of storytellers. Studying hypnosis gives one names for the various storytelling tools, names like cadence, voice emphasis, embedded commands, implied causatives, disguised suggestions, and more.

When I have taught courses on hypnosis, once my students mastered these various categories (which are arbitrary and only created for heuristic purposes), I often gave them the assignment of listening to a master storyteller. They listen to a recording of the person at work and then break down each utterance into its appropriate category. In this way, they learn that storytelling uses hypnosis and hypnosis is just effective storytelling. Then I asked them to listen to three-year-old children. These are the true experts at hypnosis, especially around Christmas time. Since three-year-olds have little or no money to buy themselves things, they must influence their parents to do so and must cultivate in their parents both the desire to buy things and the impulse to do so. Not only that, they must guide relatively stupid parents (from the perspective of the three-year-old) to buy what a three-year-old really wants.

The students recorded the stories and conversations of young children and analyzed them for techniques used. All of the techniques occurred, and with great mastery. I don't know when we lose our storytelling abilities—perhaps as our allowances increase. However, these skills return later during adolescence, when parents have bigger things that children need—permission to stay out late, to go on trips, to borrow the car, and the like.

Whatever we call the persuasive and artful use of language—hypnosis, guided imagery, storytelling, creative prayer—the idea is the same. We must get people's attention. We need their full attention. They must be totally absorbed in what we are doing. They must forget about the rest of their lives. They must leave their worries behind. They must be absolutely focused in this moment in time, not thinking back to yesterday or ahead to the appointments that come later in the day. They must be mindlessly empty-headed.

To achieve this state, I sometimes remind people of how it feels to be at the movies. We go to the movies to forget life's problems and to be entertained (with the exception of certain people, who go to art films to be depressed). I screen movies to be sure they have happy endings, because I see enough sad endings in real life that I don't consider sad endings entertaining. For this reason, I love Disney as predictably uplifting, which is what I crave.

So when we go to the movies, we prepare to be absorbed. We prepare to suspend disbelief and get caught up in the story. I want this attitude from people during our work together. I want them to empty their minds and become able to receive images from inside. Too much noise in the mind prevents us from hearing our inner storyteller. I want them to sit back, relax, and enjoy their own inner show.

Once she was in a receptive state of mind for hearing a story, I told Marianne the Dineh creation story. In this story, the characters struggle through five different worlds to emerge into this one. I thought that this could parallel Marianne's journey, one of emerging through the worlds of her own life into a brand new world.

*

"We begin as usual: This story happened a long time ago. In the beginning there was only darkness, with the sky above and water below. By some mysterious and holy means, sky and water came together. Everything began when they touched, and First World was created—a red island floating in a sea of mist. Its inhabitants were the Nilch'I Dine'e, who existed in spiritual form and could travel like the wind. They were called ants, dragonflies, beetles, bats, and locusts, but they weren't insects or animals; rather, they were spiritual beings. There were also the holy people, whose form and beauty we modern day humans eventually received. The waters around this island were inhabited by powerful guardians: Water Monster to the East, Blue Heron to the South, Frog to the West, and White Mountain Thunder to the North.

"The only light came from the sky and consisted of four sacred colors that glowed from different directions to mark the time of day. Dawn was marked by a white glow in the East, signaling the Nilch'I Dine'e to awaken and prepare for their day. The height of the day was marked by a blue sky from the South, during which the Nilch'I Dine'e carried out their daily activities. Yellow from the West marked the end of day by telling them to put things away and rest. Black from the North told them to sleep.

"The center of the First World was a place where water sprang forth from the ground, forming three rivers that flowed to the East, South, and West. The North had no river because it was the direction of darkness and death. Four groups of Nilch'I Dine'e lived along those three rivers, all in different places, making a total of twelve villages. No one lived in the North.

"Everyone lived at peace and life was good, until trouble arose because of adultery. This angered the guardians of the Four Directions, because First World was supposed to be a holy place. They saw the growth of deceit, jealousy, and envy. They gave the Nilch'I Dine'e three warnings to change. When those warnings were not heeded, White Mountain Thunder from the North told them to leave immediately, but they didn't listen to that either, causing the guardians to turn their backs and decide to punish the Nilch'I Dine'e.

"One morning the Nilch'I Dine'e saw something on the horizon coming closer and closer. It looked like a ring of snowy mountains. As it got closer, they saw that it was an unbroken wall of white—higher and wider than they could ever fly across. It was a great flood sent by the guardians of the Four Directions to punish them. Frightened, they frantically flew up toward the sky, which was smooth and solid, so hard that they couldn't even scratch it. Just as they were ready to give up in despair, a strange blue head emerged from the sky, telling them to fly east. There they flew through a narrow opening in the sky into the Second World, or the Blue World.

"The land of this world was barren and flat. They found no beings anywhere within a two day's journey, until one morning a small group of blue beings who resembled them appeared, with legs, arms, wings, feet, and bodies. The Nilch'I Dine'e couldn't understand the language of these beings, the swallows. Nevertheless, they forged a pact of friendship, which lasted until adultery started again and the angry swallows demanded they leave.

"Once again they took flight toward the solid sky, and once again, just as they were ready to give up in despair, a white head mysteriously appeared, telling them to fly south. There they found a hole in the sky that took them into the Third World.

"At first they thought this world was uninhabited, but then they discovered that grasshoppers lived there. They made friends, all was well, but then adultery happened again, and the angry grasshoppers demanded that they leave. Again they were at the edge of despair at an impenetrable sky, when a mysterious red head appeared and told them to fly west. There they found a hole in the sky and entered the Fourth World through a winding tunnel.

"The Fourth World was black and white, and there was no one there to greet them. Four great snowcapped mountains stood in each of the Four Directions. Scouts traveled in all directions looking for inhabitants. Eventually they found strange beings living in the northern mountains in pit houses, whom they called the pueblo people. These people welcomed them and taught them to grow corn, squash, beans, and pumpkins. This time the Nilch'I Dine'e behaved better for a longer period of time, and all went well.

"One day they heard a voice calling from the East. Three times it called, each time coming closer. On the fourth call, four mysterious beings appeared—the holy people. They were Talking God with a white body, Water Sprinkler with a blue body, Calling God with a yellow body, and Fire God with a black body. They did not speak but tried to communicate with gestures and motions, appearing four times over four days. On the fourth day, when the Nilch'I Dine'e still could not understand them, Fire God spoke, saying "We want to make corn, white for men and yellow for women." This was done, and on the twelfth day they returned with two buckskins and two ears of corn, one white and one yellow. Water Sprinkler and Fire God laid the first buckskin on the ground. Calling God laid the two perfect ears of corn on the buckskin, placing the second buckskin over the corn. They told the Nilch'I Dine'e to stand back, while a sacred wind entered between the buckskins. As the wind blew, mirage people appeared and walked around the buckskins. On the fourth turn, the ears of corn moved. The white ear had become a man, and the yellow ear a woman. These were First Man and First Woman. These were the first real people with five fingers and no wings, made in the image of the holy people."[3]

❋

How do I use this story as a template for a person to tell her own story?

I gave Marianne suggestions to let the story work on her, to help her bring up images that could change and heal her. The story was interspersed with suggestions for going deeper and deeper into herself, to the place where her inner healer and her inner storyteller lived. Having told the story fully once, I returned to it in an interactive mode and asked her to let her inner storyteller inform her about the creation of the cancer. We wanted to trace the birth of First Cancer Cell. Where was its precursor? When did water and sky meet to create the first hint of cancer?

Immediately she saw her first marriage. She told a story about a man she had loved deeply throughout college but knew how impractical it would be to marry him (women thought more about those considerations forty years ago). He was an artist with no prospects of gainful employment. How could he support a family? How could she relax and raise a family with him? Nevertheless, he gave her joy just by his presence. She loved his spontaneity and his creativity, overflowing whenever they were together like a bubbling fountain.

The other man pursuing her was a medical student. He planned to become a surgeon. He came from a respected family of doctors and stood to inherit money. He was serious and practical. He wasn't as much fun to be around, but he gave her a solid sense of security. With him, she imagined, she could relax and raise a family and let him worry about supporting them, which he would do admirably.

Marianne eventually broke up with the artist and became engaged to the medical student; this was her "first world." He ended up serving in the Vietnam War, which changed him, as it did many of that generation. Their first child awaited his return, but he had turned cruel. She caught a sexually transmitted disease from him, which turned out to be difficult to treat. She no longer felt affection from him or for him. As he grew more cold and distant and lost himself in his surgical practice, another child came, but each time they had intercourse, she experienced it as a kind of violation. Eventually they separated and she struggled to get child and spousal support. Her notions of security had not borne fruit.

Her second world began, she recounted, when she met Barry. She was a struggling graduate student with two young children. Barry was a successful architect, charming and suave. He swept her off her feet. They became engaged and she quit her graduate studies with a master's degree in music. That relationship also turned sour. Another child later, she discovered Barry in an affair. As time progressed, she learned that he had kept a series of girlfriends on the side and that his affection was relatively shallow. His charm swiveled according to whom he was with. She felt betrayed. She felt that her pelvis took another hit. She felt dirty, as though darkness had spread into her organs, impossible to clean. (I have heard and written about similar descriptions from other women with ovarian cancer.)

Her third world started when she fled from Barry and returned to graduate school, now a struggling mother of three. Extracting support from Barry was also difficult, and now she had two ongoing court battles over money. She eventually completed her PhD in music and met David, a successful attorney. After an eventful romance in which he took her to Paris, Bali, and Morocco, they married. This time they had dogs instead of children, but David also turned out to be flawed. He had a homosexual side that he kept in the closet. To her surprise, this surfaced when he stopped having sex with her and several months later announced that he was HIV-positive.

To Marianne's amazement, she remained HIV-negative, though how that had happened she hadn't a clue. This began her fourth world, in which she vowed to leave men alone and take care of her children. She found a job teaching music at a small college in Indiana and concentrated on work and childrearing. Anxiety-filled months passed as she continued to be tested for HIV. She felt the darkness growing and saw cancer cells emerging, fed by her bitterness and despair. Her loneliness grew. Her children thrived as her soul withered. David was eventually diagnosed with AIDS. They didn't bother to divorce, since he told her he was dying anyway and that she would be better off financially if they remained married. Eventually she found herself caring for David as he died.

Years passed, her children left home for college, and she met another man, with whom she was currently involved. They lived in different states and saw each other on weekends. He was cool and distant, but she was reasonably sure he was faithful and not gay. He taught film at a prestigious Eastern university, and they shared an interest in theater and music. Life was better, but she continued to feel empty and dirty inside—barren like the third world, she said.

She described the diagnosis of cancer as almost a relief. The darkness could be cut out. But traces remained. She felt it inside of her, and indeed, it did spread onto spots inside her abdomen. Another surgery removed those spots and chemotherapy agents were used to wash the inside of her peritoneum (the inner lining of the abdominal cavity). Then we met.

Marianne experienced tremendous relief from telling her story. The Navajo creation myth had given her a template for its rendition. Other imagery followed, including her seeing her pelvis as a desert with areas of dead, black tar clinging to the saguaro and other cacti. She was on medical leave from her job, living in Maui to try to heal herself, which worked for her partner. Though they didn't see each other as often, and he enjoyed his monthly trips to the islands as a welcome break from the drudgery of his mainland teaching job.

I wondered how she could clean the desert. The idea emerged to use bits of dead cactus, stones, and other materials I provided her to make dolls of the men in her life who had traumatized her pelvis. She constructed amazing renditions from saguaro spines and boots and found objects, including rusted tin cans, barbed wire, and stones. We ceremonially burned the dolls and then did a cleansing ceremony for her pelvis.

Two years have passed without return of the cancer, but her CA-125 antigen levels have begun to rise, and I have suggested a return to the desert for further work. We will see if she comes.

Diane was another woman who needed to tell her story. Diane came for a spiritual healing retreat because of metastatic colon cancer that had spread to her liver and several bones in her spine. She was living with constant pain and fear. Her husband was supportive but couldn't accompany her. She brought a friend to help take care of her, though I discovered that she didn't need care so much as she was afraid of being alone.

After an appropriate "hypnotic induction," I told Diane the story of Jumping Mouse.[4] I intuitively knew this was the right story. In retrospect, I think I recognized the high likelihood that Diane would die. Jumping Mouse dies in such a way that she is transformed, and death is rendered less fearful. Jumping Mouse illustrates the observation that the journey matters more than the outcome. For Jumping Mouse, the quest for the Sacred Mountain mattered more than her life. Life was secondary to the quest. I wanted Diane to be as peaceful as Jumping Mouse was with her fate, whatever it would be. I wanted Jumping Mouse to give her a sense of meaning for the transformations forced upon her by her illness.

✳

"Jumping Mouse was always curious. She lived in a family of mice who were content with their small corner of the world—avoiding eagles and hawks, foraging for food, and huddling together in their comfortable home. Jumping Mouse, on the other hand, was always pushing the limits. She went far from the nest to see what was there. She took risks running across open ground to find new places to explore. Several times hawks had almost taken her. Jumping Mouse's mother chided her to be more cautious and to act like a mouse. 'You'll be somebody's dinner if you keep this up,' said her mother.

"Nevertheless, Jumping Mouse continued to explore. She wanted to visit the distant mountain. She wanted to know what was on the other side. One day, she decided it was time to go. She would have her adventure. She took some food in a bundle and set out for the distant, purple mountains.

"Jumping Mouse's first encounter with danger was with a mountain lion who appeared to be dying. She cautiously approached the great beast. 'What is wrong with you, my friend?' she called out.

"'I am dying,' said the lion, 'unless someone can doctor me.'

"'How would I doctor you?' she asked.

"'The spirits say I will die unless someone makes a great sacrifice for me. I have lived a selfish life, and unless someone performs a selfless act for me, it is over. I have not lived so as to inspire such behavior from anyone else. My relatives have turned their back on me. They live as I did, thinking only of themselves.'

"'I have little to give,' said Jumping Mouse, 'but you can have my bundle. It holds everything that I own. It is yours.' The lion was touched by Jumping Mouse's sacrifice.

"'Aren't you afraid I will eat you anyway?' asked the lion.

"'Yes,' said Jumping Mouse, 'but that is a risk I will have to take.' The bundle changed paws and the lion felt her strength returning.

"'I will take you as far as I can on my back,' said the lion. 'Where do you wish to go?'

"'I am traveling toward the distant mountains,' said Jumping Mouse.

"'Then I will take you to the edge of my territory,' said the lion, 'and protect you from predators.' Good to her word, the lion carried Jumping Mouse far from her home and deposited her at the edge of a great prairie.

"'This is as far as I can go,' said the lion. 'Good luck.' Jumping Mouse climbed down and continued on her way.

"The journey was long and hard. Jumping Mouse became fatigued. She didn't know how she would ever make it to the purple mountains. Almost delirious, she stumbled into a big rock. But something was different about this rock. It moved. It was warm. It seemed furry. Jumping Mouse worked her way around the rock, only to discover that it had a face and horns.

"'What are you?' Jumping Mouse exclaimed.

"'I am a buffalo,' answered the creature.

"'What is wrong with you?' asked Jumping Mouse.

"'I have lost my vision,' said the buffalo. 'I am blind and cannot see. My herd has abandoned me. I can no longer keep up with them and I am left for the lions to eat.'

"'Is there no way to cure you?' asked Jumping Mouse.

"'The spirits say I can only survive if someone gives me an eye. No one will do that, so I am lost.' Jumping Mouse felt great compassion for this massive beast.

"'I will give you an eye if you will carry me to the distant mountain,' said Jumping Mouse. 'I can never get there on my own, and it would be worth one of my eyes to get there.'

"'You would do that for me!' exclaimed the buffalo.

"'Yes, if you will do what I ask for me,' answered Jumping Mouse.

"'I will,' answered the buffalo. Bravely, Jumping Mouse plucked out her eye and climbed up the buffalo's head. She placed the eye in the buffalo's empty socket, where it magically grew and grew until it was almost as large as Jumping Mouse.

"'I can see again,' exclaimed the buffalo. 'I am saved, thanks to your generosity and kindness. Now climb on my back, and I will take you to the distant mountain.' Jumping Mouse did just that and rode with pleasure, warmly snuggling into the buffalo's hairy coat, hidden from all predators.

"They journeyed far, the buffalo sleeping standing up, and finally, they reached the base of the distant mountain. 'We are here,' said the buffalo. 'I can go no further, because my hooves are not made for climbing mountains. I am a creature of the plains. You are on your own now, to climb this thing that I cannot climb.' Jumping Mouse thanked the buffalo and carefully climbed down from its massive back. She started up the mountain.

"Mountain climbing was harder than Jumping Mouse had ever imagined. Her small size prevented her from grabbing the handholds that the rocks presented. She struggled and struggled, seeming to falling backward as often as she moved forward. On one of her falls, Jumping Mouse found herself rolling into the legs of a hawk.

"'What are you doing here, little mouse?' said the hawk. 'It is rare that lunch presents itself so readily. Why do you do this?'

"'I am trying to climb the mountain,' said Jumping Mouse.

"'Why?' asked the hawk.

"'To see what is up there and what is on the other side.'

"'You are a strange mouse, but nevertheless, I am a hawk, and hawks eat mice.'

"'I would give anything to make it to the top before you eat me,' said Jumping Mouse.

"'Anything?' asked the hawk.

"'Anything,' affirmed Jumping Mouse.

"'I am missing an eye, which makes it hard for me to hunt,' said the Hawk. 'Give me your remaining eye and I will take you there. I will even spare your life, for the improvement in my vision will make it possible for me to hunt so much better that I will find another lunch.'

"'Done,' said Jumping Mouse, plucking out her other eye and giving it to the hawk, who placed it in her empty socket and regained the sharp, binocular vision that hawks are so well known for. Now Jumping Mouse's world was dark. She could only feel the hawk lifting her in its talons and carrying her skyward. Up and up they soared. Just that sensation of soaring was worth all of her sacrifice, thought Jumping Mouse.

"After what seemed like a century of time, they landed. The hawk carefully placed Jumping Mouse at the top of the mountain. 'You are here, little mouse, at the top of the sacred mountain. Creator bless whatever happens to you next.' Jumping Mouse wished she could see what it was like at the top and what was on the other side. She asked the hawk to tell her, so the hawk began to describe the magnificent view stretched before them. Jumping Mouse could see it inside her mind, just as the hawk described. She was content and ready to die.

Jumping Mouse lay down at the summit and fell into a deep sleep. How long she slept no one can say, but when she awoke, things had changed. Her body felt different. Her paws had grown extremely large. She opened her eyes and could see! The view was just as the hawk had described it, though ever so much more beautiful. She looked down at her body and was in for her next surprise. She had feathers! Her legs had turned into talons. She opened her mouth and was greeted with a shriek, like the cry of an eagle. She had heard that sound before as eagles dived to hunt for mice. When she cried out again, she realized that the sound was coming from her. She had become an eagle! Now she could truly find what was on the other side of the mountain."

※

At the end of the story, tears flowed from Diane's eyes. "I'm like Jumping Mouse," she said. "Both my mother and my father died from colon cancer. I always believed that if I got cancer, it would save my brothers and sisters from having to get it. That's why I never had any children. I knew I would get cancer, but that my sacrifice would save my brothers and sisters."

Diane finished her story of living in the shadow of certain cancer. "I've never told this to anyone," she said. "It was my secret pact with God. It's given me the strength to keep going."

Here was Diane's story of strength, courage, and meaning. How much more meaningful it became when she was able to share it! My next task was to wonder how we could create an alternate story in which she could find the same sense of meaning and purpose and still live. This was tricky business, because Diane's survival at this point would be a miracle. In her construction, her death would have meaning and purpose. I could never wish to take this away from her. Yet her presence with me in the desert meant that she wanted an alternative story, whether or not she could believe it.

Telling stories is a creative act of self, family, and community construction. In a larger sense, stories are a cohesive force in the formation, identity, and stability of cultures. Communities exist as constructions through shared stories. On the personal level, receptivity to stories allows the individual to access her own "inner storyteller and inner healer" to generate her own healing story. Stories and selves are inseparable. When we tell stories, we create a relational self that arises from our interactions with the audience. New stories create new selves. New selves have different physiologies. A radically different enough self-construction can shake off an illness that clung to the previous self.

Telling stories is therapeutic because it is creative, and creative acts change us. In all three examples I've related in this chapter, telling new stories led to great changes. Odessa continues to tell creative stories, in the form of plays about weight. Marianne tells stories about her transformation through several successive worlds of relationships. She tells these stories to members of her healing circle, to members of her prayer circle, to me, and to others. We are her healing community. We care whether she lives or dies. Diane also had a healing circle to whom to tell her stories, along with family and friends.

Today, Odessa is thriving, and Marianne is still miraculously living with cancer, years beyond her doctors' expectations. Diane died with peace, dignity, and a sense of meaning. To the end, she believed that her sacrifice would prevent her brothers and sisters from developing cancer. The Jumping Mouse story became her favorite. In her final days, she told everyone she was jumping into eaglehood, just like Jumping Mouse.

7

Stories as Psychotherapy

Everything the power of the world does is done in a
circle. The sky is round and I have heard the earth is
round as well. Stars are round. Birds make their nests in
a circle, for their religion is the same as ours.

BLACK ELK

Storytellers and healers help people make meaning in their lives. These meanings are delivered within the stories they tell. I've implicitly been demonstrating what's now called *narrative psychotherapy*, an approach to helping people change that resulted from collaborations among indigenous peoples and Anglo-European psychologists, anthropologists, sociologists, and others. As I described in both *Coyote Medicine* and *Coyote Healing*, indigenous healers work through story. They tell stories—mythical, legendary, and personal. They encourage the person who is suffering to tell his or her story. During their work with the person, through imagery ("putting them to sleep so that they dream like their asleep but they're really awake"), through community gatherings, and through ritual and ceremony, the healer helps the person change his or her story.

I learned how to do this from Native American healers and then later discovered that an actual academic tradition (albeit small) that emphasizes the healing power of stories exists within psychology and the other human disciplines. In this chapter, I wish to introduce readers to this tradition, in the hope that through the concept of "story as psychotherapy" we can all help it grow stronger and have more of an impact on mainstream practice and culture. Narrative psychotherapy is based upon postmodern philosophy, which is surprisingly similar to the philosophies of Native America (and other indigenous cultures). Narrative psychotherapy says that stories contain our experience and the meaning we make of that experience. We communicate about our world by telling stories. Stories hold the richness and the complexity that simple declarative facts can never grasp. Narrative psychotherapy states that the real object of study is the "storied nature of human conduct"—how human beings deal with experience by constructing stories and listening to the stories of others. It proposes that the "story" or "narrative" provides the dominant frame for organizing experience and for creating meaning out of that experience.

Narrative medicine and psychology also provide us with different diagnoses than the typical, anatomically based diseases from the International Classification of Diseases Annual (ICDA). That diagnosis may be made, for example, by a Dineh (Navajo) hand trembler, who reads the aura of the person and their illness, telling a story within a system of cultural symbols about what has led up to the illness to produce it and what will make it better. The hand trembler then prescribes the appropriate ceremony or healer. Within the Lakota and Cherokee traditions with which I am most familiar, the healer diagnoses the problem through careful listening and rapport building. The healer teases out the story before a ceremony is ever considered. Once the healer understands the problem (again, within a particular, culturally bound metaphorical system), a treatment plan can be constructed, usually a combination of botanical treatments, individual counseling with the healer, family counseling, purification (as in the sweat lodge), healing ceremonies for the family and the community, and sometimes massage therapy, a technique that was particularly well developed among the Cherokee (as well as the Apaches and Native Hawaiians).

A story can be defined as a unit of meaning that provides a frame for interpreting experience. We enter into stories, we are entered into stories by others, and we live our lives through these stories.

For the past decade and a half, some psychologists have been turning toward the notion of narrative with accelerating intensity, to establish a new "paradigm" or "root metaphor." They have examined other fields of scholarship to borrow or adapt concepts and notions about narrative and are indebted to literary theorists, philosophers, historians, theologians, anthropologists, sociologists, and scholars of women's, gay and lesbian, and ethnic studies for a great deal of the foundation upon which the narrative perspective in psychology is being built.

The idea of a narrative or a story becomes a root metaphor for psychology that replaces the mechanistic and organic metaphors that have shaped so much theory and research in the discipline over the past century. We can, for example, recognize Freud's narrative as just that—a story he created to explain his experience, not necessarily relevant to all other people or cultures. Freud's narrative was decidedly mechanistic—hydraulic, in fact. Drives push things up from a hidden underground source. The ego rides like a pontoon boat on top of an unconscious lake. Conflicting drives create tension. "As if" becomes more important than reality.

Another dominant paradigm of the twentieth century was the biological—the idea that behavior is genetically determined and that human will or desire plays little part in psychology. Our actions are the results of raging storms of chemicals wreaking havoc in our systems. Treatment is primarily chemical—medications to alter the balance. But biological explanations are also just interpretive stories, and not necessarily true. While biology is vitally important to our existence, it is only one level of explanation, and not necessarily the most powerful level for understanding all of our activities.

Experience affects biology and even gene expression. At the University of Miami, Dr. Tiffany Fields found that touching premature babies changed gene expression. Touching babies for fifteen minutes twice daily resulted in the up-regulation of two genes, C-MYC and MAS, producing higher levels of the enzyme ornithine decarboxylase. These higher levels allowed the babies to gain more weight on the same amount of calories as babies who were not touched, thereby leaving the hospital an average of six days earlier, with a savings of $3,000 per baby.[1] Gene expression is influenced by emotional experience. Watching horror movies changes the expression of genes that control cytokines, which are the messengers that regulate our immune system. Horror movies appear to be immunosuppressive, while comedy enhances immune function and even raises pain thresholds.[2]

Narrative psychology recognizes multiple layers of explanation. At our current level of understanding, we don't have to understand the correspondence among levels to know that each level is important. We don't have to understand all the details about how the stories that we live affect our biology, though we are beginning to appreciate some of the chemical processes involved.

We situate our experience within stories that determine the meaning of our experience. These stories determine which aspects of experience we will select to express. They determine the shape and form of that expression. They direct our lives and relationships.

A life—the totality of an individual's activities, relationships, hopes, dreams, poems, and progeny—is created through the enactment of the stories we tell ourselves, the stories we tell others, the stories that are told about us, and the cultural stories that constrain us all. Telling a story about ourselves results in our living out that story. We become who we describe ourselves to be. We perform the roles required by our stories, for particular audiences and on particular stages—the various contexts of our lives. These stages may include the home, the workplace, the hockey rink, the neighborhood bar, and others. The audience can include our immediate family, our co-workers and bosses, our fellow hockey players, or just the guys at the bar. People may have invisible audiences who are always watching—a bearded male god on a silver throne, a dead mother, the angels, the spirits, and more. The performance of a new story or role can transform a person's life, but only if the story is performed for the correct audience. If you were raised Southern Baptist, the story of discovering you are gay, falling in love, and traveling to Vermont to get married probably wouldn't play well before the Southern Baptist Church or imagined members of its congregation who you think are always watching you.

A spiritual transformation occurs when we change the role we play for a spiritual audience, however we conceptualize it (God, the spirits, our ancestors), also witnessed by a community of humans concerned about spiritual matters. The actor (the person performing a text or living out a story) must have confidence in his or her own authenticity, which comes from the feeling that he or she is correctly situated within the story, its scenery, and its other characters. A classic enactment of

Hamlet would not feel authentic if the guards wore modern combat fatigues. Everyone must fit into their roles and costumes. This congruence of roles and costumes has been called culture.

The idea that our lives are situated in our stories implies a particular notion of authenticity—a person arrives at a sense of authenticity in life through the performance of his or her stories to an appreciative audience, with a sense that the play fits what is expected. This notion of authenticity is different from romantic notions about "true personhood" or the "true self." Those beliefs suggest that, under particular and ideal circumstances of life, a person will be "released" to become who he or she truly "is," which is authentic. Narrative psychotherapy's notion is that people feel authentic when the play works, when the other characters' lines match theirs, and when the audience responds as expected. People become what our mutually shared stories expect them to become.

The classic experiment supporting this argument is the Stanford prisoner and guard experiment. One year, over the Christmas break, students were recruited and randomly assigned to play the role of either prisoner or guard. The basement of the psychology department was turned into a prison. All students were paid equally; they knew they were playing roles and would return to being students at the end of the break. Nevertheless, the experiment had to be terminated early, because the guards were becoming so cruel to the prisoners that the experimenters feared that they would do permanent damage or even kill one of the prisoners, or that the prisoners would riot and hurt one of the guards. These results were sobering and suggested that people fulfill their roles even when they have been told that the roles are only "make-believe."

In other classic experiments, students "shocked" other students with lethal levels of electricity just because they were told to do so by an experimenter. The shock was given for answering a question incorrectly. The students being shocked were acting and didn't really receive any electricity but pretended to suffer greatly and to eventually pass out. Almost all students recruited for the experiment kept increasing the shock level when told to do so, even though they could see how much suffering they were inflicting upon another.

In another study conducted in a first-grade classroom, intelligence tests were administered to children. Teachers were told opposite results from what was actually found. The top half of the class was labeled as the bottom half, and vice versa. One year later, the students were actually performing as they had been labeled and not as they had been tested, showing that the teachers' expectations were more important than the students' innate abilities.

In all of these contexts, the subjects performed the stories they had been given, and the stories shaped their lives. Their experience structured their expression of their experience, which fed back to further structure their experience. The stories changed the subjects through their enactment of the stories.

These stories that we perform are our lives. The expression of our experience through these stories makes up our lives and our relationships. Our lives are shaped or constituted through the stories we and others tell about what we are doing and why we are doing it.

Narrative psychotherapists are challenged by the notion that human activity and experience are filled with "meaning," and that stories, rather than logical arguments or lawful formulations, are the vehicles by which that meaning is communicated. This dichotomy is expressed as the distinction between modernist and narrative forms of thought, each of which is irreducible and fundamental to the other. The modernist perspective holds that there are invariant principles or rules that can be determined. The narrative perspective holds that principles are created as the result of stories that we tell and are somewhat arbitrary, depending upon the story.

Noted psychologist Jerome Bruner wrote, "a too-ready separation of scholarly disciplines such as occurred between psychology and anthropology must surely be counted as one of the most stunting developments in the history of the human sciences."[3] The concept of *social construction* is important to narrative psychotherapy. The idea is that we cocreate our world and the beliefs through which we perceive the natural world. This concept consists of three central ideas:[4]

1. The production of knowledge is a creative, interpretative process and cannot be adequately framed within logistic theories. This means that we create knowledge rather than discover it. It means that we form stories (called theories) that tie together observations and the results of experiments, and

through argument and counterargument, decide through consensus which stories to accept and which to reject. For every rejected theory or story, a small group continues to cling to it and becomes the minority in a field, or even gets rejected by the field as so blatantly unscientific as to be unacceptable. These are the deviants, who are important just in case they are right.

2. In their experiments, scientists actively aspire to produce results that accord with their theories. The work of science is to confirm theories, not to discover hidden truths. Without theories or stories to guide us, we could do nothing. The stories form the context in which experiments are performed. Science takes big leaps when someone discovers such a great inconsistency in the currently accepted story that no one can continue to ignore its holes. Then a new story is constructed that takes into account what was previously ignored.

3. Knowledge is always grounded in a background of contingent assumptions and local investigative practices. This means that we cannot escape our context, even as scientists. The way in which we perform experiments comes from a certain worldview and set of cultural assumptions. My favorite example of this is the randomized, controlled trial that is conducted in medicine to presumably offset individual differences in response to treatment. Yet what matters most to people are their individual and unique responses to treatment. Thus, the project of medicine becomes the search for the common response, rather than the search for categories of people who will respond to the same treatment quite differently. Individual differences are ignored. While useful, some pressing questions cannot be addressed by randomized, controlled trials unless major modifications are made (such as attempts to reanalyze the data for individual differences and variations that might have caused the experiment to turn out the way that it did).

When we apply the concept of social construction from within storytelling psychotherapy, we arrive at three central conclusions:

1. The subject of psychology is not an object of a natural science but an artifact, in the sense that it is imaginary and cannot be

touched. This means that the study of how people act or live does not result in a natural object suitable for dissection. While biological psychology asserts the claim that the brain can best be understood by dissecting it into smaller and smaller parts, in fact, no amount of dissecting the brain helps us explain certain kinds of behaviors in groups of organisms or even in individuals. Cutting up your dog will not tell me why he likes to play Frisbee.

2. There is a reflexive relationship between the stories people tell and the people who tell them. People tell stories to describe their psychological states and produce theories to explain their actions. These theories then inform their further actions and later psychological reactions. Theories are just stories. They may or may not be true, but they lead to action that is real. Theories as stories create our worlds even if those theories are flawed or not seen as true by other cultures. The best twentieth-century examples lie in the stories (theories) that various cultures told about race and gender and what was expected (demanded) for certain races and usually for women. Thankfully, we have rejected many of these stories and are closing the gap of inequality between men and women and among the various races. We produce stories to explain our behavior; these are all constructed after the fact and may have little or no truth value. They comfort us with the illusion of self-knowledge.

3. People, the subject of psychology, cannot be adequately analyzed in natural scientific terms. The language of the natural sciences is mathematics. Natural systems tell their stories in mathematical language. Gravity, for instance, has a story to tell about the curvature of space-time that is best expressed mathematically. However, the story about human beings is incomplete with only a mathematical description. The story about human beings requires us to listen to the stories that people tell to explain themselves and their projects, hopes, and dreams. Psychology can never be reduced to a natural science like mechanics or hydraulics or hydrogeology.

These insights have important but rarely appreciated consequences for medical and psychological research. So-called qualitative research that studies the stories people tell about their lives is always considered inferior to questionnaire research that forces people to choose among several responses to a question about their lives. Yet the qualitative studies are invariably richer in explaining human lives. It is our cultural assumptions and local research practices that hold questionnaires to be more valid than interviews.

In a classic textbook from 1963, Berger and Luckman argued that "identity is formed by social processes. Once crystallized, it is maintained, modified, or even reshaped by social relations . . . ."[5] This means that who we think we are is created by living in a context—a family, a community, a culture. We cannot readily step out of this context to comment upon the assumptions we have grown up with, because we would never think to question these assumptions as anything but truth. Here is where cultural diversity helps us. Members of other cultures can look at our beliefs and point out to us assumptions that their culture does not hold to be self-evident truths. Then we can begin to examine our hidden cultural assumptions, which restrict the story alternatives from which we can choose.

Stories contain a kind of hidden code that informs us how to handle situations with which we have no prior experience. Consider the effect of the Hawaiian story of Moki and Bufo on Rhonda, a seventeen-year-old flirting with anorexia. Her naturopath referred her to me because she met the diagnostic criteria for anorexia and was threatening suicide. The story will reveal how a creative solution emerged from Rhonda, stimulated in part by my stories, but primarily as a result of her own personal transformation, which seemed nothing short of miraculous.

The first thing I had to do was to address Rhonda's threat of suicide. Her mother attended our session, appropriately wondering if Rhonda needed hospitalization, but hoping that was not so. In talking with Rhonda and her mother, I learned that Rhonda had been more severely anorexic in the past, and had actually gained some weight under the care of the naturopath, who was treating her homeopathically with a remedy called *Aurum metallicum* (gold) and with homeopathic detoxification using low-potency remedies designed to help the body clean out toxins.

Rhonda thought this was mostly bull and was taking the remedies to please her mother. She believed that life was hopeless and just wanted to be dead. Strangely, she implied she couldn't kill herself until exams were over, because it would adversely affect her grades. I learned that she was a driven achiever. Performing less than perfectly was unacceptable.

When we had developed more rapport, I told her I was required to commit her to the psychiatric hospital if she couldn't make a contract with me and her mother to avoid suicide for a specific period of time. At first, she refused, saying that going to the hospital was fine for her. I then told her stories about my experiences as a psychiatric resident witnessing the bad things that can happen on psych wards. These included some of the stories I told in *Coyote Medicine*. I even suggested she could get the book and read about why psychiatric hospitals weren't fun places to be. I never told her that she shouldn't go to the hospital. I just described my own experiences working there. Her mother had several stories to add. I continued to say that I respected her right to choose what she wished, but I worried about that choice, based upon my experience. As we neared the end of our scheduled time together, Rhonda suddenly announced that she was willing to make a deal for one month. We negotiated a one-month moratorium on suicide to give me a chance to help Rhonda find a reason to live. Once I was sure that her mother believed in the agreement, they left for home.

I've learned that you have to trust people about suicide. Thanks to the Creator, I haven't been proven wrong yet. The only time I came close to being sorry was during my residency training in San Francisco, when my superiors refused to go along with my approach and applied their "we know better than you do" ideas to a young woman who so successfully manipulated them that they let her go, at which point she promptly took an overdose of pills. She survived, but with permanent damage to the nerves of her arm from lying on it for too long while she was unconscious. I've learned that patients are smarter about suicide than we can ever be. If they want to kill themselves, they will find a way. I've learned that building trust and rapport and sharing my own fears about them, me, and potential repercussions is more effective than bullying them.

With Rhonda, I felt comfortable that we had done the best we could, because Rhonda seemed believable and her mother agreed. I told her mother that the most conservative approach would be to admit her anyway, though I doubted she could be held if she said the right things, and she was smart enough to do that. Then we would have lost the war, since she would never trust us again. Rhonda's mother agreed, setting the stage for our one-month journey for Rhonda to find a reason to live.

In my next session with Rhonda, I told her the story of Moki the gecko and Bufo the toad.

☀

"Once upon a time, in the Hawaiian Islands, there was a young gecko named Moki. Moki was an ordinary gecko in every respect except for one thing—he had the loudest, most obnoxious laugh anyone had ever heard. Moki and his friend Owl were constantly getting in trouble for their pranks, mostly because of the after-effects of Moki's laughter.

"This story, like all stories of its kind, takes place a long time ago, 'cause that's the way it is. The story occurs in the days of the Great Choosing, when every noble family was to select an animal to be its totem of power, or *amakua*. A most serious and powerful ceremony would take place that evening, and Moki's parents warned him to behave. They stressed upon him the importance of being serious and not laughing, not even once, lest he shame the gecko family.

"Moki solemnly agreed not to laugh, tell jokes, or pull any pranks. He would be the model of decorum, as would his partner in crime, Owl. They resolved to be more serious than the serious, more perfect than the perfect, quieter than the quiet, the best of the best [which is what I suspected Rhonda was trying to achieve—to be the best student, best anorexic, and most depressed of the depressed].

"Night came and the conch shells blew to call the people and the animals to gather. All of the *ali'i*, or noble families, were present, including the greatest king of all the islands. The most powerful *kahuna* of anywhere presided over this majestic event in service to the king, in which families came forward in accordance with their rank and stature and picked their power animal for all time. One by one the animals were chosen. Pomp and circumstance was preserved until Moki noticed the fattest man he had ever seen waddling forward to choose his family's power animal. 'Oh, not us,' he thought. 'You would crush us without noticing.' That image made Moki think of a joke about a great big fat bufo toad. The more he tried not to think about it, the more it occupied his mind, until he told Owl, and suddenly the two of them could contain themselves no longer, and they burst out laughing. The ceremony came to a screeching halt. Silence reigned, except for their laughter. Soon they noticed that the drum had stopped, chanting was suspended, and all eyes glared at them. Moki's laugh was the loudest, and it was upon Moki that the *kahuna* focused his rage.

"'The gecko family has dishonored this solemn ceremony. They are to leave immediately. They will not be chosen by anyone.' The *kahuna* folded his massive arms across his chest and towered above the geckos. Moki turned and ran into the jungle, lest he be scorched by his parents' rage. He wanted to die that night right there in the jungle, he was so embarrassed. [I was picking up the theme of wanting to die, maybe to show Rhonda alternate solutions, maybe to show her how silly that response is when it comes from someone else, especially an animal, like a laughing gecko.]

"Moki ran and ran and ran. He ran so hard and so far that he had no idea where he was. He just wanted any creature to jump out of the jungle and eat him. He was so mortified he knew he could never go back. He could never face his parents or the other animals. He could never face the *kahuna* again or any of the *ali'i*. He might as well be dead.

"When he was so breathless and exhausted that he thought he would die right there on the trail, he suddenly heard a noise that did not belong to the jungle. 'What's that?' he wondered. He listened closer and discovered a young human girl, crying. He followed the sound of her sobs into a clearing, finding her sitting alone, tears pouring down her cheeks.

"'Young girl,' Moki said. 'What's wrong, and why are you out here alone? It's dangerous in the jungle at night.'

"The little girl stood as tall as she could, acting as proud as a tearful young one can. 'I'm the daughter of the great chief,' she said. 'Daddy wouldn't let me come to the ceremony. He said I was too young and made me stay home. I was going to show him and come all by myself. But I'm lost and I can't find it and now I don't know where I am.'

"'Neither do I,' thought Moki, who decided not to say that, since he had to be brave for the princess. 'Don't worry, princess,' he said. 'I just came from the ceremony and I'll figure out a way to get you back there.'

"Just as Moki took her hand to lead her back the way he had come, a dark shadow fell upon them. He looked up to see a massive bufo toad, weighing at least four hundred pounds. Sores and warts covered his skin, which oozed a slimy-looking substance. Worse, the toad stank. His eyes were glowing coals inside a malevolent face.

"'Uh, hello, Mr. Bufo,' Moki said. 'This is the great chief's daughter, and I'm taking her back to the ceremony. You could come, too,' he stammered.

"'No,' said Bufo. 'I think I'll stay here and take you both to dinner. You'll be the appetizer and she can be the main course.'

"'But what would the great chief say about that?' Moki pleaded. 'You don't want to anger the great chief!'

"'I'll anger anyone I please,' shouted the great Bufo, who was staring into Moki's eyes, making Moki feel drowsy. Moki's will was draining away. He found himself slowly walking toward the toad's gaping mouth.

"'Moki, no,' cried the Princess. 'Don't look in his eyes. He's got you under his spell. Fight it, Moki. Fight it, for my sake.' [In parallel fashion, I wanted Rhonda to fight the seductive fascination of suicide and anorexia, both of which are like the toad's eyes in that they seem to pull you into their spell.]

"Hard as he tried, Moki couldn't break free. The toad's eyes bore down upon his, forcing his will upon Moki. He was dangerously close to that gaping hole of a mouth, one bite away from annihilation, when suddenly he remembered the joke that had gotten him cast out of the choosing ceremony, and he started to laugh uncontrollably. This terribly ruffled Bufo, since the first course wasn't supposed to break out laughing.

"'What's this about?' demanded Bufo.

"'Heh,' said Moki. "Do you know where a four-hundred-pound bufo toad sleeps at night?'

"'Where?' said Bufo, puzzled.

"'Anywhere it wants,' answered Moki, still giggling. Bufo

paused for a moment to consider this. Then slowly he began to laugh, his huge body shaking and quivering with each guffaw. Before long, the toad was laughing uncontrollably also.

"You're okay, Moki,' said the toad. 'And I wasn't really going to eat you.'

"'Like heck you weren't,' thought Moki, but he wisely kept that to himself.

"'I'm really a nice guy,' said Bufo, 'with a skin problem.'

"'Help me take her back to the ceremony,' said Moki, 'and there'll be lots to eat there.' Bufo agreed, and together they set off across the jungle, taking short cuts that the toad knew. When they reached the ceremonial grounds, they were the strangest sight of all—a little girl, a huge toad, and a laughing gecko, for Moki had continued to tell jokes to keep the toad in the best of moods.

"'Stop!' cried the guards, with their spears ready.

"'No,' called the princess. 'Let them pass. The bufo toad is my friend and the gecko saved my life.' The guards recognized the princess and bowed before her. When her father saw her, he demanded to know how she had gotten there. Upon hearing the story, he welcomed Bufo to chow down, and he had more to say to Moki.

"'Little gecko,' he said. 'You have restored the honor of the gecko family. Unfortunately, all the power animals have been chosen, but one honor remains—to be the power animal for all the islands. That I give to the gecko family. From now on, you are the *amakua* for these islands upon which we live.

"Moki was proud, so proud he could look his parents in the eye without wanting to die anymore. And they happily went home."

❋

The story seemed to get Rhonda's attention. It had many of the necessary elements—wanting to die, wanting to be perfect, being embarrassed, encountering massive fat, eating and being eaten. Also, it provided some levity to our interaction. It's not a terribly serious story, in its own gecko-Coyote way. Later we would joke about snacks to befit a four-hundred-pound toad and what to do with the hallucinogens found upon its skin.

How do we pick a potentially healing story? First, we have to discover at least one character that resembles one the person is enacting. Since stories are two-dimensional, we have to reduce the complexity of another human being into a more simple character with whom she can identify. Though I will never know for sure, I guessed that Rhonda felt like both Moki and Bufo—one an outcast, the other a fat, grotesque villain. The guess was good enough, because Rhonda changed—because of the story or in spite of it. Rhonda stopped obsessing about her weight. She made having a boyfriend and a normal social life more important than being thin. She gave up on the battle between her parents, which had been raging long before her conception. Rhonda's anorexia had begun when her father moved out. After the work we did together, Rhonda found more interesting pursuits than her parents' problems.

We identify with characters in a story in accordance with our temperament and constitution. Rhonda's constitution matched these two characters. In taking her homeopathic case, I was caught by how difficult it was to decide between two remedies—*Aurum metallicum* and *Natrum muriaticum*. The *Aurum* character, for example, is an outcast in search of a task, persecuted for her intrinsic traits, while the *Natrum muriaticum* character is the rebel who only really wants to go home, just like the characters in the story.

Later I discovered that *Aurum metallicum* was more likely Rhonda's mother's constitutional remedy, and that *Natrum muriaticum* matched Rhonda better. Was that true when we met, or did it emerge as an evolving property during our group discussions? I had encouraged Rhonda's mother to surrender trying to control Rhonda and fix her problems. I tried to teach her how to just listen to Rhonda's stories and to offer her unconditional love. Mothers can try too hard to fix their daughters, I told her, and anyway, once they're five years old, it's hopeless. You've lost your last chance, so give up and listen and enjoy her unique perspective.

Hearing Rhonda's mother's story was important. Susan had married a very handsome man, who had never succeeded. In a two-dimensional reduction, Ralph was an ironic antihero. He failed at every business he tried. He resembled the Peter Pan character, the boy who never grows up. He remained this way after Rhonda's birth, while Susan became more responsible. She played a really good Wendy to her husband's Peter. She earned a master's degree in business administration and got a high-powered job. The more she succeeded, the more her husband appeared to fail. While Ralph did excellent self-care, Susan did almost none. Rhonda grew up in the midst of this struggle over self-care and taking care of the family. Her parents danced around a cycle of production and consumption. Mom produced and she and Dad consumed. Mom's resentment, bitterness, and anger grew. Rhonda and Mom became allies in complaining about Dad. The more they complained, the more inefficient and "flaky" he became.

Eventually Ralph and Susan separated and began the divorce process. Then Rhonda and Mom were left alone without Dad in the house. That's when Rhonda began to display anorexic behavior. The play had lost a character. When the play went from three characters to two, the roles shifted. The old rules stopped working.

Dysfunctional as it may have been, the old family had provided a stability that disappeared when the drama changed. For a while, the play could work with Dad missing, as though he would return at any minute. But at some point, they realized he wasn't coming back. As an absent character, he lost power. They still needed dramatic tension. The fighting shifted. Now it was between Rhonda and her mother. Now Rhonda refused to consume. Life was meaningless. She had no purpose. She just wanted to die.

Rhonda expected perfection from herself, just as Susan expected perfection from herself. Rhonda believed that she must be the perfect student. She must achieve better than an A in every course. Susan believed she must excel as an employee. She must be more than the perfect manager at every moment. Did Ralph provide the comic relief for this duo? Did Ralph's buffoonery serve to relieve tension? Did he keep the play light, tending toward comedy instead of tragedy? Was Ralph their gecko-Coyote? Without him, the play took on a dangerous quality. Fantasies about his leaving turned into fantasies about Rhonda's leaving, but through death or disappearance (anorexia). The family's source of comic relief had disappeared.

But this was only my construction. It stands as a piece of literary criticism, but is it true? I don't know. What I can say is that my feedback about these ideas and my comments on how I saw the play going seemed to help them change during the course of our interaction. I've also noticed that treating family life like a play is less threatening than directly commenting upon the family. I've found that saying "your character seems to be" is much less threatening than "you seem to be."

The other value of talking about characters and the roles people are playing is the immediate externalizing effect. If I'm playing a role, I can change that role. I can stop acting in this play. I can do a new play. The technique allows people to reconsider their roles without feeling judged or becoming defensive: I'm not saying there's anything wrong with you. You're fine. In fact, you're a great actor or actress. But the play is starting to wear on you, so we need to find a new play with new roles and characters that will be more fun, maybe even life affirming. This is easier to accept than being told one is pathological, or receiving a diagnosis, or hearing how screwed up one is, which is what much of conventional psychotherapy does.

As we continued, Rhonda eventually got disgusted with therapy. She refused to continue, instead bargaining for a car, telling her mother she would abandon suicidal threats forever if she could have a car. Her mother got her a car. Rhonda got a job, acquired a boyfriend, ate appropriately for her weight, and stopped contemplating suicide. Her grades continued to be excellent. The process of therapy, if we can call it that, consisted of a negotiation of story. More daunting is my developing awareness that there are no intrinsic, underlying principles to be gleaned from this story. My story about what happened, while valid for me, might bear no resemblance to Rhonda's or Susan's story about what happened. Would they recognize themselves in reading this description? Probably not, because it's my description, not theirs. Nevertheless, because of our muddling through this together, the story line changed. Maybe I became the annoying but silly character to replace Ralph. I continued to remark to Rhonda that I was no expert. I couldn't heal her or make her eat. All I could do was tell her some stories, give her a homeopathic remedy that might or might not help, and otherwise muck about with her. We did agree that I could help her mother learn better self-care skills and how to be interested in Rhonda's life without meddling. For that goal, Rhonda was enthusiastic.

I doubt the existence of any single story about anorexia. I think it's simply an attribute of a character. Many different characters can don the anorexic cape. It's just a prop, and one that drifts in meaning as the culture changes. As anorexia has become more recognized, it has become more valid as a long-term identity. Its meaning can change over time. The degree to which it can be embraced as an identity can also change. This is because no social construction is static. Everything is in motion.

People typically cannot see the story they are living. The help of someone else is required to sufficiently tease out its elements, fictionalize it (meaning simplify it so that it is understandable), identify the characters and the audience, point to the archetypal themes, and wonder what values are being pursued. When invited playfully to join this project of "literary criticism," most people enthusiastically join in. The storytelling paradigm is largely void of the blame contained in the dominant culture's "defective people" paradigm. The exception to our inability to see our blinders comes in the form of the occasional divine or spirit guidance that patients may receive in dreams or visions, telling them how healing can best be accomplished.

Telling a story is more effective than lecturing or interpreting. We identify with characters in a story in accordance with our own temperament and constitution. In telling the stories that inspire and provoke healing, the world's traditional healers demonstrate an implicit awareness that we don't have to explain how someone got sick or how they will get well to stimulate healing, and sometimes, to cure. The world's healers seem to recognize that people and families are what systems science calls a self-organizing, creative, problem-solving whole. These whole systems do need to be fixed, but sometimes they just need the necessary inspiration or a gentle nudge to "fix" themselves—meaning that they self-correct to return to the path they seem to want to follow. Illness severity doesn't always predict what kind of effort will be required to initiate change. Sometimes just one innovative story provides the inspiration for total transformation.

8

Archetypes as Agents of Change

Any claim to objectivity is an absolute
demand for obedience.

HUMBERTO MATURANA

What are the constraints of the stories we concoct? Are we who they say we are? Or do we tell stories to inspire ourselves to move toward who we wish to become? The Russian philosopher Bakhtin stressed the importance of being "unfinalized and becoming," stating that we can never truly become who we think we are or who we want to be.[1]

The human condition has limits. A finite number of stories continually recur. A finite number of roles exist—hero (wounded, reluctant, supernatural, ironic), fool, lover, princess (distressed, captured, enchanted), adventurer, victim, shrew, courtesan, and witch, to name a few. The themes and plots of our lives are limited by culture and biology. The stories we need to hear for transformation have already appeared in the world's myths, legends, epic poems, songs, plays, and novels. Many cultures exist, but there are only so many codes to decipher for information about how to transform. Even evil is limited in its forms of expression.

Despite our lack of control over the stories of our lives, by becoming aware of the story characters we are enacting, we can coauthor new stories in conjunction with therapists, healers, family members, and communities, thereby changing our character and plot. We can find easier paths and new endings, new rivers to navigate to unexplored territories.

An archetype is a model, pattern, or theme that finds consistent and recurrent expression in human life. Archetypes found their way into the earliest forms of literature—stories, myths, songs, and poetry. They are the recurrent themes intrinsic to human life and relationships. They represent the potential for what people can do and the range of possibilities for their stories. They contain the limits of the human condition, limits that were well established even by the kings of old.

Archetypal patterns are the themes that persist with variations from age to age and that correspond to a pattern or configuration of emotional tendencies in the minds of those who are stirred by the theme. Carl Jung believed that these patterns are "inherited in the structure of the brain" and are "stamped upon the physical organism."[2] When forms are assimilated from the environment upon slight contact, predisposing factors must be present in mind and brain. These forms can be glimpsed in the world's sculptures, from Rodin's garden pieces to the great works of Michelangelo.

Cultural patterns are the preexisting configurations or arrangements of tendencies that determine the response of members of a group to a new element. Culture resembles the unique topography of a landscape, like a small altar with candles in a Mexican living room.

Myths and stories contain enduring human concerns. Our stories unfold from our lives. Our stories are constrained by our biology, by our psychology—in essence, by our brains and the interaction of our brains in social life. All of our personal experiences are unique, but the archetypes represent broader categories or dimensions of that personal experience. The stories also connect us with our ancestors and the themes of their lives.

Two major themes of human culture come from changes of the seasons and from the journeys of heroes. Historically, it has been easy to link the cycle of human life with the succession of the seasons. Springtime is linked to birth and childhood and to the East, where the sun rises to give birth to the new day. Summer is linked to adolescence and to the South. Fall is linked to adulthood and to the West. Winter is linked to old age and to the North. The myth of Demeter and

Persephone is the quintessential seasonal myth, with the regular descent into the underworld when the plants wither and die, followed by the return to the surface world when the plants flourish and blossom again.

I use the cycle of seasons to generate ideas of birth and rebirth, renewal and regeneration. Within the broader cycle of a life come smaller cycles of emergence, flowering, harvest, and decline. Similarly, illness can be seen as a time of decline. In an earlier story, we linked perpetual winter upon the Earth with an illness and the theft of summer from the sky people with the restoration of wellness. Cycles of change are important inspirations because otherwise, the illness experience often feels like one of stasis and stagnation.

My use of the term archetype is different from that associated with Carl Jung and his analytic psychology. Jung thought of archetypes as essential underlying forms that do not vary from culture to culture. I think of archetypes as common themes forged from the interaction of biology, culture, and geology. To me, archetypes represent the realm of the possible. The theme of the hero is one such archetype. The hero represents a theme of overcoming obstacles to prevail, sometimes against overwhelming odds. The hero's story is easy to link to recovery from illness. The situations and obstacles are similar. We can readily link the stories told about heroes to the stories told about healing. Through this linkage, we can inspire healing through the telling of heroic stories.

Heroes may be born under mysterious or unusual circumstances. A special sign may mark the hero for greatness. He may descend from great men or deities. Hercules was the Son of Zeus; Jesus was the son of Yahweh. While young, the hero may be exiled or placed in harm's way (like Orestes, Moses, Hamlet, and Snow White). The hero must prove himself by a task or feat. He accomplishes great deeds for the people, like King Arthur establishing Camelot or Beowulf killing the Monster. If he dies, his death may be mysterious or ambiguous. Arthur disappears into Avalon. Christ is crucified. This suggests that the hero is not dead. He may be reborn or return at a later time of great need.

What are the potential characters people can play? Jung's notion of archetypes as underlying forms that exist independent of the people who use them is perhaps unnecessarily romantic. I suspect these forms change regularly with the evolution of culture, biology, and history. The definition of hero may also change regularly, in synchrony with cultural changes, just as warfare changes with the progress of technology.

The hero is a most inspirational character for therapeutic stories. At some time in our lives, we all want to be a hero, and we are all the heroes of our own lives. We cocreate ourselves through the stories that we enact in the world, though sometimes we repeatedly tell stories whose outcomes seem inevitable, leading us to believe that we have no choice in the matter. Sometimes we are born into a family with a strong need for a particular character and no one else to fill that role but us.

I use Steven Barnes's description of the stages of the hero's journey frequently.[3] Once we understand the creation of the illness, we are ready to steal fire (consciousness, perspective, the capacity for self-reflection), rewrite our stories, and become heroes. Barnes's description of the heroic adventure resembles such stories of healing. Here is how it goes:

1. The story begins when the potential hero is confronted with challenge. For the hobbit Bilbo Baggins in J. R. Tolkien's *The Lord of the Rings*, Gandalf asks him to use his talents as a thief for the benefit of Middle Earth.[4] The challenge can also be a diagnosis of cancer or rheumatoid arthritis or bipolar disorder. Like the hobbit Frodo Baggins, people with illness are invited to step up to the challenge of taking the ring to Mount Doom, meaning that they must accept the idea that they can make a difference in the course of their illness and take action to do so.

2. The hero initially rejects the challenge, often because of fear. Any challenge large enough to force heroism has to be frightening, or it wouldn't be heroic. Bilbo tries to stay home in the comfort of the Shire. Mulan hesitates before grabbing her father's armor to join the war. Perhaps she would prefer the matchmaker to succeed in making her a bride?

3. The hero eventually accepts the challenge, or we would have no story. Not all sick people do this. Some give up or are otherwise unable to rise to the challenge. We often call this depression or despair. The Little Mermaid in Hans Christian Andersen's story accepted the challenge when she made her pact with the evil sea witch to allow her to become human for twenty-four hours. The sick person accepts the call to heroism when he accepts the idea of personal agency—that he can do something to impact the course of the illness. Of course, doing something to impact the

course of the illness does not always mean cure or even survival. Sometimes just finding meaning where none seemed possible before is enough.

4. The hero experiences a road of trials. The places we visit trace out the story. A long story requires several destinations to be interesting. If the hero triumphed immediately, the story would be pointless. Our life narratives seem to need an element of struggle before success comes to us. Frodo Baggins struggles through Middle Earth carrying the ring, encountering allies and scoundrels, good and evil, crisis and challenge. In his "dark moments of the soul" he hears Gandalf telling him, "All you have to do is to decide what to do with the time you are given." In each of these moments, he decides anew to continue the hero's journey. Mulan struggles to learn how to act like a man and a soldier, eventually triumphing when she climbs a tall pole with her bare hands.

5. The hero finds allies and powers along this road of trials. Frodo has Gandalf, the walking trees that defend the forest, and the elfin princess to aid him. He has Samwise Gamgee, who has promised not to leave him. Mulan is helped by a comic family dragon, who draws out the best in her each time she confronts the enemy. I often serve as ally for my clients. I help them find hidden resources and talents lying within. I invite them to bring forth their unique strengths and assets.

6. The hero confronts evil or the obstacle at least once unsuccessfully. The hero tastes defeat. The evil can be outside of the person or can be some insufficiency that exists inside the self, as in a lack of honesty or other weakness. Mulan's weakness is her sex (in the cultural context of medieval China). The Little Mermaid's weakness is her lack of voice. The evil in *The Lord of the Rings* is the power of the ring to breed greed and evil within the person holding it. In the state of weakness, nothing can be accomplished.

7. The "dark night of the soul" occurs when the hero feels that all of his or her innate capacities are insufficient to meet the challenge. All is lost. Mulan collapses in the snow while the army marches away. The Little Mermaid is ready to give up and become the property of the sea witch. Frodo is riding on the tree

in the direction of the Shire just before he is inspired to convince the tree to change directions back toward the war and Mount Doom.

8. A leap of faith and a transformation follow the dark night of the soul. Mulan transforms when she gets up from her despair to ride to Beijing to save the Emperor.

9. The hero must confront evil again and emerge victorious. Mulan overwhelms the Mongol Khan. The Little Mermaid succeeds in getting the prince to fall in love with her. The sick person gets on the road to recovery and is transformed.

10. Finally, the student becomes the teacher. Mulan is celebrated by the entire Forbidden City. The Little Mermaid marries the prince. Everyone applauds. We move to a higher level and start the process again.

This entire process can be linked to the healing journey. We can link the steps of healing to these same ten steps, which give people a sense of how to construct their own healing journey as they pick and choose elements from each heroic story they hear.

To prepare someone to become the hero of his or her own life, we must first elicit the story he or she is currently living. Then we wonder about plausible alternate stories incorporating better health. What type of heroic story could bring this person back to health? We ask what character the person plays, who is the audience, who are the supporting characters, what is the plot, what values are being pursued, and how we can transform the story to include heroic recovery.

We generate a cluster of questions about the story. What is feared? How is faith lacking? How could allies or new abilities help the person accept the current challenge? How could the manner of accepting the challenge lead to victory? How does the person relate to life's major areas of concern, including love, the body, family, and work? We all spin out of control in one or more areas of life at some time. How does this person accept or reject challenges in these areas? How does he develop his power? How do allies and powers relate to the rejection of the challenge at an earlier time? How can the allies now serve the main character?

Each character in a story represents or highlights different aspects of the hero. Mulan's captain is crucial to her character. His moods set the stage for different sections of the story. What's happening in the story for other characters casts a better view on what's happening for the main character. Scrooge could not exist without Bob Cratchit.

Unless the hero enters the terrifying dark night of the soul and accepts the challenge, he cannot be victorious. We need to ask questions about what will allow victory. We need to know what our character's personal, intimate, dark night of the soul will be like. How will he experience despair? What will his leap of faith look like? Will it be figurative or literal?

By addressing these questions together, we learn about the story and the hero. How will our hero confront evil? Will the evil be external or internal? Will it be like the evil in *The Lord of the Rings*—magical, diabolical, vicious, bloodthirsty, and completely amoral? By discovering how the person sees his or her illness, together we are able to construct a shared story of heroic transformation with a greater potential to lead to wellness.

Options available for types of heroes include numerous variants—the god-man combination, the prophetic hero, the military or action hero, the priestly hero, the leader hero, the reluctant hero, and the anti- or ironic hero. Each version may have different appeal for individuals.

The story of Jennie provides us with an example of how story can function as an agent of change. The stories I told Jennie helped inspire her to get out of her house and go to college, since she couldn't tolerate high school. We will see how Jennie transformed her life from failure to dramatic success in almost the blink of an eye.

When I met Jennie, she had stopped attending high school for the past six months. She was sitting at home, depressed and bored. Her brother had set the stage by dropping out of school and staying home one year previously. Their parents were Romanian immigrants who had never quite adjusted to America. Jennie's father had fallen into the black market. He had gone to prison for three years for his deeds but had been released and was now pursuing his work. His cover was that of a machinist. He made frequent trips to Florida, though tools were not the only items in his kit. He never flew, only drove. Jennie liked going with him to Florida but felt strange at the way he would disappear for days at a time, leaving her with money for food in a condo beside the ocean. This had started when she was fourteen. Jennie's father was obsessed with the idea that Jennie's mother had cheated on him, though no evidence supported this. He did everything possible to keep from giving her any money, consequently depriving Jennie. His court-ordered child support was minimal, since his business was entirely cash and undeclared.

Sixteen-year-old Jennie stood at a crossroads when I first saw her. She was being presented with multiple options, as in the Navajo creation story I described earlier. I approached Jennie by telling her stories to inspire her to believe in her intrinsic worth. I wanted her to cast off the idea that her inability to tolerate high school meant that she was defective and inferior. I offered her the idea that her difficulties with high school were actually signs of superiority. After hearing many stories and through other discussions, Jennie decided to skip high school and just go to college. The stories helped her to arrive at the conclusion that she was too advanced already for high school.

I told Jennie my story, in which I started college during high school and took medical school courses while still in college. I used the Navajo creation stories for their moral values and my story to inspire Jennie that she could pursue a course of learning different from the usual. I spent agonizing hours negotiating with her father about how she would pay for her courses. She attended her local state university and finished the semester with all As. Then she wanted to attend a summer program at Columbia University in New York City. After further arduous negotiation, her father paid half and her mother borrowed the rest. Again, all As. After one more semester at the local university, Jennie discovered that she could take courses without being a matriculated student at Stanford University. She worked hard on both of her parents to find the money, and she went. She finished her GED and applied to Stanford based upon her academic record. At the time of this writing, Jennie has just graduated from Stanford and is applying to graduate school in international law. She spent a year abroad at The Hague, studying at the World Court, and wants to eventually practice international law in The Netherlands.

What was Jennie's story? Initially she had great potential to be an antihero. She hadn't been able to fit into several high schools. Her father was a criminal. Her mother had failed at several businesses and was chronically depressed. We transformed her story into one in which she was a positive hero, a Phoenix rising from the ashes. Telling Jennie stories went far beyond storytelling. The stories provided an opportunity for a dialogic relationship between Jennie and me, in which she could experience my sense of value of her as a human being. Through my presence with her, Jennie "borrowed" my words and values. Over time, she reworked and reworded these words and values so that they became her own. She reauthored the stories I told to make them uniquely hers.

Powerful stories contain an element of transformation. Their central character often undergoes a dramatic change. Great story always places this change in the context of change occurring in larger entities (institutions, families, governments). The kingdom is being transformed in *Macbeth*. Middle Earth is being transformed in *The Lord of the Rings*. Because we are interconnected, as discussed in earlier chapters, change on any level is associated with change on every other level. When the larger group changes, we also change. If enough of us change, the larger group changes. Jennie's narratives about herself changed to become more heroic. Her changes were embedded with cultural forces questioning our methods of education. Jennie is an example of the success (from multiple perspectives) of alternate stories about education.

Stories often arise to address a problem. Most of my stories arise to address the problem of illness. Other stories arise to address problems of displacement, homelessness, disempowerment, discrimination, and more. Stories contain hidden advice about how to address a problem. The problem is the central event of a story and is a prerequisite of most great stories. The problem represents the obstacle standing between us and the achievement of our value goals. Stories about solving problems allow us to borrow new ideas for how to solve our problem to attain our goals.

Even though the presenting problem is usually the illness, we often come to understand the illness as a partially successful solution for pre-existing problems. Initially, the illness is the problem that must be overcome. It is the obstacle to enjoying life. It appears to be the cause of suffering. But suffering may precede the illness that comes to help solve the suffering. Illness may be a partial answer. Jennie's depression was a partial answer to her inner turmoil. Depression allowed her to better tolerate her incredible frustration. It quieted her creative drive sufficiently to tolerate a social situation in which no solutions could be found. When different stories showed her solutions, she forgot to be depressed. The excitement of a world of possibilities for learning offset her sadness and weariness.

Consider Freda. Freda's problem involved three years of progressively worsening asthma and high blood pressure, to the point that the conditions interfered with her ability to conduct her nationally syndicated radio broadcasts. It's difficult to make sense over the air when every sentence leads to a paroxysm of coughing. Freda was seventy-one years old and recognized as an international expert in her field. She had experienced asthma and high blood pressure as a young adult but had cured herself.

One of my goals was to establish that Freda's prior success in overcoming asthma and high blood pressure established her as a hero. I asked Freda to tell the story of how she cured herself in the past. Her rendition revealed her force of will. She had willed herself to be well. She was so busy and so passionately involved in her activities that she could not be slowed down by illness. She accepted an arduous journey of nutritional and lifestyle change, much as Frodo accepted the burden of the ring, and succeeded in throwing those illnesses into the fires of Mount Doom. But had she? Why had they returned? Having defined her as a previous hero, we needed to understand how the world had shifted since her youth. What was different now from the time in which she had cured herself and from the ensuing time in which she was free from health problems?

Freda saw herself as recently having put enormous pressure on herself to finish a series of tasks before she died. She was approaching the age at which her mother had died. She needed to finish several books before that time. Questions brought her awareness to a set of hidden assumptions centered on the notion that she would die at the same age as her mother. My questions helped her to see that she was physiologically more like her father, who had lived into his nineties. I wondered if she would care to relax and give herself more time to complete her opus.

She had used her tremendous will to change her life already once. Why couldn't she do it again? With Freda in a trance so that she could be completely absorbed in her internal movies, I told her the Hopi and the Navajo creation stories, interwoven into an imagery designed to help her see the creation of her villain. We watched the growth of HTB, which stood for "hard to breathe." HTB became a character in his own right. He had needs, demands, and desires. An illness takes possession of our bodies. For physical creatures, our bodies might as well be our galaxies. Once we have an illness, we struggle with how to overthrow the "evil empire" (as the rebels did in the movie series *Star Wars*). Freda and I began a process of negotiating with HTB for relief. Over time, Freda succeeded in transforming herself and her world into one in which HTB no longer held office. She had usurped his power. In the process, she had reclaimed her former power of will and was directing herself toward more healthy behaviors and a healthier lifestyle.

Heroic stories provide a multiplicity of ideas about how to conceptualize illness and potentially overcome it. In *Macbeth*, for example, a usurper has killed the king and taken over the kingdom. This theme is easy to link to problems such as diabetes, in which immune factors have destroyed the pancreas and taken control. Without insulin, the kingdom will die. The problem becomes how to unseat the usurper. While we may never bring back the healthy pancreas, we can prevent the usurper from destroying the kingdom.

In Homer's *The Iliad*, the larger story is the seduction of Helen and the war waged to get her back. The foreground story is that of the Greek army being decimated because Achilles, its best warrior, has dropped out of the fight. It's easy to see how we could create a parallel between the fight to recover Helen and the fight to recover health. The resignation of Achilles could be used to parallel immune system sluggishness or the onset of depression. We would then need to find a way for Achilles, the immune system or "fighting spirit," to rejoin the fray. Naturally, this parallel would not work for everyone. An important aspect of storytelling or narrative practice is the art of matching a story line to the interests and proclivities of the recipient.

Regardless of which stories we use or what cultures they come from, the process of storytelling envisions a world of multiple meanings. Everyone involved participates in a dialogue that creates meaning. This dialogue identifies people as the authors of their stories, narrators of their desires, and contributors to what comes to be called "the truth." The person suffering continuously borrows from the words and discourses available to him or her, from the language and relationship with the storyteller and other important people in the healing environment. Storytelling is permissive. It allows multiple truths to emerge and eventually intertwine into a shared vision of how healing can take place. This differs markedly from conventional medicine's monologue, in which medical experts speak "the one truth" as if there were no others. Our health care system proceeds on the "one truth fits all" paradigm. The permissive, storytelling approach to transformation quietly offers to overthrow that somewhat totalitarian approach to defining what is possible.

For conventional medicine, the hero is the doctor, and it is his or her magic that makes the patient well. Many doctors grow addicted to this role. The narrative approach returns the role of hero to the one who suffers. The doctor is the mentor or ally—always a supporting role. Imagine *The Lord of the Rings* if Gandalf were the hero instead of Frodo! How much less rich and interesting that would be!

Because we have all been heroes at one time and place, stories about heroes draw us into their experience and inspire us to emulate them. Heroic role models can have powerful influences on our lives. They inspire us to transform. Their stories communicate a hidden code through which we learn how to change, as surely as the Navajo code talkers communicated important messages at the front of World War II. In all stories of heroism, a problem-solving force has emerged triumphantly and is worthy of detailed study.

Different heroes have different skills that can be brought to bear on solving a problem. These varying skills are specialized aspects of being human. Doctors, lawyers, and detectives specialize in different functions needed to solve particular problems. Artists specialize in creativity. Our inner doctor takes care of us when we don't feel well. If someone is suing us, our inner lawyer takes over. Our inner detective solves mysteries. Our inner investigative reporter seeks out the truth. The profession of the hero brings a different set of skills and resources. Each profession encompasses another set of skills. A great story or a healing story isolates one of these skills and examines it in detail.

Thus, healing stories contain core values for transformation, a dominant character who displays particular skills that can be used to solve problems, a plot to keep our interest and create parallels with our own lives, the main emotional traits of the character, the handicap of the character, the threat and the antithreat, the hero's profession, and the problem to be solved. The principle action is made up of smaller component actors with various emotional, physical, mental, or spiritual characteristics. These are the subplots of the story. The dominant action gives the story its genre and is determined by how the story ends. Mysteries end in enigmas. War stories involve physical action and end in victory or defeat. Spiritual stories end in transcendence or descent, with the elevation or the fall of the central character to a higher or lower plane. A great story isolates the plots and subplots, separating and examining in detail these dimensions of our lives. It isolates the feelings associated with its particular genre, whether it be thriller, mystery, or love story.

Both heroic and healing stories often contain a "marvelous element," which is the unique thing without which the hero cannot accomplish his or her task or goal. These include vast, unconscious spiritual, emotional, mental, or physical powers waiting to be awakened or released. They can include animal helpers, nature elements, spirits, and ancestors (all common in Native American stories), as well as extraordinary abilities, such as a profound capacity to love, the power to transcend duality, or the ability to experience ultimate truth. These marvelous elements render transformation more likely.

Other marvelous elements include magic potions or objects, ultimate weapons, fantastic places; they may also be swords, shields, a lady's handkerchief, or other ordinary things that have marvelous symbolic meaning. In *The Lord of the Rings*, the marvelous element is the ring of power. That whole story builds around this ring and the desire to gain power over those who would possess the ring. Every character is tested to see how he or she will react to the opportunity to possess the ring as a means to power. In Charles Dickens's *A Christmas Carol*, the marvelous element is Scrooge's money. The marvelous element of a story corresponds to the unique talent or hidden resource that allows the person to transform and improve, reframe, or solve the problem. We tell stories with marvelous elements to stimulate an internal search for what will catalyze or facilitate personal transformation.

In many great stories, one marvelous element often dominates and becomes the subject of the story, but this is not necessary. When these marvelous elements are explored in depth, they can become an ultimate source of unity, or of clarity, meaning, and power. The ultimate source of unity in *The Iliad* is Achilles's anger, his dominant trait. *The Iliad* is virtually a complete description of everything known about anger—how it is transformed, transferred, processed, expressed, and metabolized. Achilles starts out angry at Agamemnon and ends up transferring that anger to Hector, who has killed his friend. Its clarity of purpose has kept the story alive for more than three thousand years. Its perfect description of anger remains relevant even today. All the other elements in the story support this unity and reveal the place of the story in the larger scheme. Similarly, Freda's dominant element was her force of will, set against the context of her feelings about the pressure of time. In chapter 1, Dana's dominant element was her drive for perfection. For Tom in chapter 5, the dominant element was his need to serve his family.

In *The Lord of the Rings,* the dominant subject is the ring of power, also a fascinating and marvelous object. In *A Christmas Carol*, the dominant subject is Scrooge's greed, also the dominant trait and the threat. The entity being transformed is London. The big problem is poverty. Each of these stories contains puzzles that contribute more information to the whole, which is the life cycle we go through from birth to death.

Stories have healing power in every culture. The need for stories is universal, as is the power of story to change our lives. Stories precede every ceremony and contain the logic for why that ceremony is done the way it is. The Navajo creation story that we have visited contains the sacred colors, mountains, directions, spirits, and other important knowledge that is part of every Navajo ceremony. In *Coyote Medicine,* I told the Lakota story of how the Four Directions were set and also the story about how the sun removed the scar from Burnt Face. Together, these stories contain all the symbolism of the sweat lodge ceremony.

Native American stories also contain cultural images or archetypes that serve as agents of change. Native American images are not familiar to most English speakers as European images but include various animals or local geographic landmarks—like Shiprock in Dineh stories, or Devil's Tower, Wyoming (the Bear's home for the Kiowa people who formerly lived there), or Bear Butte in South Dakota, or other landmarks mentioned in the various stories I have told in this book. These shared images and the stories that contain them also hold cultures together and contain the implicit wisdom of healing.

Stories are told during ceremony—sometimes sacred stories, sometimes testimonials. Then, when the ceremony is done, people tell stories of personal transformation resulting from the ceremony. Story is the glue that holds cultures together, explaining why the elders say that every story has a spirit and that the spirits speak to us in stories or parables. Ceremonies are the means of enactment through which we make our stories heard by the spirits, who can then choose to intervene on our behalf. Ceremony elevates our stories to the level of cosmic myths, the type of stories that the spirits are used to hearing. Once we are cast in this form, the spirits can act on our behalf. Stories are the sorcerer's stone, the magical talisman that contains the mystery of transformation.

9

Stories of Miracles

Miraculous stories inspire us like no others. Miracles present us with the tantalizing possibility of transcendence. The miracle of Christ's Ascension is the fundamental basis of Christianity. It establishes an irreconcilable difference from its Jewish predecessor. Miracles help us to challenge our hidden assumptions that limit our expectations for what is possible. Since we often get what we expect, the overthrow of expectations is a crucial step toward social, cultural, and physiological change. Stories of miracles are empowering and enabling. They are not "how-to" stories. Instead, they inspire the listener to find the qualities that make sense within the story and to seek and develop those qualities within him- or herself.

Anna's story is miraculous in its own way. Modern psychiatry, like modern oncology and the other branches of biomedicine, discounts healing that takes place in the absence of or despite medication. Anna shows us how the power of belonging to a community of meaning can offset the biology of bipolar disorder, leading to healing. For those of us who have been conventionally trained in medicine, this is miraculous. For the members of that community, it didn't seem unusual at all.

The green grass hills seemed to stretch forever, limited only by the bright blue horizon. It was not hard to imagine those hills covered with buffaloes, or eagles circling overhead. The occasional eagle still graced us with its presence, but the buffaloes had long since disappeared. We had come to Ben Standing Bear's spread for sun dance. One year ago I had brought Anna to see Ben, a local traditional healer, for help with what had been diagnosed as bipolar disorder. She had never left. I looked forward to seeing her again, having kept in touch by letter and having seen her two other times during the year at other ceremonies.

Anna was part African-American, part Cherokee, a product of slavery in the Deep South. Anna had been hospitalized every year for as long as she could remember. She had been tried on every medication known to psychiatry. All gave her side effects, some life threatening. Anna was labeled with bipolar disorder, which used to be called manic-depression. The term implies extreme ranges of mood, from elation to the deepest depression. Unfortunately for them, people with this diagnosis spend 85 percent of their time being depressed. And, when they become elated, their behavior can be bizarre enough to lead to hospitalization or jail. Anna's elation was not without consequences. She would become paranoid and hypervigilant, on constant alert for threat. She felt pressured to talk but would reveal so much that her listeners became uncomfortable. As her mania progressed, she would become psychotic, misinterpreting the world around her and its intentions so severely that she would end up in restraints in a psychiatric hospital. She could bitterly describe the trauma of being tied up in seclusion. The mental health care system was brutal to her. She came to me for an alternative, since medications had never contained her. She would eventually spiral out of control, in spite of whatever drug regimen she was given.

Anna felt her paranoia growing, so she knew something had to be done before she lost all reason. She didn't want more medication. Her past doctors had been encouraging a drug called Clozaril, which had potentially serious side effects, to accompany her lithium, valproic acid, and olanzapine.

Anna had spent the last year with Ben, who had taken her into his home. He provided her with structure to contain her mania and bipolar disease, just as Melvin had done for a schizophrenic patient in *Coyote Healing*. Anna was welcome to stay as long as she wished. Ben was willing to patiently wait for her to become ready to craft a different life story. Initially, Anna acted very crazy. She talked all night. She would wander into the hills and get lost until someone rode out to find her. She misperceived people's intentions, alternating between incorrectly perceiving sexual advances and incorrectly perceiving threat. In most communities, including Tucson, where I live, a petition would have been filed with the court for involuntary commitment of Anna for evaluation and eventually for court-ordered treatment. In Ben's Native American community, Anna's behavior was lovingly tolerated and gently redirected. In a community where everyone knew everyone else, communication was rapid. Everyone quickly came to understand Anna's behavior as temporary and changeable. When they understood that, Anna's behavior changed.

Anna was led to participate in every ceremony that took place in that community. She was tolerated like a child, and her outbursts were accepted as spirit-driven. Verbalizations that would have been considered meaningless and bizarre in conventional culture were carefully studied and respected as possibly coming from spirits speaking through Anna. What was the effect of being respected versus ignored or ostracized?

Over the course of her year, Anna became more and more calm. Her bizarre verbalizations became less frequent. She behaved as she was treated. By the time of my visit, while clearly eccentric, Anna could no longer be described as manic. She fit in a palpable way into the community. She helped cook for postceremony feasts. She made long strands of prayer ties. She learned the sacred songs and practiced them around kitchen tables. Of course, alcohol and drugs were strictly forbidden in this community by virtue of Ben's powerful presence, and so these were not even temptations.

On the day of my return, Ben was inside the tipi, in the midst of a story. He seemed to always be in the midst of a story, having melded his life into the art of never actually starting or ending. Ben was surviving into the twenty-first century in the patchwork way common to most modern day shamans. On the weekends he led ceremony. During the week he worked as a printer.

Ben told all kinds of stories. He borrowed freely from all cultures, changing names to fit his audience. What Ben knew was priceless, for it was his own unique amalgam of everything that had ever crossed his awareness, and he had the gift of semantic mutation. His consciousness treated stories the way viruses treat DNA. As he heard and recalled stories, he would make substitutions, deletions, and recombinations until something resulted that had never been heard before. Maybe all healers work this way.

Ben was telling a story about an ancient one who gave up his voice so that his family might never go hungry. This man was a great healer and storyteller but was perpetually poor. A spirit had appeared to offer him a trade—his voice and his ability to heal in exchange for prosperity.

"The healer's wife was overjoyed," Ben said. "Finally she would always have meat on their table and the things in life which she felt she had deserved for all these many years of living with a healer. A deer brought itself to their lodge and lay down for their food. The choicest roots began to grow behind them. Barren bushes grew berries.

"But things were worse for the healer than he could have ever imagined," Ben continued. "He had not realized how many little things we do in life that are healing. He could not make the softest touch, for these are often more healing than the grandest ceremony. He could not reassure or comfort his wife and children. In fact, there was little he could do, for most of what we do in life is healing to someone.

"Unfortunately, his wife soon tired of prosperity. What is wealth without love? What is prosperity without comfort or joy? What is the satisfaction of hunger and thirst without gentle companionship? Soon the healer and his family were more despairing than they had ever been.

"This is sort of a variant of 'the grass is always greener,'" Ben said. "The man was now helpless, for he had lost the capacity to heal, and that is what makes us human. His wife vowed to help him, but what could she do? She vowed to take him to healers in distant lands, to do whatever it took to make things right again. Through her prayers, their healing poverty returned, but with a new found appreciation."

Within several days, it became clear to me that this kind of transformation had happened to Anna. She was so much less paranoid and better able to engage in the softness of healing that Ben described.

Each year that I returned to visit Anna, her behavior continued to improve. Her paranoia gradually abated, now that she was embedded in a community that served to regulate her feelings and provided her with sufficient feedback to ameliorate her suspicious tendencies. After four years, her mood extremes had virtually disappeared. "I felt the grace of God descending upon me like one of those blankets we throw on the sweat lodge," she said. "When you are touched by grace, all else falls away."

Are stories of the healing of bipolar disorder miraculous? My psychiatry training would suggest so. My desire to become a psychiatrist began with reading British alternative psychiatrist, Ronald D. Laing, while still in high school. Laing illuminated the world of madness for me by showing that it had meaning. To him, madness was a creative response to living with insane conditions and inside impossible families and cultures. Life within these contexts was unbearable. Madness allowed unbearable emotions to leak out and be expressed, even if cryptic and in gibberish. Laing believed that psychiatrists and psychotherapists should help the individual, family, and society become more aware of emotional, experiential, and existential needs in a way that increased meaning and authenticity. Psychotherapy should improve quality of life and allow individuals to live within families and societies in a life-affirming manner.

Laing explained why madness was often found in the more intelligent patients. They were able to comprehend the impossibility of their lives, generating all the more suffering and desire to communicate their condition. He wanted to legitimatize and validate experience, allowing people to reconstruct a sense of worth and meaning for their lives within a saner context. Laing's psychiatry emphasized the use of self healing over medications and the use of one's own authenticity in a community healing effort.

During medical school, as I began to study my Native American heritage, I discovered that traditional medicine people treated insanity in much the same way R. D. Laing did, but with one essential difference. Their treatment was more compassionate and supportive than that proposed by Laing, who sometimes seemed to leave his patients adrift in their unbearable emotions with little direction and few guideposts.

Through their reliance upon the sacred, Native American medicine people could work miracles, quietly disclaiming responsibility, achieving a kind of transparency so that the credit for their work passed through them to the spirits who stood behind them. Through the philosophy of the Seven Directions, a safe path for life could always be found. Through the intervention of the spirits, unbearable feelings could be contained. Native American medicine people seemed able to work within the domain of intense emotions experienced by those suffering severe mental disorders. Ben was able to do this with Anna. He could tolerate and bind the profound emotions of her major life experiences and transitions. He was used to these intense emotions, because they are frequently stirred up and activated by ceremonies. These emotions deeply affect the entire family and community and are the fuel that drives therapeutic change.

Intense life events open portals into the intense emotional world that we humans are capable of entering, yet so rarely do. It is the same profound emotional experience that occurs whenever deep and exhaustive therapeutic work gives birth to a new sense of integration. More than twenty years ago, neuroscientists at the Langley Porter Neuropsychiatric Institute of the University of California at San Francisco conducted a randomized study at Agnews State Mental Hospital in San Jose, California, now closed, that convincingly showed that new-onset schizophrenia could be effectively treated without medication. The unmedicated patients remained in the hospital longer, for up to six months, but fewer than 10 percent had future breakdowns that required rehospitalization. The medicated patients left the hospital sooner, but 90 percent had future breakdowns that resulted in chronic rehospitalization and disability.[1]

The recovery of the unmedicated schizophrenics did not prove that schizophrenia is a psychological and not a biological illness. It proved that biology responds intimately and immediately to one's surroundings and to the treatment that can be provided in that environment. My own research on the facilitation of labor with behavioral methods and the prevention of labor complications with hypnosis and other psychosocial interventions has similarly shown that psychology and biology are two banks of the same river.[2] Native American medicine people never lost the "primitive" understanding so common in traditional and preliterate cultures: that mind, body, spirit, and community are one, and that our modern boundaries between self and others, self and nature, self and spirit are artificial constructs of a restricted materialistic vision.

Swedish anthropologist Ake Hultkranz studied Native American attitudes toward conventional medicine. He wrote, "The general Indian attitude to white physicians is that they are clever in curing mundane diseases, although not quite reliable. Many are found to fail in their efforts to help out the patients, but so do the traditional medicine men;

so the dilemma is the same as in traditional society."[3] One Navajo nurse whom he interviewed said, "The problem with white doctors was that their cures affect only symptoms and not the causes of disease. Physicians are, however, respected when their efforts relieve suffering and restore health."[4]

Psychiatrists, on the other hand, are not respected. Psychiatrists and other mental health professionals who come onto reservations are accused of looking down on people, not understanding the language and customs of the reservation, staying only temporarily and remaining ignorant of Native values. They are often young and inexperienced. William Powers wrote about the distaste of the Oglala people of South Dakota for psychotherapists; they believed that the psychotherapists interfered with the medicine person's proper activity.[5] The Oglala believed that medicine people cured more quickly and effectively than psychotherapists. The yuwipi ceremony, for example, could potentially cure illness within the day of the ceremony. Horn Chips, an Oglala Lakota healer and the ancestor of the very-much-alive Chips family of South Dakota, received this ceremony in 1876 as a cure for "white people disease." In the ceremony, the medicine person is tied up. The room is completely dark. In that darkness, the spirits release the medicine man from his bonds. Then he doctors the sick people.

Hultkranz also wrote:

"It is today not uncommon to find Indian medicine men at work in white people's homes. For instance, Lakota medicine men from South Dakota are active in white districts in nearby Rapid City. Some medicine men take more extensive journeys. The Crow medicine man Tom Yellowtail, for instance, has visited patients as far away as California, Wisconsin, and New York. It is obvious that this expansion would have been impossible without an enhanced susceptibility to the efficacy of Indian medicine on the part of the white population. People who in other connections turned to white folk healers have included Indian curing in their health program. While formerly this happened now and then when white trappers and explorers were out alone in the wilderness with Indians as their closest neighbors, today the medical trade takes place on a more general and businesslike level. The inclusion of Indian medicine at hospitals has strengthened this transaction.

"To the Indians, this is not only a national victory. It is the sign of a more meaningful medicine where the connections between medical etiology, social care, and religious faith are tied closely together. The white man is caught in an Indian religious universe that is nonetheless wide enough to include his own religious values, or nearly so . . . ."[6]

Anthropologist Wolfgang Jilek summarized Native American criticism of Western scientific medicine as follows:[7]

1. Lack of holistic concepts and practice
2. Overvalued focus on physical, biochemical aspects, paired with neglect of psychosocial and cultural aspects of ill health and treatment
3. Superiority of indigenous therapies in the utilization of dissociative mechanisms and in effecting positive personality changes

Russell Willier, a Cree healer from northern Alberta, wants to revitalize Cree society so that it can take its place in the multicultural Canadian world.[8] A medicine man who inherited his medicine bundle from his great-grandfather, he has tried to incorporate ideas and techniques from the white society. He thinks that his medicine craft is good for everybody and therefore offers it to the whites. This has provoked both protest and approval in the Indian communities, and in white circles as well. Willier is quite open about his methods. He has been filmed in action, and academic doctors are welcome to watch his medical procedures.

Willier's methods include diagnosis with the help of guardian spirits and treatment with herbal teas and ointments according to the directions of these spirits. It happens that the spirits in his dreams change old traditional herbal compositions. All treatment is accompanied by tobacco offerings. Willier does not think that his herbal medicine would otherwise be efficacious. The diseases he takes care of are multifold. Psychosomatic diseases take a prominent place, but organic diseases like cancer also fall under Willier's treatment.

This Cree medical activity has had such a successful result that Willier has instituted his own health center, where other Indian healers are also at work. He is aiming at cooperation with Western doctors. He is convinced that he can do what they cannot achieve, and that they can do what for legal reasons he cannot achieve. Although some orthodox doctors refuse to have anything to do with him, he persists in his conviction that cooperation between the two medical worlds is necessary. Cooperation, not integration.

This is only one example of an attitude among modern Indian medicine men, but in my experience it is very characteristic of the interaction occurring between traditional and modern medicine just now.

In pre-European America, when healing was required, the patient or a relative would ask the healer or shaman for assistance. The shaman would consider the request and the proposed fee, often requesting a commitment from the supplicant to fast or to undergo a vision quest, sun dance, or other personal odyssey, along with holding a feast for the community. It seems that then, just as today, the cost of healing was not cheap, although perhaps generosity was more common then.

Among the Lakota, preparations for healing might begin with a sweat lodge ceremony to purify the participants and start prayers on the road to the Creator. The sick person would be inside the lodge if sufficiently strong or would rest outside while a relative entered on his or her behalf. A very ill patient need not even be in the vicinity. After the sweat lodge ceremony, the patient or the relative acting on his behalf might be taken "up on the hill" for a vision quest. Those waiting below would continue in ceremony for the benefit of the patient. Another sweat lodge concluded the process, in which the vision was interpreted and plans were made to fulfill its guidance. Later, the patient or relative might fulfill a commitment to be pierced in the sun dance or to perform another ordeal of service on behalf of patient and community.

Among the Navajo, similar processes were applied, with the family or a relative visiting a diagnostician (a hand trembler or crystal gazer) to learn the proper ceremony needed to cure the sick family member. Next the family would seek a person who knew that ceremony, arrange the fee, and notify relatives and friends, and the ceremony and accompanying feast would commence.

How different this is from modern Anglo-European medicine, in which the patient is delivered to the medical arena to be cured, bereft of the involvement of friends and family in the healing process. The materialist doctrine of medicine has taught that the body *qua* machine can be repaired by trained servicemen cognizant of its structural workings. Drugs and surgery will return the patient most effectively to a state of pre-illness functioning.

Why does Native healing work so well for its believers? What conditions must be met for a "miraculous" healing to occur? I have arrived at the following answers:

1. A shared system of beliefs exists, permitting forgiveness, reconciliation, and miraculous (to this society) transformation.
2. We rely on a belief or emotional commitment to a world of Spirit with the power to intervene to better our lives.
3. We have complete trust in healing, in the healer, and in nature and have faith that the prescribed rituals (treatments) will lead to the desired outcome.
4. We make a deep, emotional commitment to the idea that our thoughts and actions can improve our health.
5. We hold a belief that anything is possible for the Creator (the Divine) and that divine intervention in human affairs can be requested and obtained.

Mary was a thirty-year-old woman with migraine headaches. She had tried many therapies, none effective, at substantial cost. She was the mother of one child, lived in an expensive suburban house in New Jersey, and was married to an investment banker. Four weeks after our first meeting, we were standing in the dark outside of Tucson. A brilliant fire was burning. Our sweat lodge stood silently to the west, covered with blankets and tarps. The sky was dark, clouds obscuring the moon. Flakes of snow began to fall. The wind blew hard. It was cold outside the reach of the fire.

I was leading a sweat lodge dedicated to Mary's healing. Two friends came with her from New Jersey. I had brought a helper to carry the stones—a firekeeper. When the fire had sufficiently heated the stones, we would pray to the Great Mystery and to Dakuskanskan, the Creator, to heal what modern medicine and psychology had not budged. The intensive work had begun three days earlier, after Mary arrived in Tucson. I had seen her on three previous occasions while passing through the Newark area. We had discussed her problem. She had come to the desert to resolve it.

On the first day, I began laying the groundwork for the sweat lodge, for a transformative ceremony to change Mary's life. My work was to remove all doubt that she would be well, thereby creating a bridge between the modern world and Native tradition. I began conventionally enough by connecting her to a range of biofeedback machines, devices she had already unsuccessfully encountered. I did not want to teach her to control her physiology. I wanted to monitor her hidden responses as we began a hypnotic process to prepare a groundwork for faith in healing. Storytelling would play an important role in this.

William Lyon wrote that "absence of doubt among participants is a . . . prerequisite to success in shamanic rituals. A single participant's doubt can cause failure."[9] Doubt can be destructive. Wellness requires inculcating faith as complete knowledge of wellness, as if the healing had already happened. With Mary connected to biofeedback, I began the process of trance induction. With instructions for slow and deep breathing and for the progressive release of tension, I began to tell Mary the story of the sacred beings. Mary knew about the sweat lodge. She was afraid of the power and the heat. I told her about Skan, the Creator, to help her rest and relax, to prepare herself to give her troubles to Skan.

"We'll be talking about certain characters in the sweat lodge ceremony," I told her. "While you're relaxing and resting, I want you to just enjoy yourself, to let yourself go a little, to listen to my words without having to think about them too much. I want to tell you about the beginning, about Inyan, the rock, who was here first, when there was no other. Created first, he began the legacy of the sacred beings. You will meet Inyan, the rock," I said. "He will enter with the hot stones. Parts of him bring heat to doctor us. Han will be there, also. Han is the dark, the shapeless and formless, there with Inyan from the beginning in the dark, the proper milieu for spirits. It will be dark inside the sweat lodge. We will close the door to honor Han, to let the spirits into her milieu. You will feel the fullness of the darkness as we honor her in the heat. First Inyan and Han—those two will begin our journey.

"Inyan longed for companionship," I told Mary. "He was lonely. He wanted another being with whom to relate. Not Han who was shapeless, formless, and everywhere, but another, whom he could touch. He consulted with Skan and was given permission to labor and give birth. He struggled long and hard with that birth. He lost much blood, the blue blood of the rock. Finally, Maka was born, the earth, that which covers the rock almost everywhere, except for those high places where we still see him.

"You have given birth," I told Mary. "You can relate to the pain of the rock as he gave birth to the earth. You will drink water, the blood of the rock, in the sweat lodge," I said. "It will have been transformed. It will have become medicine for you. It will be *wakan*, or holy.

"So we start with the three elements, the first three of the sacred beings, the rock, which we will bring into the lodge and place in the center of the pit to give us warmth, the earth upon which we will sit, who gives us the very materials from which we build our lodge and form our bodies, and, finally, the water, the blood of the rock. When we place it on the rock, it will sizzle and make steam to purify us. The sweat will pour off our bodies. When we are purified, we will drink sacred water for inner purification, for internal sanctification."

Mary was moving toward a deep trance. Her breathing was becoming regular and slow. I would continue telling her about the sacred beings whom she would honor in the sweat lodge, about the living reality of nature.

I told Mary about an old Lakota saying, that men are content with anything. They will sit around the fire and eat or talk or sleep. It is women who are always trying to better the world, to improve the world for their children. "It was the same situation for Maka and Inyan, the rock," I said. "Right away, Maka wanted to improve things. She didn't like that it was always dark. She wanted to be able to see herself. How could she know if she were ugly or beautiful if there was no way to see herself? She took up the matter with Inyan, her companion. He was stumped. He couldn't see a way to resolve her dilemma. How could he? The world was perpetually dark. So Inyan and Maka called upon Skan, the Creator, for help with their problem. This began the tradition of prayer, of asking for help from a higher source for problems we cannot solve for ourselves.

"Skan heard their prayers and resolved the question by creating light out of darkness. 'Let there be light,' he said. Han, the darkness, parted to separate herself from Anp, the light. Skan asked Han to hide where Maka could not see her, while she adjusted to Anp. From the light, Maka looked at herself, and decided woefully that she was ugly. We will be keeping Anp out of the sweatlodge," I joked. "That way no one can think they are ugly.

"But Maka saw herself as cold and ugly, so she asked Skan for permission to take the waters, the blue blood of her companion, and adorn herself with that blue as a kind of jewelry. Skan liked the idea and blessed it. Then Maka took the water and placed it strategically to form lakes, rivers, streams, and ponds. They become beautiful jewels upon her skin. Maka was happy, as were Inyan and Skan.

"Soon, however, Maka complained again. Maybe it's like that at your house," I said. "Maybe you're always improving things, but your husband would be content with things just the way they are."

Mary laughed. From deep within her trance she muttered slowly that her husband expected her to improve things while he was away working. I sensed a hint of resentment in her voice and stored that for later discussion.

I continued. "Maka complained to Skan that everything was always the same. She was cold. She wanted variety and she wanted warmth. She begged Skan to make something to warm her and soften the blazing light. Skan reflected upon this and decided to make a warming spirit to sit in the sky. Skan made what we now call the sun, what the Lakotas call Wi, formed from parts of rock, earth, water, and Skan. Skan put Wi in the sky and there was warmth upon the earth. Maka was satisfied. But after a time, she was uncomfortable. The constant heat was too much. Skan had decreed that the sun give all material things a shadow to provide variety of light for the pleasure of the earth. No spirits were to have shadows. But Maka said that not even this was sufficient. Bring back Han, she begged. Let me have some time without the heat of the sun. Let me have some time in darkness to recover from the heat of the sun and to enjoy the softness of the darkness.

"Skan reflected upon this and felt that it was good. They had been living in the First Time, which was perpetual and unchanging. Now Skan created the Second Time. Skan decreed that the Second Time would consist of regular cycles between Han and Wi. Maka indicated her pleasure as to the length of each. One complete cycle was to be called a day. Wi was instructed to rest underneath the world when Han returned. Anp was to precede him each day to announce his return. Thus light always precedes sunrise. Maka experienced this cycle and was well pleased. All returned to harmony.

"Within the lodge," I said to Mary, "Wi will enter through the heat in the stones. Wi shines upon the trees, who absorb his heat. We cut the trees and transfer the energy of the sun into the stones through the process of fire. Fire comes from the sun. When we light the fire, the sun walks among us. We will light the fire in the time of Han, or darkness. In this manner we will honor both.

"These four—the sun, the moon, the light, and the darkness—are the Wakantankan," I told Mary. "Part of the great mystery is that they are four but also one. Even they cannot understand this, for Wakantankan remains a mystery to any one of them. We will pray to Wakantankan in the sweat lodge. You might say your headaches are like Wakantankan," I said to Mary, kidding her, "for they are a great mystery to you. But we will ask the real mystery to solve your headaches. You do not need to know what to do to make them go away. That will be revealed to you. But then you must do it, for what comes in a sacred manner must be obeyed. Otherwise you would be trampling on your prayers, an unpleasant sight in the eyes of the spirits. So we want to be sure you will do what you are told when the instructions come." We finished the day's story with those four beings. The remainder of the day was spent on an inner journey, during which Mary traveled to the territory of her headaches to learn what had created them. Skan creates everything and gives it a purpose. "We must not ask your headaches to be removed until we understand that purpose and can honor the Wakantankan without the need for headaches. Please," I asked Mary, "do not even try to send them away until we have that learning."

As we progressed into the wilderness of her brain, Mary realized that the headaches had brought her out of her suburban existence in search of spirituality. She had tried every medical, psychological, and holistic alternative. None had worked. All that was left was a spiritual path. I asked her to honor the spirit of the headaches, for its gift was substantial.

On the second day of Mary's intensive spiritual retreat, I began with a ceremony, praying to the spirits of the Four Directions, the Sky, the Earth, and All our Relations to help Mary. We returned to working with the biofeedback machines and trance while I told Mary the story of the companions of the four sacred beings mentioned the day before. As she relaxed her tension, slowed her breathing, and entered more deeply into the trance zone, I told her about the companions of the four.

"Skan had established domains and dominions for each of the four. Throughout each day, they remained there with nothing to do. The sacred beings were bored. They were lonely. They longed for companionship, so Skan assembled them and gave each the power to create a companion in whatever manner was desired.

"Wi created a disk like himself, only more lovely, which is called Wi-win (feminine sun) or Han-wi (sun of the darkness). He made her less bright than himself so he could constantly gaze upon her. Together they governed the two times of day and night. Maka created an alluring and seductively beautiful being to whom she imparted her ill nature. Maka called her Unk (which means passion). Unk was so beautiful that Maka became jealous of her. She and Maka quarreled violently, and Maka threw her into the waters and remained without a companion.

"Skan created the wind for a companion. The Lakota word for wind is Tate. Tate is formless, like Skan. Tate was created to carry the messages of the Creator to whoever should hear them. Listen to the wind," I said, "for there you will hear the voice of the Creator."

Mary stirred. From far away in trance she murmured that she had always been afraid of the wind. She feared the wind would tell her things she did not want to hear. She hadn't known anything about the wind but worried when she heard it, went indoors when it blew strong, and generally avoided it.

"Listen to the wind," I urged her. "Fly with the wind. Let Tate whisper into your ear. He will tell you what you need to know about your headaches. He will tell you what you need to know to heal your headaches." Mary traveled with the wind. The wind carried her to the home of her mother, dead three years now. Mary saw herself standing in her mother's bedroom, aware of a rage at her mother that she could never express. She heard the wind whispering, "Forgive yourself. Forgive yourself." She saw her mother's pain. She had seen her mother as a vain, mindless, alcoholic recipe hustler. The wind told her to look deeper. Beneath the surface flowed a river of pain. Beneath the surface hid the demons her mother could never confront. These demons eventually killed her mother as she gave up all desire to live.

Mary cried softly with this realization. Her biofeedback machines indicated profound physiological change taking place. I encouraged her to remain in the hands of Tate. "Let him help you see all that you need to see about your mother," I urged her. Mary saw herself refusing to admit the death of her mother, fighting to make her mother want to stay alive from her own guilt at the rage she felt. The wind asked her to breathe out the guilt, to release it for the wind to carry to the Four Directions, to disperse it across the heavens.

Later that day we learned about Wakinyan, the Thunderbeings. I told Mary how the Thunderbeings could cleanse her pain away. I told her how they were created by Inyan to be his companion. "They have a form so terrible that they must conceal themselves within a cloud, or you would go insane from a mere glance at them. But their purpose is noble. They are here to rid the world of filth. They are here to wash away the demons, like the ones who destroyed your mother and who would destroy you.

"They bring life-giving rain with the thunder and lightning," I said. "The old ones say that lightning will never strike a cedar tree, because the cedar is our symbol for life everlasting. People used to stand beneath a cedar tree for safety in a thunderstorm. I don't know if that will work for people who have doubt," I said. "Maybe it works only for the ones who know its truth. We will throw cedar upon the stones," I told Mary. "We will fill the lodge with the sweet smell of cedar once it is purified."

I told Mary that we would pray to the Thunderbeings, the Wakinyan, for cleansing during the lodge. "They come from the West," I said, "the direction to which we must look for help with our fears. Give the Thunderbeings your pain. Give the Thunderbeings your fear. Let them help you release the toxins and the sickness that give you your headaches."

When we finished the imagery, I did bodywork with Mary. I used a combination of techniques I have learned from Apache and Cherokee practitioners, as well as methods of my own that I have discovered to be effective. I worked with Mary to release tension inside her neck and to decrease the tension surrounding her rib cage so that she could step out of a path of restriction.

We talked about Mary's insights from the imagery. Now that she knew about the sacred beings, I asked her to imagine them helping her. I asked her to imagine that we could call upon them and that they would come to provide help. The sun had shown her the game she played with her husband, of not expressing herself to him, of not expressing her anger, until she grew more and more enraged. When a migraine came, she could legitimately withdraw and care for herself. "This is the same pattern you followed with your mother," I remarked. Mary was shocked with the realization. We finished our day together with a ceremony. We smoked tobacco and thanked the spirits for their help, asking for their added protection as she prepared for the sweat lodge.

That next morning was cold and bright. A storm front seemed to stand on the Rincon Mountains to the East. I worried that we would have rain and quickly made prayer ties to the Thunderbeings, asking them to hold back the rain until we could cover the sweat lodge and make a roaring fire. When Mary awoke, we rushed to cover the lodge—first with sheets, then blankets, then tarps. We placed black and white flags on the altar with cherry sticks to honor the Thunderbeings. Then we started our day's work for the sweat lodge, which would take place that evening.

I told Mary about several other sacred beings and the feast of the gods that we would be recreating in our ceremony. "You should know about Ksa, or wisdom," I said. "Ksa often travels with Wohpe, the daughter of Skan. Wohpe is also known to the people as the White Buffalo Calf Woman. Ksa is the son of Inyan and the Wakinyan. The opposite of Ksa is Iktomi, also son of rock and thunder. Ksa is proud, but Iktomi is not. Iktomi spends his days trying to thwart the Creator's desires and serves as an obstacle for all change and improvement. Both have queer shapes. Both invoke laughter when they are seen. But Ksa is honored by laughter, where Iktomi vows to humiliate all who laugh at him." We called upon Ksa to help Mary to explore her inner world for the parts who needed help.

I told Mary the story of Wohpe, the White Buffalo Calf woman, which is such a famous story that I will not repeat it here.[10] "Wohpe is always present in the lodge," I told Mary. "Her qualities are love, compassion, and forgiveness. She comes from the South. Look to her for beauty and love." I encouraged Mary to see herself through the eyes of the White Buffalo Calf Woman, to see herself as a beautiful creature to be loved, cherished, and honored.

I told Mary about the creatures who are the opposite of Wohpe—the offspring of Unk. They are Iya and Gnas. Iya means "devil" and Gnas means "evil one." I told her about the tricks of Gnas, and how these two travel the world to deceive and manipulate for their own gain. We journeyed inside to learn if she had been touched by Iya or Gnas, for most have. We asked the Wakinyan to help with the cleansing of that wound.

Last I told her about the star people. Tate had approached the Creator with a problem. When he traveled at night to do the wishes of Skan, darkness was everywhere. He could not see where he was going. He asked Skan to help him travel at night as easily as during the day. The Creator thought this over and took some of the spirit of water. He put it into the sky and created beings that could provide some light for the night, but not enough to disturb Maka, who wished to rest from the heat of the sun. He called these new beings star people. He charged them with watching over the world at night and reporting to him what they observed. He made one their chief and put him in the North. The place of the chief was fixed, so that anyone could look toward him to determine where they were at night, as they looked to the sun in the daytime. In this manner, Tate could have light and direction for his night sky journeys.

This brought us to the feast of the gods (sacred beings). I wanted to give Mary this way of understanding the sweat lodge. I said to Mary, "Ksa wanted to create good things for taste and smell. Food had not yet been invented, since sacred beings need not eat for survival like mortals. Ksa told Wohpe about his idea. She liked it but could not decide where to plant these foods, since whatever domain was chosen would cause one to resent another. Ksa suggested the underworld, beneath the Earth. In those days this was considered neutral space, where councils were held and where Skan deliberated about the conflicts and desires of the sacred beings. Wohpe excitedly agreed, and the fruits were planted.

"Then, from material he created, Ksa made a lodge in the shape of the sun, with the entrance where the sun's light would shine inside the moment he arose in the morning. He made the place of honor at the West. Whoever sat in this spot would be the first to be greeted by the sun when he rose in the morning. A seat was created on each side of the door for those who were to lead the feast. Toward the North was the seat of the host. Toward the South was the seat of the one who would serve the food and drink. Heat was borrowed from Wi and placed in the center of the lodge. This was the first lodge and is the model for all lodges, including our sweat lodge. All the sacred beings were invited to the feast, and all agreed to come. Gnas encouraged Iya to become a tempest and try to blow down the lodge. Iya tried and failed. Because of this, it is said that evil cannot destroy the lodge. Nor can evil enter the lodge without losing its power. Because Iya attempted to defile the food that was to be served to the gods, Skan decreed that Iya could no longer enter the lodge.

"Skan, the Creator, came to be in the seat of honor, with Tate at his right. The sun and then the moon sat at his left. Maka was to the right of Tate. To the left of the moon was Inyan, followed by Heyoka (the Thunderbeings, when they allow themselves to be seen) and Unk. Gnas was placed to the right of Maka. Ksa sat in the place of the server, and Wohpe in the place of the hostess. In the same manner," I told Mary, "we will place you in the seat of honor, where the Creator has sat. I will sit in the seat of Wohpe, and my friend, Sanjay, will sit in the place of wisdom. He will serve us the stones and the water as Ksa served the sacred food and drink to the gods. I will tend and honor the stones, as Wohpe honored the fire in that first feast.

"I wanted to tell you this," I said, "so that you will know how sacred this sweat lodge is. All of those sacred beings will be there. Whenever we build their lodge and hold their feast, they walk in our midst. They will hear your prayers, and your prayers will be answered. They will come true."

The point of my story was to indoctrinate Mary in how to view prayer. I wanted to give her faith that her prayers would be heard and would come true when we smoked the sacred pipe, just as the White Buffalo Calf Woman said.

William Lyon writes, "Prayers are acts of personal sincerity that require a great deal of effort and will on the part of the individual . . . . The efficacy of prayer . . . lies in its ability to call forth communication between [person] and spirit. This act is a sacred undertaking filled with importance."[11]

Thus I used story to give Mary this idea for prayer, to implant the idea that the spirits would be right there with us, taking every word that came from her mouth.

We placed the stones upon the fire, which burned brightly. We smoked for the fire, speaking to the spirits already gathered of our intentions for this sweat lodge. Then came the snow, at first a gentle series of flakes that enlivened the night, but before long, sheets falling thickly around us. The peacefulness imparted by the snow was astounding. The spirit of winter had sent us a most exotic gift. Before the night ended, eight inches would cover the lodge and the desert. What a gift to see snow in a desert winter! What a sign that our prayers were being answered!

None wanted to leave the fire. We were transfixed by the pristine beauty of the snow. It covered coats and coated hair. We continued to sit beside the fire, praying quietly. Occasionally the wolves and the coyotes howled. The horses came closer to discover what we were doing.

Time came to enter the lodge. The wood had burned down sufficiently to remove the first set of stones for the first round. In my tradition, sweat lodges are done in rounds of four, though many tribal variations exist. We sat inside the lodge while snow fell in gusts outside. My friend, Sanjay, brought the coals inside. I burned sage to dispel any evil we may have brought inside. We blessed ourselves and then the pipe. I activated the pipe by connecting the bowl and the stem.

The bowl represents the Earth and the feminine; the stem, the sky and the masculine. When the two are joined, the pipe is activated. It is ready to work. I prayed to each of the directions, taking a pinch of tobacco and offering it to each in turn. Slowly the pipe was filled. When this was done, we brought the first seven stones inside. We touched each stone by the pipe with a prayer. We placed each stone in its unique place, for the particular direction of the Seven Directions that it represents. (In addition to East, South, West, and North, the other three directions place us as three-dimensional beings and are up, down, and center.) We placed cedar on each stone to welcome it into the lodge. When all seven had arrived, we placed the pipe upon the altar, and the remainder of the rocks needed for the first round entered. Then came the water, which is blessed upon the stones. Sanjay closed the door and slid inside beneath its thick blankets. I thanked each person for coming, we thanked the Thunderbeings for the snow, and we began the songs for the first round.

In the second round, Mary had a chance to pray. Her prayers were strong and clear. She asked for her migraines to be healed. She gave thanks for being led to these ways of healing and asked to be guided more directly, without recourse to head pain. She prayed to the North for strength in speaking directly to her husband, which she knew was required for her wellness. She prayed for her mate and her child. She asked the spirits to help her husband adjust to the new woman she was becoming. Her prayers were thoughtful and sincere. After the third round, the pipe entered. We smoked and knew through faith that her prayers had come true. After the fourth round we crawled out into the snow, lingering around the fire before we departed for the warmth of the house.

In the morning, Mary had organized her thoughts. She had encountered within the lodge her blocks to letting go, to relaxation. She remembered using chemicals to loosen up. Without chemicals she had progressively grown more uptight. With her mother's death and her marriage, she had released her last hold on spiritual connectedness that had lingered from her college days. She had found her wall, that concrete fence that kept her tension inside and people outside. I told her a story about the book by C.S. Lewis, *Out of the Silent Planet,* in which the protagonist discovers through a journey to Mars that all the planets sing in celebration of the Creator except ours. Ours is silent, overly consumed by evil. I talked about the need to open the wall to let the song of the sun enter, to let the angels come to roost inside her. We spent time just feeling what she had hidden for so long. Certain words became more meaningful to her—betrayed, sad, angry, bitter. She had not considered these words for years. They had been locked inside her.

"I used to be so open," she said. "Like my son. Then I was really shocked." I asked her to remember when she was shocked. She recalled a big house in New Orleans. Things were harmonious. Peaceful. Then boom. Overnight, it seemed, her parents were divorcing. The house was being sold. We returned to that time with spirit eyes. We saw her parents fighting. She wanted to yell at them about their betrayal of her, that they were really screwing up her life. The Thunderbeings cleansed the scene. She felt the breath of compassion surrounding her. Her child consciousness changed. Wisdom entered the scene. That child in New Orleans could cope more easily with so much spirit help to back her up.

I asked about other betrayals. Mary traveled to her mother's diagnosis of cancer. She had not seen it coming. She had not suspected. She let herself be caught up in the drama of her mother's death. Then boom. At the same time, her husband was having an affair. She had recovered her strength but had not healed the wound. She related feeling as if an ax murderer were waiting around the corner. She feared another tragedy.

I turned the tables by mentioning faith. "We are all out of control," I said. "From our level we cannot control our destinies. We must ask for help from higher realms. All must relinquish that hope of control to be humble before the spirits, who will help us if we ask."

Mary's physiological monitors showed how profoundly her biological responses had changed. To complete the day, she made a shield to contain the most important images from the sweat lodge and her trance journeys.

We concluded our work the following day with a ceremony. After talking and using imagery together, we went outside into the darkness to light the fire. We sang to the spirits, asked their help, made our prayers, and concluded our week's work. Mary left the next morning.

Back at home, Mary rapidly absorbed the concepts and used them to find wellness. The lifting of her pain was gradual and progressive, and the headaches diminished in frequency. Four months later she was pain-free, and her migraines have not returned.

Testimonials like Mary's are told at every ceremony. Some are miraculous; some are ordinary. All inspire us. Success stories present us with the tantalizing possibility of transcendence and a hidden blueprint for how to make another person's transformation our own.

Why do I study the miraculous? And why does this make so many people uncomfortable?

To me, the miraculous explores the limits of what is humanly possible. These are limits that I do not truly grasp. The stories in this chapter have hinted at areas in which people achieved more than conventional medicine could believe. This is the beauty of miraculous stories, that they show us where we can and do transcend. Conventional medicine's goal of predictability—as well as the conventional nonspiritual worldview—are destroyed by these miraculous stories.

Like the characters in this chapter, hearing miraculous stories inspires us to take stock of our lives and wonder how we could and should change. This is what stories are about, to inspire us beyond our wildest dreams. And this is what excites me—exploring the limits of the human condition. What are the impossible dreams that we can realize? I don't know, but I know that skepticism and doubt block the realization of these dreams. I believe we can say that what we expect has a powerful impact upon what will happen, and I believe that an active effort is required on our part. Much more than that may be suspect. We do not know, except to say that perhaps God heals. Perhaps states of grace exist. Perhaps, in the blink of an eye, everything changes. But I suspect the hard work must always be done by someone. Sometimes I contribute. Sometimes the person does all the work him- or herself.

So long as a single candle can burn, we will take back our night, expanding beyond the shadows cast by that lone candle. Stories of miracles are important reminders. They let us know what is possible. However rare, their existence serves as an inspiration. The fact that some few individuals have scaled Mt. Everest inspires those of us who would never climb a mountain to do so in our own unique ways. We must nurture and preserve stories of miracles as inspiring us to reach for the stars in everything. Like Cervantes's don Quixote, we must dream the impossible dream if we ever wish to wake up within that dream of healing and cure.

10

Reauthoring Therapy

Through many sunrises have I struggled with misty
chains of fear,
hardly able to jump even three feet into the sky,
afraid of falling were I to go higher than that.
But now the fog has burned away,
revealing fertile ground
instead of the scorched earth I imagined.
Can we move forward into a summer of renewal and
redemption,
planting trees of recovery and transformation—
mighty oaks, tall palms, and hibiscus groves?

The final process in healing and in curing is to reauthor the story
about who we are to include being a person who has been healed.
I like stories that make it hard to go backward. The stories we tell
about ourselves have spirit. This spirit is in dialogue with ours. We need
a plausible story that is believable to our audience, which is usually our
community. Cancer survivors and other remarkable patients often have
to leave their doctors because the doctors will not support the new story
of healing, countering with stories of relapse that support the doctor's
belief that healing is an illusion, that diseases are more powerful than

we are, and that biology is unaffected by meaning. The new stories told by people who have been healed are generally less contradictory and more respectful of the narrator, and represent paths of greater joy and peacefulness. The new stories include more possibilities than the old stories. Pamela's story provides a good example.

Pamela came with the problem of feeling lost. She needed a sense of home. Her surface reason for consulting me was to help her decide whether or not to keep an apartment in Georgetown and a Maryland country home. Georgetown was trendy and chic, but her country house outside of Annapolis was spacious, isolated, and surrounded by nature—foxes, sycamores, and willows in the lowland by the river. She thought of moving into Georgetown to have more community, since so many of her friends lived there and so many of her activities took place in Washington, but she had not been able to let go of her country house. She wanted hypnosis to help her resolve where to live. But, as with most good stories, the plot thickened.

Pamela had been seeing a married man, who couldn't leave his wife. They met at an event sponsored by one of the arts boards to which she belonged. He was educated in art history and had his own impressive collection. She immediately recognized him as a teacher and clung to his every word. They went to galleries and museums together, took walks in the park, climbed the Washington monument with the tourists, and rode bikes around Jefferson's tomb. Their sex was extraordinary. But for all that, he wouldn't leave his wife. "Because of my children," he said.

Pamela recognized hers as a common experience, especially for women of her age (forty plus). Nevertheless, when they were together, she felt "at home." Without him, she felt homeless. Rain drizzled for days during the week he relocated his workplace to Philadelphia. The stream flowing behind her house flooded her backyard as she contemplated their diminished opportunity for meetings. He continued to live in Maryland, on a high bluff overlooking the river, half an hour from Pamela's home, but with his wife and children. Driving to Philadelphia to see him seemed unreasonable. Pamela knew she had to let go of him but felt vertigo whenever she thought of doing so. She thought she would drown without him.

How do we make sense of Pamela's story? The psychoanalyst of the past assumed absolute authority for knowledge about the other person's psyche and soul, creating elaborate descriptions with fanciful terms from Greek mythology, a wonderful contrivance to sound erudite. Many psychotherapists assume knowledge of a person that they don't have. "Pamela is acting out," one might say, stringing together an elaborate beaded necklace of poorly defined technical terms that make the storyteller appear quite smart. How can we make sense of the story of a life without those crutches, without pretending that we have an objective understanding of another person's world? How can we proceed if no one has privileged access to the naming and interpreting of life?

I proceed from my own stories, by comparing the story I am hearing to stories I have told in the past about my life. Or I think about how I would feel if I were telling the story I am hearing. Sometimes we are guided by intuition, even perhaps by the occasional telepathic reception or spirit communication, but we can never be certain about such matters and must structure an understanding from the story heard. To be therapeutic, I must tell Pamela a story about the story she told me that provides her with diversity of perspective. I must tell a story that allows her to see her story as only one of many and not the only reality. Then she can consider reauthoring her own story (which means re-creating herself).

To understand someone else's story, often we need to ask them about the terms they use. I wanted to better understand Pamela's use of the word "homeless." Homeless is not a primary emotion. So when Pamela said she felt homeless, she was describing a complex set of emotions combined in that one word. "What do you mean by homeless?" I asked her.

"I mean lost, without direction or guidance, alone, lonely, outside looking in, excluded, and grieving." She proceeded to tell me about numerous people among her family and friends who had recently died. In fact, her biological family now consisted of her adult daughter (also living in the District) and her older sister, who lived in Denver. Her tears about the death of her parents contrasted with her stories about feeling isolated and lonely while growing up with them. She described her childhood as "being the only living person in a family of robots." It reminded me of another story I had heard from a woman who poetically described her family as a collection of appliances—a refrigerator mother, a television father, a toaster brother. What a powerful way to describe a cold and aloof woman, a man lost in himself and his diversions, and a hyperactive brother.

I asked Pamela to tell me what "feeling at home" would be like. She told me a story of an Italian man in Annapolis whom everybody knew. He owned a small family restaurant on a busy corner—a little trattoria. He ran the cash register and supervised the dining room, greeting the regulars with the insults they had come to lovingly expect from him, while his wife cooked in the kitchen and his children waited and bused tables. Pictures of him with important local people and celebrities, including John Wayne, decorated the walls. Pamela described the experience of eating in his restaurant as coming home.

"Have you ever felt at home?" I asked. Then came one of those intuitive moments in which I suddenly had an image of her sitting in a house by the water, at a wooden desk, writing, and looking up at a lighthouse. It felt very peaceful. I described this image to her and got the typical "oh my God" response that people give when an intuition is correct.

"That's the house where I lived before moving to my current one. I loved to sit at that desk and feel the warmth of the sun stream through the window. I really felt good in that house. The river flowed down to the ocean past short trees buffeted by the wind. I was renting the second floor in this house where the river met the ocean, beneath a lighthouse. I used to love to sit at my desk overlooking the water and write in my journal. When I got tired, I looked up at the lighthouse for inspiration. Sitting in my second floor window, I would wave at people walking on the sidewalk down below. That's when I felt at home."

"How does being with a man make you feel like you have a home?" I asked. Tears filled her eyes.

"Terry is such a kind, warm, loving man. Being with him made me feel so good. It made me forget all my cares and concerns."

"But he's not available," I said.

"But he might be, someday," she countered.

"Is it okay to stay out in the cold waiting for someday?" I reminded her of the characters from *Waiting for Godot*.[1]

"Not really," she responded.

"So what stops you from dating other men and finding an available life partner?" I asked.

"I don't do that," she answered. "Women of my age don't do that."

"Do what?" I countered, playing Coyote-sly.

"Go looking for men," she said. "They have to find us."

"And how do they find you, sitting at home?" I asked.

"God has a plan for all of us," she said, "and He sends The Right One, no matter what you do."

"I heard that God helps those who help themselves."

"If God wants me to be happy, God will send me someone. If not, He won't." As we continued to talk about her ideas of God and men, I noticed that Pamela's tone led me to believe that she made herself seem unavailable to the men who did come her way. By now, the definition of homeless had changed to being lonely, without a life partner. The place where she lived was less important than who she spent time with, as was self-care. When Pamela became involved with Terry, she moved at the same time to her new house and abandoned her prior self-care rituals (yoga, meditation, exercise, chi gong). She was experiencing what sociologists call *binding social practices,* in terms of having an affair with a married man and adhering to her own concept of how women and men meet and pair up in general. Pamela's ideas about how men and women relate—the binding social practices to which I refer— came from her cultural and family upbringing. She expected God to provide her with an ideal man without any effort on her part but pushed away all the men she met. When I gave her several examples of how I had come to that conclusion, spoken in her own words from sto- ries she had told me, Pamela realized that an external observer might make that conclusion about her.

What would an alternate story sound like? I suggested she needed a more playful view of dating. Perhaps she'd like to try on a new set of beliefs, since hers didn't seem to be working. What if God is relatively neutral and just wants to give you what you want, and what if you're communicating ambivalence about what you want? Or what if God is afraid to help you find a man, for fear you'll give away the few self-care skills you have left? I proposed a new idea to Pamela. I suggested she think of herself as a strong, independent woman who does her self-care rituals everyday and plays with men the way eighteen-year-old women do. I suggested she could have fun with men without having to commit to them, think about them as life partners, or even see them again after one date. She could go places with the idea of communicating to the environment, "Hey, I'm a beautiful woman. Don't you all want to rush up to me and talk to me?"

Pamela tried this at a benefit dance, and the handsome drummer from the band flirted with her all night. When she asked her friend who had brought her to ask him to ask her out, she learned that he already had a girlfriend. She felt crushed, drowned even. We continued to refine this new narrative. "Why feel crushed?" I asked her. "You just got validated. Even a guy who already had a girlfriend found you irresistible. That's great feedback from the universe. Now you have to practice taking life and dating less seriously. It's just fun." I told her stories overheard from my nineteen-year-old daughter about the dating habits of her and her friends. "Pretend you're nineteen again, but in this culture. Not the one in which we grew up."

Pamela kept working at this. Slowly but surely, she reworked her concept of herself as a person who dates. She started having fun with men. Little did my daughter know what a role model she had become. Pamela went out with lots of men, had fun, and rarely slept with any of them. Over time, a romance developed with one of the men whom she would never have initially considered as a life partner. She felt less alone. She accepted my suggestion to practice her self-care for one hundred consecutive days. (Chinese philosophy says that whatever you do for one hundred consecutive days, you will do for life.)

As part of this work, I prescribed Katherine Hepburn movies. The great Hepburn "never met a man she couldn't step on." One of her memorable quotes was about confronting men head on during an era in which women were supposed to be demure, cunning, and conniving. The daughter of one of the early suffragettes, Katherine Hepburn took no bull from men but was also an elegant, sexy woman. She clearly enjoyed men, her sensuality, and her sexuality in a way that was transformative for her times. She became Pamela's role model. Pamela began to remodel herself as "Hepburn-esque." She imagined herself as the heroine in the movie *Out of Africa*.

Pamela did eventually marry her new romance and created a wonderful home for herself as the Katherine Hepburn of greater Annapolis. Her new story encompassed a character radically different from the dysfunctional dater I first met.

Her new (reauthored) story added the pursuit of autonomy and self-sufficiency to the pursuit of love, making it more empowering. Her initial archetypal character was the passive princess, Sleeping Beauty, waiting to be kissed. Her new archetypal character was closer to an Amazon, initiating the kisses herself.

Stories enable us to link aspects of our experience through the dimension of time. There does not appear to be any other mechanism for the structuring of experience that so captures the sense of lived time, or that can adequately represent the sense of lived time.[2] Through stories, we see our lives changing. Through stories we gain a sense of the unfolding of events in our lives as recent history. This sense is vital to our perception of a future that will be different from the present.

Stories construct beginnings and endings; they impose beginnings and endings on the flow of experience. According to University of California at Los Angeles educational psychologist Jerome Bruner, "We create the units of experience and meaning from a continuity of life. Every telling is an arbitrary imposition of meaning on the flow of memory, in that we highlight some causes and discount others; that is, every telling interprets experience."[3] In considering the vital role that stories have in helping us organize our experience, we see that the stories in which we situate our experience determine:

1. The meaning that we give to experience
2. The selection of those aspects of experience to be expressed
3. The shape of the expression that we give to those aspects of experience
4. Real effects and directions in our lives and in our relationships

All stories are "indeterminate" in that they carry a degree of ambiguity and uncertainty, even contain inconsistencies and contradictions. This fact will be appreciated by those who have read a novel that was particularly engaging and then have gone to see the movie made from it, only to find to their dismay that the movie director got it all wrong! Literary texts are full of gaps that readers must complete for the story to be performed. In likening the interaction of readers and literary texts to the interaction of people and the stories through which they live their lives, we become more aware of our need to fill the gaps in daily interaction. Just as the gaps in literary texts recruit the lived experience and the imagination of the reader, so do the gaps in the stories that are "lived": recruit the experience and the imagination of people, as they engage in performances of meaning under the guidance of the story. This recruitment is the process through which people learn how to transform and to be healed.

With every performance of a story, people reauthor their lives and relationships. Every telling encapsulates the whole story but is more than the previous telling. The evolution of lives and relationships is akin to the process of reauthoring our stories, the process of entering into stories with our experience and our imagination, and the process of taking these stories over and making them our own.

Stories are, in the first place, given. One person tells them. Another person hears them. But stories are not lists of defined instructions. They do not give you the eight essential steps to creating the perfect life. They are engaging and occupying, but indeterminate in the sense that it is up to the listener to set one of many possible meanings. It is through this relative indeterminateness—the ambiguity and uncertainty of all stories—that we can construct our own meaning, negotiating it through recourse to our lived experience and our imagination. This requires us to engage in a process of origination. We originate the story within ourselves and make it our own.

I conclude with a story about a young woman's death from cancer. The story began traumatically. Through working together, we reauthored it to give meaning to a life that seemed all too short. The strictly biological story is one of tragic bad luck.

Tiffany was a twenty-two-year-old woman just starting graduate school in anthropology, diagnosed with a rare form of bladder cancer that had already spread well beyond the bladder. She was only diagnosed when the cancer shut off the urine from her kidneys, requiring a dramatic surgery to correct.

Tiffany's parents had resources and spared her no possible conventional or alternative therapy. Tiffany continued to decline despite everyone's efforts. In our early work, we used guided imagery, acupuncture, bodywork, energy work, hypnosis, and other techniques to control her discomforts (nausea, vomiting, bloating, pain). Tiffany was a fast learner and quickly mastered these techniques, achieving a comfort unique for advanced cancer patients. When this threshold had been passed, we began to consider spirituality. We began to seek meaning for her life, what had transpired and what was left of it. Like Frances from *Coyote Healing*, Tiffany had considering going to divinity school but had decided instead to study the anthropology of religion. When her cancer was diagnosed, she had been intensively studying the German theologian and Christian mystic, Meister Eckhart. Once we had overcome her chemotherapy symptoms, she decided that we should create our own course on his readings as part of our work together. I was not that familiar with Meister Eckhart but had been introduced to him in the writings of Matthew Fox, so this sounded exciting.

I had come to understand that Tiffany's sense of meaning came from her pursuit of holiness. I had an image of Tiffany trekking in a desert of ideas, metaphorically following Christ's path to wander alone, hungry and thirsty, for forty days and nights. Like Frances from *Coyote Healing*, Mother Teresa was her ideal, the person she most respected. During college she had visited Mother Teresa in Calcutta and aspired to be like her. Jesus was her other hero.

Why did Tiffany develop cancer? As I have mentioned before, I want to resist simplistic psychological or spiritual causative explanations for cancer. Everything is so much more complicated than we imagine. I did come to understand that Tiffany's pursuit of holiness through the course of her cancer brought meaning to her suffering and to her death that no one could dispute. Tiffany became a Mother Teresa or Christlike character, and this made all the difference for her.

Tiffany's goal was to completely empty herself of will and desire. She believed that "only the empty can be filled by Spirit. If you are full, Spirit has no room to enter. Spirit is attracted to the empty spaces within the soul, not to the sites of fullness." She believed that emptiness would allow her to enter into the kingdom of heaven.

In one of our readings, Meister Eckhart wrote:

So long as a person has his own wish in him to fulfill the ever-beloved will of God, if that is still a matter of his will, then this person does not yet possess the poverty of which we want to speak . . . . For a human being to possess true poverty, he or she must be as free of his or her created will as they were when they did not yet exist.

Tiffany aspired to become nothing but the pure will of God as she died, to be empty of all else but God. For her to aspire to the kind of

emptiness that predated our creation would create the profound emptiness that would allow God to enter. Not to guide us to do His will, like
puppets to the puppeteer, but rather to enliven our souls so that we *are*
the will of God, Tiffany told me. She explained to me how different it
was to imagine doing God's will in actions planned based upon our
reading or our understanding of God, as compared with "doing without mind," with Being God.

Poverty was a goal for Eckhart, as it was for Tiffany. Though her
family was wealthy, she abstained from any demonstration of consumption. She spent her summers working in the inner city in the most
abject poverty imaginable. More than anything else, Tiffany wanted to
serve God. She wanted to make a difference in the world's suffering. She
seemed to feel guilty for having anything. Was she emulating Eckhart in
saying that she must be as free of these life supports as if they did not
exist? Must she walk alone through the valley of the shadow of death?
Her mother would have gladly taken her place on any challenge. But
would that have been desirable, if it could have been done? I wondered
if Tiffany's wish to be empty could have contributed to her illness. Did
she feel that she had no right to live, considering how much more others suffered than she?

Next, Tiffany showed me the writings of a Thai monk, Venerable
Ajahn Chah, who wrote:

About this mind, in truth there is nothing really wrong with it. It
is intrinsically pure. Within itself it is already peaceful. That the
mind is not peaceful these days is because it follows moods. The
real mind doesn't have anything to it. It is simply an aspect of
nature. It becomes peaceful or agitated because moods deceive it.
The untrained mind is stupid. Sense impressions come and trick it
into happiness, suffering, gladness, sorrow, but the mind's true
nature is none of these things. That gladness or sadness is not the
mind but only a mood coming to deceive us. The untrained mind
gets lost and follows these things. It forgets itself, then we think it
is we who are upset or at ease or whatever.

But really this mind of ours is already unmoving and peaceful,
really peaceful, just like a leaf which is still as long as no wind
blows. If a wind comes up the leaf flutters. The fluttering of the
leaf is due to the wind—the fluttering of the mind is due to those

sense impressions. The mind follows them. If it doesn't follow them it doesn't flutter. If we know fully the true nature of sense impressions we are unconcerned.

Our practice is simply to see the original nature of the mind. So we must train the mind to know those sense impressions, and not get lost in them.

To make it peaceful—just this, is the aim of all this difficult practice we put ourselves through.

Therefore, we must cultivate emptiness. We must actually dwell in God as God dwells in us, not even knowing what we do or are doing. It must be done so matter of factly that it is not even noticed.

We must make a radical Letting Go in order to be sufficiently empty and therefore able to be God. God enters the emptiness.[4]

Eckhart writes that God is nothingness, which is more properly hyphenated as no-thing-ness. To be full of God we must meditate or contemplate no-thing-ness, since that is God. God is not a thing.

I wondered how Tiffany could become no-thing, when she was the oldest, favorite child of a family that was everything—the perfect family, the most respected family, the most successful family. Within her lay the desire for no-thing-ness, as expressed in all of her good works with the poor. I had the sense that Tiffany aspired to selflessness, as in having no self, as in being completely empty. This was the gist of the stories she showed me. (I sensed another Tiffany from her imagery, a wild girl who wanted to sell hats in a "throwback from the sixties" store or buy a Harley-Davidson and set out across Route 66. That path would be unique and iconoclastic. These choices were constrained by her family and her religion. My stories about these versions of her were too frivolous to be believable, but they made her laugh.)

Was this the pivotal point, to empty Tiffany of the sense of fullness her family provided her, the sense of fullness her culture provided her? Her own attempts at emptying had been serious, planned, careful, thoughtful, and safe. When she finally was empty at times during our sessions, she came alive with a vivacity she didn't often reveal. Spirit was clearly in her then, but I think that level of passion and excitement went against her definitions of acceptable religiosity.

In one exercise, we found seven versions of Tiffany who were well.

One, as I mentioned earlier, sold hats. Another rode a bike down Route 66. Yet another taught school in an impoverished neighborhood but as a vital member of that living community. This brought forth Tiffany's satisfaction at worship in the gospel church of an inner-city black community, in which the sermon is a dialogue between minister and congregation and the music smacks of vitality compared with the staid, conventional, quiet realm of Protestant Sundays. It was this surrender to the passion of life that attracted the versions of her who were well.

Another of Tiffany's favorite Eckhart quotes said:

> One must be so free of all knowledge that he or she does not know or recognize or perceive that God lives in him or her; even more, one should be free of all knowledge that lives in him or her. For, when people still stood in God's eternal being, nothing else lived in them. Hence we say that people should be as free of their own knowledge as when they were not yet, letting God accomplish whatever God wills. People should stand empty.

While this paragraph could profoundly connect Christianity and Buddhism and Native American spirituality, I believed that Tiffany was using it to make meaning out of her disappearance from life.

I think Tiffany did achieve, as Buddhist monk Thich Nhat Hahn said, "awareness of no-thing."[5] She set about letting her little bottle of self drain out. She pulled the plug and let her personality and will spill out into the sand, so that only empty remained. Did God enter? Together Tiffany and I had profound spiritual experiences that I will never forget. We experienced Christ. We experienced God's entry into the soul. We felt that spark of life that enlightens and enlivens us all. Together we experienced wise, kind, compassionate, loving, enlivened, and all-encompassing energy, whether you call it Christ, Spirit, or bodhisattva. When we are filled with spirit, we are no longer ourselves, but a hybrid human-spirit being, thing and no-thing simultaneously. Working with her through the dying process became one of the profound events of my life.

Tiffany's miracle bore no relationship to the health of her physical body. I believe she achieved sainthood in this life. She achieved the state of human empty–spirit full. She eventually stopped returning to the state of being only human, moving on to her own kind of sainthood.

During our time together, through collaborative dialogue, we succeeded in reauthoring Tiffany's story from one of a tragic young life cut short to a story of spiritual transformation and transcendence, a journey from graduate student to saint, accomplished within the frame of one short year. I began with a different story in mind, one of miraculous physical cure. That wasn't to be. But what emerged was full of beauty and a reminder of both the fragility of human existence and the potential each of us has to rise above our mortality to become more than anyone ever thought we could be. This is what Tiffany did in her own Christian way, inspired by the mysticism of Meister Eckhart with a liberal sprinkling of Vietnamese Buddhism.

Another Eckhart quote said:

[T]here is something in the soul from which knowing and loving flow. It does not itself know and love as do the forces of the soul. Whoever comes to know this, knows what happiness is. It has neither before nor after, and it is in need of nothing additional, for it can neither gain nor lose. For this very reason, it is deprived of understanding that God is acting within it. Moreover, it is that identical self which enjoys itself just as God does. Thus we say that people shall keep themselves free and void so that they neither understand nor know that God works in them. . . .

The masters say that God is a being, an intelligent being, and that he knows all things. We say, however: God is neither being nor intelligent nor does he know this or that. Thus God is free of all things, and therefore he is all things.

Therefore it is necessary that people desire not to understand or know anything at all of the works of God. In this way is a person able to be poor of one's own understanding.

This understanding in physicality was what Tiffany achieved through the experience of cancer. Dying young from cancer and making it meaningful is a miracle in itself. Though she died, Tiffany had a healing. She attained holiness, from the perspectives of everyone who knew her. She taught me that writing about healing and the suspended state of grace entailed in healing is difficult. The location of healing is never quite available, as implied by Heisenberg's uncertainty principle. It happens through the creation of emptiness and the infiltration into that emptiness of a mysterious force that is free of all things, because it is all things. So this emptiness is a metaphor for giving up our will and surrendering to the larger good, to the larger cell or organ or being of which we are but a miniscule part. Thinking that God controls us like a puppeteer, as is popular in fundamentalist religions, is like thinking that we control one mitochondrion in one liver cell. We do not, and God does not, because we are God and God is us.

Tiffany was quite fond of the "five touchings of the earth" meditation, which we did often together. In the first meditation, we contemplate that whatever we think we are is but one wave in the ocean. Each wave is a manifestation of the greater whole. The waves come and go. They are impermanent. But the ocean remains forever. This body that I have, it is a wave. It will come and go. But knowing that I am truly the ocean and not the wave, I can feel peaceful.

In the second meditation, we consider that we have been many times and will be many times, and all these beings are manifestations of that which we truly are. Again, we are the ocean and not each wave.

In the third meditation, we consider that we are all of our ancestors and all of the offspring yet to be born. Again each of us is a wave in a greater ocean. My mother, my father, they are in me as I was in them.

The fourth meditation is on our beloved, while the fifth is on finding loving kindness and compassion for one whom we feel is our enemy. We embrace the enemy and feel that we are the enemy and the enemy is us.

When we are the ocean, there is no death, no disease. In this state, healing has already happened because illness never was.

Tiffany gave me the following quotation during the week that she died. It was Eckhart's sermon on his concept of breakthrough, so important for his spirituality. Perhaps it was also Tiffany's way of telling me she was ready to break through, to achieve the greater union with God she sought. She had found what really mattered to her—the sacred.

> In the breakthrough . . . where I stand free of my own will and of the will of God and of all his works and of God himself, there I am, above all creatures and am neither God nor creature. Rather, I am what I was and what I shall remain now and forever. Then I receive an impulse which shall bring me above all the angels. In

this impulse I receive wealth so vast that God cannot be enough for me in all that makes him God, and with all his divine works. In this breakthrough I discover that I and God are one. There I am what I was, and I grow neither smaller nor bigger, for there I am an immovable cause that moves all things. Here, then, God finds no place in people, for people achieve with this poverty what they were in eternity and will remain forever. Here God is one with the spirit, and that is the strictest poverty one can find.

Tiffany's story provides a worthy ending to this book, because she taught me more than I taught her. When I met her, I had some ideas about how to approach her chemotherapy side effects. Once they were resolved, I did not know how to proceed. What next? Only Tiffany could guide us where we needed to go, since her construction of meaning and purpose had to come from her unique needs and point of view. I could not have guessed that we would spend six months delving into Buddhist philosophy, Meister Eckhart, mystical Christianity, and Tiffany's evolving sense of herself in her successful spiritual quest. In the end, that was what mattered. And this is what occurs for each person who transforms—through the incorporation of multiple stories, in the context of social relationships among a community of listeners, tellers, and other audience members, a new story emerges, a story with elements that can be traced to the many, but that has become uniquely the person's own.

Sometimes, through dialogue containing multiple tellings and retellings of our stories, we arrive at strategies associated with physical curing, and sometimes we do not. I haven't been able to develop a formula for how to reliably cure illness on command. Curing remains a great mystery to me. At first, I was incredibly frustrated by this. I thought the job of an academic (which is what I was striving to become) was to figure out the underlying rules. I have come to realize that there aren't any. Nature is plastic. Nature changes with us, as we change with nature. Everything is connected. Genetics changes with social interaction. Culture influences biology. Even enzyme kinetics drift with social movements. I mean to make the radical claim that there is no biology apart from culture. Our efforts to carve the world into separate academic disciplines have been futile and need to be reversed. I believe more sensitive future research will begin to reveal how cultural beliefs shape physiological responses and modulate the expression of genes, even turning some on and off. I believe we will come to see that genes are exquisitely responsive to what we do and how we live in community with others. I predict that this discovery of a new field of cultural genetics will be a hallmark of the twenty-first century into which we have now embarked.

This dependence of biology upon culture (of the family and the larger society) is why any attempt to create a formula for constructing miracles will fail, because no such formulas can exist. We are each unique and must arrive at our own solutions. We do so better when we come together in community. But in the end, we are left only with uncertainty and the opportunity to interact together to create shared meaning and understanding. Stories are the glue that holds our social relationships together. The stories we tell about ourselves contain our images of self, which give us a sense of continuity in the world. Within the new narrative medicine, stories contain the clues to understanding illness, for they describe our internal, biological, and social relationships as well as our connections to other aspects of the universe.

One Lakota healing elder said, "While we can never know what's possible (only the Creator knows that), we must always do the best we can do." And that best sometimes leads to miraculous cures, personal and spiritual transformations, and the experience of connectedness or "at-one-ment." So, in spite of uncertainty, and without formulas or maps for how to proceed, what is marvelous and amazing and so wonderfully human is that we proceed in the dark, that we construct stories of healing that become true, despite the fact that we "don't know what we are doing."

Stories do present the problem of a multiplicity of meanings, which are not always obvious and must be deciphered. Through listening carefully to the stories of others and by telling stories of our own, we come to an awareness that is beyond words. Every attempt to articulate our understanding in language is so simplified as to be incorrect. Only the story in its wholeness can convey the wholeness of our understanding. This is why stories are the unit of meaning for life and medicine. This is why stories can heal.

Notes

Introduction

1. Among the many studies on this topic are S. Saxena, A. L. Brody, M. L. Ho et al., "Cerebral Glucose Metabolism in Obsessive-Compulsive Hoarding," *American Journal of Psychiatry* 161 (2004): 1038–48; L. R. Baxter, J. M. Schwartz, K. S. Bergman et al., "Caudate Glucose Metabolic Rate Changes with Both Drug and Behavior Therapy for Obsessive-compulsive Disorder," *Archives of General Psychiatry* 49 (1992): 681–89; S. E. Swedo, P. Pietrini, H. L. Leonard et al., "Cerebral Glucose Metabolism in Childhood-onset Obsessive-compulsive Disorder. Revisualization During Pharmacotherapy," *Archives of General Psychiatry* 49 (1992): 690–94; A. L. Brody, S. Saxena, D. H. S. Silverman et al., "Brain Metabolic Changes in Major Depressive Disorder from Pre- to Post-treatment with Paroxetine," *Psychiatry Research* 91 (1999): 127–39; S. D. Martin, E. Martin, S. S. Rai et al. "Brain Blood Flow Changes in Depressed Patients Treated with Interpersonal Psychotherapy or Venlafaxine Hydrochloride: Preliminary Findings," *Archives of General Psychiatry* 58 (2001): 641–48; and K. Goldapple, Z. Segal, C. Garson et al., "Modulation of Cortical-Limbic Pathways in Major Depression Treatment-Specific Effects of Cognitive Behavior Therapy," *Archives of General Psychiatry* 61 (2004): 34–41.

2. Studies comparing cognitive behavioral treatment with antidepressant therapy in recurrent depression include G. A. Fava, S. Fabbri, N. Sonino, "Residual Symptoms in Depression: An Emerging Therapeutic Target," *Progress in Neuro-psychopharmacology and Biological Psychiatry* 26 (2002): 1019–27; G. A. Fava and C. Ruini, "Development and Characteristics of a Well-being Enhancing Psychotherapeutic Strategy: Well-being Therapy," *Journal of Behavior Therapy and Experimental Psychiatry*

34 (2003): 45–63; G. A. Fava, C. Ruini, N. Sonino, "Treatment of Recurrent Depression: A Sequential Psychotherapeutic and Psychopharmacological Approach," *CNS Drugs* 17 (2003): 1109–17; M. E. Thase, "Antidepressant Treatment of the Depressed Patient with Insomnia," *Journal of Clinical Psychiatry* 60, suppl. 17 (1999): 28–31 and discussion, 46–8; M. E. Thase, "Antidepressant Treatment of Dysthymia and Related Chronic Depressions," *Current Opinion in Psychiatry* 11 (1998): 77–83; M. E. Thase, "Psychotherapy and Psychological Assessment," *Current Opinion in Psychiatry* 10 (1997): 486–93; M. E. Thase, D. J. Buysse, E. Frank et al., "Which Depressed Patients will Respond to Interpersonal Psychotherapy? The Role of Abnormal EEG Sleep Profiles," *American Journal of Psychiatry* 154, no. 4 (1997): 502–9; M. E. Thase, A. D. Simons, C. F. Reynolds, "Abnormal Electroencephalographic Sleep Profiles in Major Depression: Association with Response to Cognitive Behavior Therapy," *Archives of General Psychiatry* 53, no. 2 (1996): 99–108; M. E. Thase, S. Dube, K. Bowler et al., "Hypothalamic-pituitary-adrenocortical Activity and Response to Cognitive Behavior Therapy in Unmedicated, Hospitalized Depressed Patients," *American Journal of Psychiatry* 153, no. 7 (1996): 886–91; M. E. Thase, M. Fava, U. Halbreich et al., "A Placebo-controlled, Randomized Clinical Trial Comparing Sertraline and Imipramine for the Treatment of Dysthymia," *Archives of General Psychiatry* 53, no. 9 (1996): 777–84; M. E. Thase, A. R. Entsuah, R. L. Rudolph, "Remission Rates During Treatment with Venlafaxine or Selective Serotonin Reuptake Inhibitors," *British Journal of Psychiatry* 178 (2001): 234–41; S. D. Hollon, "What is Cognitive Behavioral Therapy and Does it Work?" *Current Opinion in Neurobiology* 8 (1998): 289–92; D. Chambless and S. D. Hollon, "Defining Empirically Supported Therapies," *Journal of Consulting and Clinical Psychology* 66, no. 1 (1998): 7–18; and K. Goldapple, Z. Segal, C. Garson et al., "Modulation of Cortical-Limbic Pathways in Major Depression Treatment-Specific Effects of Cognitive Behavior Therapy," *Archives of General Psychiatry* 61 (2004): 34–41.

3. Ashok Gangadean, "Meditative Logic" (lecture, Greater Philadelphia Philosophy Consortium's Symposium on Spirituality and Health, Haverford College, Haverford, PA, March 27, 2004). See also Ashok K. Gangadean, *Meditative Reason: Toward Universal Grammar between Worlds* (Honolulu: University of Hawaii Press, 2000).

4. J. Barth, "Night-Sea Journey," *Lost in the Funhouse* (New York: Doubleday, 1966).

Chapter 1

1. See the last chapter of Lewis Mehl-Madrona, *Coyote Healing* (Rochester, VT: Bear and Company, 2003); and also watch www.drmadrona.com for upcoming published papers in these areas, all currently under preparation.

2. E. Laszlo, *The Connectivity Hypothesis: Foundations of an Integral Science of Quantum, Cosmos, Life, and Consciousness* (Albany, NY: State University of New York Press, 2003), 79.

3. E. Goffman, "Footing," *Semiotica* 25 (1979): 1–29.

4. R. Sheldrake, *A New Science of Life* (Rochester, VT: Park Street Press, 1995).

5. E. Goffman, *Frame Analysis: An Essay on the Organization of Experience* (New York: Harper and Row, 1974).

6. I originally read the Hopi creation story in Robert Boissiere, *Meditations with the Hopi: A Centering Book* (Rochester, VT: Bear & Company, 1986), though I took the storyteller's prerogative and modified it extensively. I had heard other versions from Hopi friends and present a version that is an amalgam of all the versions I have heard.

7. P. McNamara, "The Motivational Origins of Religious Practices," *Zygon* 37, no. 1 (2002): 143–60; A. Newberg, E. d'Aquili and V. Rause, *Why God Won't Go Away.* (New York: Ballantine, 2001); and A. Newberg, A. Alavi, M. Baime et al., "The Measurement of Cerebral Blood Flow During the Complex Cognitive Task of Meditation." *Psychiatry Research: Neuroimaging* 106 (2001): 113–22.

8. J. Hermann, *Trauma and Recovery* (New York: Basic Books, 1999).

9. W. H. Kaye, G. K. Frank, and C. McConaa, "Altered Dopamine Activity After Recovery from Restricting-type Anorexia Nervosa." *Neuropsychopharmacology* 21, no. 4 (1999): 503–6.

10. R. T. Barrett, "Making Our Own Meanings: A Critical Review of Media Effects Research in Relation to the Causation of Aggression and Social Skills Difficulties in Children and Anorexia Nervosa in Young Women," *Journal of Psychiatric and Mental Health Nursing* 4, no. 3 (1997): 179–83.

11. R. J. Holden and I. S. Pakula, "The Role of Tumor Necrosis Factor-alpha in the Pathogenesis of Anorexia and Bulimia Nervosa, Cancer Cachexia and Obesity," *Medical Hypotheses* 47, no. 6 (1996): 423–38.

12. S. Sohlberg and M. Strober, "Personality in Anorexia Nervosa: An Update and a Theoretical Integration," *Acta Psychiatrica Scandinavica, Supplementum* 378 (1994): 1–15.

13. S. Guisinger, "Adapted to Flee Famine: Adding an Evolutionary Perspective on Anorexia Nervosa," *Psychological Review* 110, no. 4 (2003): 745–61.

14. E. Stice, "Risk and Maintenance Factors for Eating Pathology: A Meta-analytic Review," *Psychological Bulletin* 128, no. 5 (2002): 825–48.

15. Lewis Mehl-Madrona, *Coyote Medicine: Lessons for Healing from Native America* (New York: Firestone, 1998).

16. Lewis Mehl-Madrona, *Coyote Healing: Miracles of Native America* (Rochester, VT: Bear & Company, 2003).

Chapter 2

1. A. J. Cunningham and K. Watson, "How Psychological Therapy May Prolong Survival in Cancer Patients: New Evidence and a Simple Theory," *Integrative Cancer Therapies* 3, no. 3 (2004): 214–29; A. Cunningham, "A New Approach to Testing the Effects of Group Psychological Therapy on Length of Life in Patients with Metastatic Cancers," *Advances in Mind Body Medicine* 18, no. 2 (2002): 5–9; A. Cunningham, "Adjuvant Psychological Therapy for Cancer Patients: Putting It on the Same Footing as Adjunctive Medical Therapies," *Psychooncology* 9, no. 5 (2000) 367–71; A. J. Cunningham, C. Phillips, G. A. Lockwood et al., "Association of Involvement in Psychological Self-regulation with Longer Survival in Patients with Metastatic Cancer: An Exploratory Study," *Advances in Mind Body Medicine* 16, no. 4 (2000): 276–87; A. J. Cunningham, "Mind-body Research in Psychooncology: What Directions Will Be Most Useful?" *Advances in Mind Body Medicine* 15, no. 4 (1999): 252–55 and discussion, 275–81; and C. V. Edmonds, G. A. Lockwood, A. J. Cunningham, "Psychological Response to Long-term Group Therapy: A Randomized Trial with Metastatic Breast Cancer Patients," *Psychooncology* 8, no. 1 (1999): 74–91.

2. Lewis Mehl-Madrona, "Predictors of Success in a Complementary Medicine Treatment Program for Uterine Fibroids," *Evidence Based Integrative Medicine* (in press).

3. C. Barks. *Delicious Laughter: Rambunctious Teaching Stories from the Mathnawi of Jelaluddin Rumi* (Athens, GA: Maypop Books, 1990), 12.

Chapter 4

1. H. Markus and P. Nurius, "Possible Selves," *American Psychologist* 41 (1986): 954–69. In addition, Barbara Konig wrote a novel, entitled *Personen–Person* (Frankfurt: Karl Hanser Verlag, 1981), that illustrates the concept of possible selves and may be inspirational for those learning to work therapeutically with this concept. The story is about a narrator who realizes she may soon be meeting an attractive man and is composed of a dialogue among her many internal voices, all residuals from past relationships.

2. E. Laszlo, *The Connectivity Hypothesis* (Albany, NY: State University of New York Press, 2002).

3. Originally published as W. Schneider, "Do the 'Double Slit' Experiment the Way It Was Originally Done," *The Physics Teacher* 24 (1986); 217–19. Retrieved November 9, 2004, from
www.cavendishscience.org/phys/tyoung/tyoung.htm
and "Thomas Young's Double Slit Experiment,"
www.micro.magnet.fsu.edu/primer/java/interference/doubleslit/(accessed November 9, 2004).

4. J. A. Wheeler, "Bits, Quanta, Meaning," in *Problems of Theoretical Physics,* eds. A. Giovannini, F. Mancini, and M. Marinaro (Salermo, Italy: University of Salermo Press, 1984).

5. L. Mandel, "Quantum Effects in One-photon and Two-photon Interference," *Reviews of Modern Physics* 71, no. 2 (1999): S274–82.

6. S. Dürr, T. Nonn, and G. Rempe, "Origin of Quantum-mechanical Complementarity Probed by a "Which Way" Experiment in an Atom Interferometer," *Nature* 395 (1998): 33-37; S. Dürr, T. Nonn, and G. Rempe, "Fringe Visibility and Which-way Information in an Atom Interferometer," *Physical Review Letters* 81, no. 26 (1998): 5705–9; S. Dürr and G. Rempe, "Can Wave-particle Duality be Based on the Uncertainty Relation?" *American Journal of Physics* 68, no. 11 (2000): 1021–24; S. Dürr, "Quantitative Wave-particle Duality in Multibeam Interferometers," *Physical Review* 64, no. 4 (2001): 42–113.

7. A. Einstein, B. Podolsky, N. Rosen. "Can Quantum-mechanical Description of Physical Reality Be Considered Complete?" *Physical Review* 47 (1935): 777–80.

8. A. Aspect, J. Dalibard, F. Roger, "Experimental Test of Bell's Inequalities Using Time Varying Analyzers," *Physical Review Letters* 49 (1982): 1804–7; A. Aspect and P. Grangier, "Experiments on Einstein-Podolsky-Rosen Correlations with Pairs of Visible Photons," in *Quantum Concepts in Space and Time,* eds. R. Penrose and C. J. Isham (Oxford: Clarendon Press, 1986).

9. D. Bohm, *Wholeness and the Implicate Order* (London: Routledge, 1980) and http://members.lycos.co.uk/bohmcomment/ (accessed on November 14, 2004).

10. R. Nadeau, *The Non-Local Universe: The New Physics and Matters of the Mind* (Oxford: Oxford University Press, 1999).

11. Visual Math Institute, Chaos References, www.visualchaos.org/refs/ (accessed on November 14, 2004).

12. T. Kuhn, *The Structure of Scientific Revolutions* (Chicago: University of Chicago Press, 1962).

13. J. L. Borges, *Labyrinth* (New York: New Directions Paperback, 2002).

Chapter 5

1. J. L. Griffith and M. E. Griffith, *The Body Speaks: Therapeutic Dialogues for Mind-Body Problems* (Jackson, MS: University of Mississippi Press, 1999).

Chapter 6

1. Rumi, *Images of the Unseen,* Mathnawi III, 2785–804. See also www.dar-al-masnavi.org

2. *Shrek* is an animated Disney movie.

3. I. Morris, *From the Glittering World: A Navajo Story* (Albany, NY: State University of New York Press, 2002).

4. I first heard this story from Hyemeyohsts Storm in a different version and subsequently read it in his book *Seven Arrows* (New York: Ballantine Books, 1972).

Chapter 7

1. T. M. Field, "Massage Therapy Effects," *American Psychologist* 53, no. 12 (1998): 1270–81.

2. N. J. Bell, P. E. McGhee, N. S. Duffey, "Interpersonal Competence, Social Assertiveness and the Development of Humour," *British Journal of Developmental Psychology* 4 (1986): 51–55; L. S. Berk, S. A. Tan, W. F. Fry, "Humor Associated Laughter Modulates Specific Immune System Components," *Annals of Behavioral Medicine* 15 (1993): S111; L. S. Berk, S. A. Tan, W. F. Fry et al., "Neuroendocrine and Stress Hormone Changes during Mirthful Laughter," *American Journal of the Medical Sciences* 298 (1989): 390–96; L. S. Berk, S. A. Tan, B. J. Napier et al., "Mirthful Laughter Modifies Natural Killer Cell Activity," *Clinical Research* 37 (1989): 115A; L. S. Berk, S. A. Tan, S. L. Nehlsen-Cannarella et al., "Humor Associated Laughter Decreases Cortisol and Increases Spontaneous Lymphocyte Blastogenesis," *Clinical Research* 36 (1988): 435A; J. Itami, M. Nobori, H. Teshima, "Laughter and Immunity," *Japanese Journal of Psychosomatic Medicine* 34 (1994): 565–71; N. Cousins, "Anatomy of an Illness (as Perceived by the Patient)" *New England Journal of Medicine* 295 (1976): 1458–63; N. Cousins, *Anatomy of an Illness* (New York: Norton, 1979); O. Nevo, G. Keinan, M. Teshimovsky-Arditi, "Humor and Pain Tolerance," *Humor: International Journal of Humor Research* 6 (1993): 71–88; and R. Cogan, D. Cogan, W. Waltz et al., "Effects of Laughter and Relaxation on Discomfort Thresholds," *Journal of Behavioral Medicine* 10 (1987): 139–44.

3. J. Bruner, *Actual Minds, Possible Worlds* (Cambridge, MA: Harvard University Press, 1986) 180-82. See also www.psy.pdx.edu/PsiCafe/KeyTheorists/Bruner.htm (accessed November 15, 2004).

4. K. J. Gergen, "Social Psychology and the Wrong Revolution," *European Journal of Social Psychology* 19 (1989): 463–84 and K. J. Gergen, "Constructionism and Realism: How Are We to Go On?" in *Social Constructionism, Discourse and Realism,* ed. Ian Parker (Thousand Oaks, Calif.: Sage, 1998), 147–56.

5. P. Berger and T. Luckman, *The Social Construction of Reality* (New York: Anchor Books, 1967).

Chapter 8

1. K. Clark and M. Holquist, *Mikhail Bakhtin* (Cambridge, MA: Harvard University Press, 1984), 2–3.

2. C. G. Jung, *Memories, Dreams, Reflections,* recorded and edited by Aniela Jaffé (New York: Pantheon, 1961).

3. Steven Barnes, Winter Brain Meetings (workshop, Palm Springs, CA, 2004). See also www.fantasticfiction.co.uk/authors/Steven_Barnes.htm (accessed November 14, 2004).

4. J.R.R. Tolkien, *The Lord of the Rings Trilogy* (New York: Houghton-Mifflin, 1954).

Chapter 9

1. L. R. Mosher, "Soteria and Other Alternatives to Acute Psychiatric Hospitalization: A Personal and Professional Review," *The Journal of Nervous and Mental Disease* 187 (1999): 142–49 and www.oikos.org/antipsychiatry/2004dendrite09.htm (accessed November 14, 2004).

2. For more information on hypnosis and labor outcome, see my paper: Lewis Mehl-Madrona, "Randomized, Controlled Trial of the Use of Hypnosis During Pregnancy," *American Journal of Clinical Hypnosis* (March-April, 2004).

3. A. Hultkranz, "Interaction between Native and Euro-American Curing Methods," *Shaman's Drum* (Spring, 1993): 23–26.

4. Ibid.

5. W. K. Powers, *Beyond the Vision: Essays on American Indian Culture* (Norman, OK: The University of Oklahoma Press, 1987), 126–46.

6. A. Hultkranz, "Interaction between Native and Euro-American Curing Methods."

7. W. G. Jilek, "Native Renaissance: The Survival and Revival of Indigenous Therapeutic Ceremonials among North American Indians," *Transcultural Psychiatric Research Review* 15 (1978): 117–47.

8. D. E. Young, G. Ingram, L. Swartz, "A Cree Healer Attempts to Improve the Competitive Position of Native Medicine," *Arctic Medical Research* 47, suppl. 1 (1988): 313–16.

9. W. S. Lyon, "North American Indian Perspectives on Working with Sacred Power," *Shaman's Drum* 16 (1989): 32–39.

10. E. Curtis, "Legend of the White Buffalo Woman," *Shaman's Drum* 16 (1989): 27.

11. W. S. Lyon, "North American Indian Perspectives on Working with Sacred Power."

Chapter 10

1. Samuel Beckett, *Waiting for Godot* (New York: Grove Press, 1954).

2. P. Ricoeur, *Time and Narrative* (Chicago: University of Illinois Press, 1983).

3. J. Bruner, "Experience and its Expressions," in *The Anthropology of Experience*, eds. V. Turner and E. Bruner (Chicago: University of Illinois Press, 1986), 7.

4. Venerable Ajahn Chah, *A Taste of Freedom* (The Abbot, Wat Pah Nanachat, Bungwai, Warinchumrab, Ubolrajadhani 34110, Thailand, 1991), for free distribution only. The entire book is online at www.buddhanet.net/pdf_file/taste-freedom.pdf (accessed November 14, 2004).

5. Thich Nhat Hahn, *Living Buddha, Living Christ* (Los Angeles: Riverside Books, 1997); and Thich Nhat Hahn, *Finding Our True Home: Living the Pure Land Here and Now* (Berkeley: Parallax Press, 2003).